THE
DREAM
GATE

Understand Your Dreams, Empower Your Life

Awaken spiritual
understanding,
creative inspiration,
and healing

DR. JANET PIEDILATO

REDFeather™

MIND | BODY | SPIRIT

Printed in China

Cover design by Brenda McCallum

Type set in Minion/ Helvetica
ISBN: 978-0-7643-6491-4
Printed in India

Published by REDFeather Mind, Body, Spirit
An imprint of Schiffer Publishing, Ltd.
4880 Lower Valley Road
Atglen, PA 19310
Phone: (610) 593-1777; Fax: (610) 593-2002
Email: Info@redfeathermbs.com
Web: www.redfeathermbs.com

For our complete selection of fine books on this and related subjects, please visit
our website at www.redfeathermbs.com. You may also write for a free catalog.
REDFeather Mind, Body, Spirit's titles are available at special discounts for
bulk purchases for sales promotions or premiums. Special editions, including
personalized covers, corporate imprints, and excerpts, can be created in large
quantities for special needs. For more information, contact the publisher.

We are always looking for people to write books on new and related subjects. If
you have an idea for a book, please contact us at proposals@schifferbooks.com.

Always and forever,
You continue to fill my dreams.
All I do is for you, my beloved Iggy.

FOREWORD   6

INTRODUCTION   8

PART 1

CHAPTER 1
Dreams as a Source of Inspiration,
Guidance, and Healing   16

CHAPTER 2
Dreaming: It Is Not Just Something
That Happens When We Are Asleep!   26

CHAPTER 3
Dreams Elusive, Dismembered
from the Dream upon Waking:
How to Capture Dreams   48

CHAPTER 4
Serious Dreamwork, Journaling   56

CHAPTER 5
The Dreaming Mirror: Dreaming
Connections, Synchronicities
with Physical Reality . . .   64

CHAPTER 6
Special Attention:
The Characters in Dreams   74

CHAPTER 7
The Waking Dream Revisited   82

CHAPTER 8
Setting Up the Personal Dream
Dictionary, First View: Perception   94

CHAPTER 9
Personal Dream Dictionary, Second View:
Amplification/Cultural/Mythic/Historical   102

CHAPTER 10
Personal Dream Dictionary, Third View:
Apperception / Personal Association   109

CHAPTER 11
Empowering the Dream
through Artistic Expression   120

CHAPTER 12
Meeting the Images, One by One . . .   126

CHAPTER 13
Using Tarot Card Imagery to
Empower Dream Interpretations   130

PART 2

CHAPTER 14
Dream Incubation via
the Waking Dream   138

CHAPTER 15
The Journey to Charonium,
the Dream Incubation Cave   150

CHAPTER 16
Approaching the Temple
of Telesphorus: The Healing
Asklepion for Personal Healing   158

CHAPTER 17
Approaching the False Door for
Afterlife Communication: Incubation
Dreaming for Special Intention   166

CHAPTER 18
Pilgrimage to the Great Clearing
in the Hidden Forest of Possibilities   174

CHAPTER 19
Journey to the Mansion of Many
Rooms on the Isle of Remembrance   182

APPENDIX
Additional Travel Guide Prayers
for Your Waking-Dream
Incubation Pilgrimage   193

BIBLIOGRAPHY   198

FOREWORD

In recent years, a plethora of books about dreams have been published, but *The Dream Gate* is not just another book about dreams. In it, Dr. Janet Piedilato has shared her own unique insights on the topic. The very title of her book makes connections with a variety of eminent writers who have used the term. To begin with, Dr. Piedilato cites Homer's differentiation, in *The Odyssey* between "the gate of horn" and the "gate of ivory." This was a clever play on words, since the Greek word for "horn" was similar to the word for "fulfill," while "ivory" resembled the word for "deceive." Plato attributed this usage to Socrates in the Charmides Dialogue. Virgil used the same dichotomy in *The Aeneid*, as did several other authors of that era. In more-recent times, the "gates" appear in works by Alexander Pope, W. H. Auden, T. S. Eliot, and Ursula LeGuin. John Wesley cited the gates in his last sermon, delivered in 1791, as did a popular song, "Gates of Ivory," which appeared in 2015. The irony is that in *The Odyssey*, Penelope, waiting for the return of her husband, Ulysses, relates having had a dream about his safe return but dismisses it as coming from the deceptive "ivory gate," not realizing that her dream was absolutely correct.

Dr. Piedilato relates how working with her dreams has been a family tradition, one passed down from generation to generation. This is a fascinating dream odyssey. And it recalls the likelihood that dreaming itself evolved over millennia, or at least something like dreaming that occurs during rapid-eye-movement (REM) sleep. During mammalian evolution, it was adaptive for the brain to be periodically activated—both to maintain the organization and activity of the brain and to be of service for environmental vigilance. The psychiatrist Montague Ullman relates how mammals had to remain vigilant, even during sleep, and that REM activity helped the organism retain its ability to be aware of possible threats and initiate protection upon awakening. Ullman connected the primordial role of vigilance to the emotional vigilance of modern humans, noting how dreams are a safe way to prepare for threats and to cope with waking-life issues.

The psychologist Deirdre Barrett suggests that the REM sleep of such mammals as cats and dogs may be helpful, giving them a chance to retain useful memories. She also describes how dreaming appears to have been adaptive, assisting human evolution, especially in regard to retaining important memories and solving current problems. Over the millennia, dreaming among humans became fine-tuned to assist important psychological purposes and even to foster creativity.

Barrett has studied numerous examples of creative problem-solving in dreams, including the cases of Elias Howe and August Kekule, also discussed by Dr. Piedilato. Indeed, Dr. Piedilato's historical surveys are a highlight of this book, especially her rendition of the dream incubation rituals of ancient Egypt and Greece. When in Cyprus, I made a special trip to see the ruins of an ancient dream temple, the purpose of which is described in *The Dream Gate*. Dr. Piedilato also takes her readers through the procedures utilized by the Delphi oracles in helping their supplicants follow the dictum to "know thyself." When in Greece I visited the ruins at Delphi, remembering the central role that the temple played for so many centuries.

Dr. Piedilato has traveled to many of the sacred sites of ancient Egypt and writes knowledgably about this topic. In addition to the special places where dreams could be initiated and discussed, it was not uncommon for Egyptians to arrange a special chamber of their own homes in ways that would facilitate peaceful sleep and instructive dreams. Dr. Piedilato has done something similar in *The Dream Gate*. She has given instructions to her readers on how to incubate dreams, how to recall dreams, and how to interpret their messages. Rather than dictating a "one size fits all" recipe, she empowers her readers to write their own "dream dictionaries" and to discover the ways in which dreams can add a valuable dimension to their lives. This is a gift that can change readers' lives or, at the very least, enrich them. Dreams and dreaming, the product of millions of years of evolution and thousands of years of social evolution, are a valuable resource for the complex times in which we are living. By opening *The Dream Gate*, readers will enter a world of wonder, a dimension that will become wider, deeper, and higher in the years to come.

—Stanley Krippner, January 2021

INTRODUCTION

That which the dream shows is the shadow of such wisdom as exists in man, even if during his waking state he may know nothing about it. . . . We do not know it because we are fooling away our time with outward and perishing things and are asleep in regard to that which is real within ourselves. —Paracelsus (1493–1541)

It is simple heredity, just not the kind I ever studied in my genetics classes. I was born of a long line of dreamers, destined to thread dreaming through my entire life. The heredity I speak of is not something etched onto codons, the units of DNA that determine hair, eye color, and human traits. Rather what I speak of is something that flows from one generation to another, embedded through ritual enactments that ensure survival. Thus, when it comes to being born into a family of dreamers, I speak of the respect, attention, and continual importance placed upon dreams in my family, especially on my maternal side. Now, since I am an original, such is this theory of mine that is absent from the halls of formal science. Dreamwork is something we adapt to, through our environmental support. If it is a ritual for a particular family to eat a particular dish upon rising, breaking fast each day with it, the process is simply passed on from one generation to another until something interferes with its survival, challenging or dismissing it. Perhaps a change in location, the diffusion of the original family over a wider territory, or the entry of new ideas simply births something new and different. Dreams and the importance of dreams in a particular culture or individual family are thus either embraced or dismissed in this manner. In my family, for generations, dreams were simply a way of life; their importance and significance in influencing waking reality were carried from one generation to another. Despite the changing views of modernity, which would challenge the importance of dreaming, the ritual of sharing and talking about dreams was sewn into the fabric of our nature, connecting us with our past and possible future. Such an environment was for me fertile ground to plant the seeds of my lifelong romance with dreaming. And romance it is that continues today. The big questions of life fill me each night prior to going to sleep. It is this deep interest that has me expanding the dreaming state to include any altered state that ushers me into what I call the *imaginatio*, the territory where I experience a world outside my proximal waking environment. Whenever I enter an imaginal state of mind, a dreaming state, I see through the faculty of the imagination, something that is not perceived through my physical senses but that is experienced through my imaginal viewing. This is true for all of us, and thus I wish each of us to embrace this wondrous idea. Let us view entering this imaginal state, dreaming, as far more than the sleeping dream that manifests after the head is upon the pillow and darkness surrounds us. This idea of seeing the possibility of dreaming as expanding to periods when we are partially awake expands the dream territory to include daytime reveries. Since we all experience daytime reveries, we can all move beyond the horn of ivory to access deeper, more-rewarding imaginal experiences.

My own history helped me early on, yet we can all play catch-up if we are really interested in understanding our dreams. Thus, while the genetics of my family rituals put me in the dreamer category quite naturally, anyone can begin by paying attention. It takes intention and devotion. That is what the Dream Gate is about. Since the trip beyond the Dream Gate is about traveling onto a strange landscape, naturally all tourists need a guide. I feel it is important right at the beginning to present my qualifications.

It was evident even prior to my birth that dreams were to play an important part in my future. My birth was announced through a dream, or rather through the absence of a dream, to my mother, a gifted mistress of dreams. The myth of her own birth was that as last born in a family of seven, it was she who was born with the veil, apparently a sign of her nature as dreamer and seer. As a biologist I believe that the amniotic sac, which usually follows a baby as afterbirth, must have wrapped itself around my mother as she arrived from the birth canal. How this would be a prediction of a child's psychic abilities remains a mystery. Yet, in my mother's case I can confirm the validity of her paranormal abilities, due or not due to the presence of that veil or sac. My mother was simply a seer. She knew things that most of us were unaware of, and in the case of my three brothers and myself, this impressive knowledge certainly did keep us in line. There were consequences to pay that were best avoided if we chanced breaking any house rules, for Mother would always know our actions. We respected her and saw her as something incredibly special, gifted beyond anyone else in our little world. Most of Mother's visions came through nighttime dreams. The instance of my birth and the prediction of my sex in dream were something of a legend in our little family. The telling of the story formed a solid ground for my own personal mythology. Annually during my birthday week, Mother would tell that story as though it were part of a sacred text of being. Since I was born on Labor Day, September first, my birthday was celebrated from the first of the month until that first Monday, the official celebration of Labor Day. Along with the preparation of a special birthday feast cookie tray came the story of the prediction of my birth. It always began with the years of Mother's pregnancy dream visits in anticipation of each child. During the first trimester of her prior pregnancies, Mother was visited in dream by a tailor who quietly sat sewing a new pair of pants. My mother, a gifted dress designer, interpreted his actions as predicting the male sex of the child. She took up her own needle and fashioned heirloom christening gowns for her future sons. The dreams correctly divined each pregnancy. Three boys were born. A fourth boy was prematurely miscarried. When the tailor neglected to show up during the first three months of her pregnancy with me, she knew her daughter would finally arrive. So secure in the validity of this absence, she fashioned a rag doll to give to the boys in preparation of my arrival. She named the rag doll Janet. The boys took their baby sister doll everywhere, loving and tenderly caring for her. Each year the story flowed easily until this very moment. With a flair for the dramatic, my mother moved on, slowly preparing for the great crescendo. First she would moan, remembering my difficult breach birth. Anxiety followed, with the great rush to get me home so she could prepare the boys for school, which followed immediately after my Labor Day arrival. She was building up to the climax, the greatest of mysteries. She would describe the arrival home, and I remember it well. There is an old black-and-white photo of my three adorable brothers all dressed up, sitting on our front steps waiting for me. So strongly imprinted upon my memory is the visual image painted by Mother—she, stepping from the car holding me, a 10-pound baby, in her arms, displaying me to the welcoming glee of these excited little boys. There is a moment of happy reunion before silence falls, and we all hold our breath in anticipation of what comes next. My mother dramatically glances around, her eyes searching for something, scouring each direction. She then explains she was seeking my rag doll surrogate. Silence greets her questions. Janet, the rag doll, a true family member, is missing from this family reunion. She asked the boys for Janet, suggesting they properly present her to their new baby sister. No one responds. The boys scurry into the house. The search was on. Yet, no one could find that rag doll. Janet had simply vanished. And so the story ends with mystery. Everyone would laugh and my cake would appear with the appropriate candles for my wish. That was that until my next birthday, when the ritual story would rise again.

I do not remember how old I was when I solved this mystery, possibly around four years of age. Yet, solve it I did, with an unshakable attitude. *How could they not see what had happened?* I apparently inquired indignantly. *Was it not plain enough? I was that rag doll come to life!* Apparently, my saucer eyes widened with such seriousness that none could contradict me! They were probably bursting with contained laughter, yet none spoke, allowing me center stage. From that day on, the story concluded with my imaginal ending. It was incorporated into the annual telling of the Dream of Janet, the rag doll come to life! From the absence of the tailor in Mother's dream to the disappearance of that rag doll, my life seemed set on course with the world of unseen mysteries, the hidden dimension of the world within. While most spend their time getting accustomed to viewing the external world, navigating the physical roads, my sights were reversed, my journeys within. My birth home was the perfect school for my training.

Lesson here? Even now, decades later, I smile thinking upon my innocent childhood leap into the imaginal! Here, a story repeated over and again, like the ancestral myths orally transmitted from one generation to another, not only touched me but transformed me. I did not just accept the tale as merely a lovely dream story, but I enthusiastically added to it, deepening its mystery by bridging its culmination by virtue of my own imagination. From the mystery of the tailor who announced by his silence and absence the coming of my female self, to the doll created upon that dream message, the dreaming tale birthed my creation story: my birth from mystery and void. It holds a bit of the philosophical here, for while my physical self, that 10-pound flesh of the baby, was born of the flesh of egg and sperm, something in my beginning lay far beyond that. It is no wonder that dreams would continue to weave the space in between for me, since I considered myself one who seamlessly dwelled in two worlds, both important. Some might look at this as an overactive imagination of a young child. Yet, that imagination widened the scope of my reach, eagerly sending me to investigate and to study more deeply the imaginal experiences that continue to enrich my life.

Mother's predictions through dream were routine, continuous occurrences in my childhood home. She simply had a connection through her dreams, one that helped her navigate through her waking life. I well remember one dream that haunts me still. It was more of remote viewing through dream rather than a simple prediction. My mother woke one morning and told us she dreamed of a lovely old woman, knotted gray bun in the back of her head, embroidered apron upon a rather rounded shape, standing greeting Mother at the door of her lovely two-story colonial home. In the dream, Mother looked inside the house, noticing a small table with a blue-and-white gingham cloth in the corner of the front hall. There was an old, polished wood staircase behind it. At the far end of the hall was a large room with a grand piano. The woman spoke gently to Mother, welcoming her, telling her she was happy to see her and wished her well. She spoke and, in the dream, welcomed my mother with the comment *I am here to give you directions.* My mother simply knew the woman and her house; the entire place was real. She was certain we were meant to find the woman and her house. She looked at us and, in an incredibly determined and serious voice, told us that this dream came to show her that sometimes we travel in dreams to real places. None of us thought it strange; after all, we lived with my mother, whose dreams defied waking explanations. Her dreams had merely presented us with a different type of schooling, one most exciting. This dream would expand our view of what happens during a dream.

For the next many weeks, our family of six piled into my dad's bottle-green Hudson and traveled around the different streets on the island where we lived. Sunday after Sunday, it was our task to find that house my mother saw in her dream. We never gave up hope, because we believed in Mother's dreams. Our patience finally paid off. I shall never forget that day. It was in an area called Travis, an out-of-the-way, rural, quiet village where we came upon the house. My mother had no doubt. This was the house she saw in the dream. My father stopped the car after going around the neighborhood block several times. A plan was hatched. *I am here to give you directions.* The friendly dream woman had spoken these words. She had given us the key to open her door. My brother was sent up the steps to knock on the door to ask for directions! The old woman with her knotted gray bun and wide apron around her waist opened it. Behind her, the table, the blue gingham cloth, the polished wooden staircase, and the grand piano. The woman had a lovely smile, so welcoming. My brother apologized for his intrusion. He told her he was looking for a particular address. She stepped out of the foyer and outside onto the top step to point in the direction she wished him to go. The address was on the next street. Naturally, we knew that, having circled the block several times. My brother thanked her and came down to the car. The lovely lady watched him pile into the back seat, waving before turning back to her home. My mother sat quietly in the front seat, mesmerized by that face. Every detail of mother's dream was real. We had never been to this section of the island. We certainly never went into that house. Yet, in dream my mother had traveled there.

New lesson learned. We can travel to real places and visit real people in dreams. Our bodies may rest in bed sleeping, but "something" travels to visit, see, and experience people, places, and things distant both to our body and to our personal memory banks. I would study this later in life, but my earliest experience was firsthand, compliments of Mother. I share this with you, the reader, since I wish to impress upon you that there is truly no limit to the territory of the dream. It is the fertile ground waiting for our discovery.

From prediction to remote viewing to creativity, my mother's dreams flowed unobstructed. One of her most exciting creations manifested one spring night. My mother would always place her easel by the front door so she could catch the northern light. In spring she would watch my father with the difficult task of taking off the heavy glass winter storm windows that surrounded her studio room. Replacing them with the summer screens was a noisy and dangerous chore. My mother would always fret, worrying about the slant of the ladder and the often-clumsy task of carrying the very heavy winter glass. More than once the glass met an unhappy end. Thus, one night in sleep my mother saw a wonderful new type of combination window/screen. She woke and drew an image. Her solution was an all-in-one replacement for what now took two windows. The glass would occupy one track, and the screens another. Once the replacement was in place, my father would never need to change another window! She spoke to a neighbor, a lawyer. He thought her idea was good but that it would take lots of money for her to obtain patents. Feeling it was unrealistic, my mother let the idea go. The combination window did manifest. Yet, we never forgot our thrill at Mother coming up with the idea long before their appearances.

Another lesson learned firsthand: dreams allow our creativity free flow. Since waking reality is too often limited by perceived dogmas, we may be able to work out problems, solve puzzles, and create novel ways of doing things by watching our dreams. They simply open our view to amazing new creations, practical as well. Just like Mother's idea to free her beloved from the laborious yearly window chores.

Perhaps one of the most significant and fascinating dream connections my mother made was with someone who had died, someone she never met in life. I should mention that my mother was an incredible artist. She painted in oils and in watercolor as well as doing beautiful black-and-white sketches. She was self-taught, simply a natural in all things. One night in dream, she had a visit from a stranger. There was such a glow about him that Mother pronounced him a saint. Yet, it troubled her that she did not know his name. From a deeply religious family, this was strange since we visited churches and monasteries often, seeing the vast display of statues of different saints. So strong was the dream visitor that Mother took out a pencil and drew his image. Wire-framed glasses on a gentle face, and his shirt carried a number. So strange, one wondered, since he appeared to be a prisoner. We all looked at the image Mother drew, yet none of us could add any intelligent comment in the direction of an identity. Mother was driven to find out who this was.

We belonged to the Franciscan monastery, and my mother often cooked for their special third-order events. Their presence as well as Franciscans from the Brown Franciscan monastery in Manhattan brought a full table to our house for my mother's beautiful home-cooked dinners. It was at one of those dinners that Mother brought out the sketch of her mysterious dream visitor. There was a unanimous reply. Maximilian Kolbe! They assured Mother that there were no statues of this holy man, for he was not yet canonized. They looked at my mother, who then supplied the story of his visit in her dream. Their story came quickly. Friar Maximilian Kolbe was in Germany during Hitler's reign. His anti-Nazi publications brought him into Auschwitz, where in time he volunteered his life in place of a fellow inmate when five in his cell were condemned to suffer starvation and death as punishment for five inmates who had successfully escaped. He was nominated for sainthood in Rome. My mother bowed her head. Quietly she spoke. "I felt he was a saint. He was radiant, with an undefinable light emanating from him." The Franciscans asked for her sketch, and a copy was sent to Rome along with her story. Fr. Maximilian Kolbe died on August 14, 1941. Mother's dream was in the late 1960s. It was not until 1982 that Maximilian Kolbe was declared martyr and saint. From the afterlife, he had stretched his being to connect with my mother in dream. Over the years, a statue was placed in our Franciscan monastery, and I visited it frequently, remembering the brave saint and my special mother, born the seer and dreamer. I would recognize him anywhere, since my mother's dream image matched exactly his life appearance.

Lesson learned: Not only may our dreams introduce people and places we are unacquainted with in our waking life, but they may connect us with individuals who have passed away. How many of us wish to visit with beloved family and friends who have passed over? Many of us seek help outside ourselves, visiting specially gifted mediums to connect us. Yet, who would not welcome a personal visit? Who would not wish to know it is possible, all compliments of our ability to dream? Mother felt a real-life visit with this saint. As I would learn much later in life, consciousness is nonlocal, and thus we can connect beyond the perceptual limitations of our waking physical limitations. I will share other afterlife communications compliments of dreaming, along with offering the tools that each of us may use to access our own personal experiences.

The universe planted me in a home where the paranormal was the normal, where my daily life was filled with the magic of visions and dreams. It was a fitting beginning for me, since my education began with Mother and was quickly joined by my childhood personal experiences. It was precisely this foundation that fed my interest in studying dreams on a more formal basis. Although I believed that this was the norm for everyone once I was in the world, I quickly discovered the truth was just the opposite. And opportunity did seem ripe for me, when in freshman year in college I was invited to be part of an experimental honors seminar. One student from each discipline was invited to partake. Each of us could choose our field of study and work independently, presenting seminars and reports. I represented the premed department. My chosen field was parapsychology. If that was not exciting enough, very early on I gained the support of an external mentor par excellence, Dr. Stanley Krippner, who was conducting dream research with the esteemed Montague Ullman at Maimonides Center in Brooklyn. The rest is history—a solid grounding of personal experience and professional studies, the thread that was woven by the Fates, winding through each era of my life until now and beyond.

I hope by the above that you, the reader, shall see that the passion of my interest in dreams is founded in deep personal experience. I believe that any guide should be one who knows well the pilgrimage territory. Thus, while my years of study have empowered my passion, my experiences are the key to my real understanding. Like a visitor to a cherished land, I never tire of the dream visits, which continue to open new vistas expanding my view of myself and the world. I hope to share this passion, lighting the fires that awaken each of you to begin your path at deepening your connection with dreams.

My mother's experience of dreams demonstrates the great reach of the dreaming capabilities, running from divinatory through creativity into afterlife communication. On the following pages I shall share more stories of dreams expanding our insights on the incredible experiences beyond the waking mind. Most of all, I provide all of this in the hopes of leading each of us into the extraordinary experiences that truly provide guidance, inspiration, and support for living a fully awakened life.

I wish each of you an amazing adventure through the Dream Gate as I invite you to come along with me and share in my passion, attaining, I hope, your certification as frequent flier.

Blessings and abundant dreams!
Janet Piedilato
July 2020

ONE

CHAPTER ONE

Dreams as a Source of Inspiration, Guidance, and Healing

I believe in everything until it's disproved. So I believe in fairies, the myths, dragons. It all exists, even if it's in your mind. Who's to say that dreams and nightmares aren't as real as the here and now?

—*John Lennon*

My childhood is filled with dream stories. Yet, these experiences are only one moment in the centuries of amazing narratives of the importance of dreams to generations of our ancestors, who placed a great deal of confidence on dream interpretation.

Moving through time and visiting societies of the past, we easily see that dreams influenced religious beliefs, guiding waking decisions and actions. Prophets, magicians, sorcerers, seers, and professional dream interpreters watched, recorded, and interpreted dreams as Otherworldly guidance. Dreams were taken with absolute seriousness, playing an enormous role in the lives of the powerful and guiding future actions, wars, and migrations. Dreams predicted cosmic events and shaped the destinies of entire peoples. While today many might dismiss dreams as irrational fantasies of the night, dreams in more-ancient groups were considered flights beyond the body. Shamans were especially honored for their abilities to enter the dream state voluntarily during ecstatic trance, where they encountered spirits, bringing back precious information and healing on behalf of others. To the ancient people, dreams facilitated communication between humans and higher spirits. Rituals were created in which individuals were encouraged to seek sleep in sacred places in order to communicate with healing deities and spirits. Dreaming mattered to our ancestors. Dreaming was considered the realm of the gods and our place of communication with them.

Around 17,000–20,000 years ago, one branch of our prehistoric ancestors lived along the Dordogne River valley in southwestern France. Their artwork is scattered along the countryside on the walls of caves. Some of the most impressive art is displayed in the Lascaux Cave, where exquisite murals demonstrate a high degree of expertise, the ancient artists taking advantage of the shapes of the stone to bring alive their bison and ancient herds. Most interesting is the inner cave painting of a human, a male with a prominent erection, lying next to a horned beast, an ancient bull. Beneath his hand is a totem, a bird perched upon a staff. The prominent erection is typical of REM sleep (Schmidt and Schmidt 2004:170–78). The male cave image is referred to as the Shaman of Lascaux. Since this cave represents a period of prehistory, there is no document to explain his presence or actions in this deep sanctuary. Paleolithic caves such as Lascaux survive as sort of dreaming temples for our imagination. These subterranean landscapes seem to be where one entered the darkness to awaken something beyond the physical;

a place of communion with the unseen, with the otherworldly. It is not unreasonable for us to just imagine the experiences that filled the men and women who sought entry.

I would like to present the Shaman of Lascaux as the dreamer who entered the sacred womb of the cave in order to communicate beyond the physical. The totem perhaps represents his flight beyond form into the world of spirit. His full erection may indicate his state of ecstasy. As in dreams where the image is the language of communication, these images left in the cave remain, the voice of the artist speaking to us, calling us to enter the sacred space to find our bliss.

THE SHAMAN OF LASCAUX

In my waking dreamwork I seek a quiet space to shut out the external world and focus inwardly. Like the ancient Shaman of Lascaux, I close my physical eyes to visualize an internal mental landscape. Imagining the totem bird upon the staff, I fly in search of healing, of communication in service of receiving information and guidance. Shamanically I travel while I am awake, not sleeping, yet I enter the same imaginal space that I enter during the nighttime dream. At night I experience another world, with beings moving along outside time and space. This is the same imaginal landscape, dreamscape, I experience when I enter the waking dream. The difference is that while awake, I am more aware of the dreaming and less in danger of forgetting my experience. Some might call this an "out-of-body experience" as consciousness stretches beyond physical proximity to view distant places. Language attempts to pin down this experience by using various terms. The shaman calls it journeying, since it does imply moving one's sight from the physically proximal environment to something distant, perhaps strange and unknown. A medium may refer to the shifting of focus to a distant unseen realm as varying degrees of a trance state. I collectively gather all these experiences under one term, "imaginal." For it is by the faculty of the imagination that we form mental imagery, upon which rests each of these experiences.

In some cases, we may be sleeping or in deep trance, where we are not actively aware of the experience, while at other times we have a critical observer in our mental awareness that alerts us to being physically present in one place while imaginably present in another. While our senses connect us with the external proximal world, it is our imagination that stretches beyond it. It is this ability to imagine that does birth inventions and discoveries, and while we connect these words with the world-changing big events in science and technology, is not our personal life enriched by uncovering our own hidden resources? Who would not gain from such empowerment? While many may not remember dreams that come at night, the dreams that are invited during waking can remedy their connection with the imaginal and open the Dream Gate to the inner world.

One of the ways we can expand our dreaming visits is by learning from our ancestors, who used what we commonly call the shamanic journey as a means of accessing the imaginal world. I sought to investigate the shamanic experience decades ago. Since my personal experiences were generated quite spontaneously, I wished to compare this one aspect of what is called shamanism.

It remains beyond the scope of this work to enter a full discussion of shamanism, which deserves at the very least an entire library. Yet, for our purposes, I will merely give a quick summary, focusing narrowly on the shamanic journey. The very word "shaman" is derived from *saman*, a term used by the Siberian Tungus, loosely translating to "ecstatic one." For our early ancestors, the shaman seems to be the artist, priest, storyteller, physician, psychologist, and communicator between the world of the human and that of the divine. He or she worked in a territory hidden from waking landscape, bridging the world seen and unseen. The shaman had the abilities to dream, imagine, and enter states of trance. These abilities placed the shaman in an honored position in his or her community. Mircea Eliade, in the classic work on shamanism, *Shamanism: Archaic Techniques of Ecstasy* (1992), called the shaman the "first technician of the sacred." Eliade saw shamanism as a highly developed religious phenomenon. The shaman had access to the world of spirits as well as ancestors. He or she would connect through rituals to solve problems, improve health, aid in hunting, predict the weather, bond the community, and facilitate negotiations, as well as to access solutions and healing. These otherworldly, non-ordinary-reality shamanic experiences birthed the sacred mythologies of shamanic communities. Much is written on individual tribal communities and their well-respected shamanic rituals. The one element I choose to focus on here is the shamanic journey, the altered state experience in which a shaman experiences what is commonly referred to as "nonordinary reality." Later on, I shall use the term *waking dream* to refer to this same state of consciousness. By altering consciousness with the aid of repetitive drumming or rattling, the shaman turns to focus inwardly, accessing the landscape of "nonordinary reality," an imaginal plain where he or she communicates with the altered dimension of being, which I refer to as *dream reality*. Carlos Castaneda first used this term "nonordinary reality" in his groundbreaking work *A Separate Reality* (1971). Nonordinary reality can be looked at as a dimension that is parallel to, yet outside, the linear time-space ordinary consciousness. Thus, entering a shamanic state of consciousness, or what I like to call an *imaginal state*, the shaman travels and enters this nonordinary reality, connecting with spirits for knowledge, healing, and help for specific problems of his or her community. In the imaginal state, compliments of the faculty of the imagination, the shaman can see, interact, and gain healing information.

I think of my experiences as a child when I would enter my childhood toy closet, telling my mother where I was going so she knew where to find me. Yet, while I gave the ordinary-reality coordinates of the location of the closet in my room, I always added that I was entering the closet so I could go far away! I had no knowledge of exactly what I was doing, but by the faculty of my imagination my consciousness shifted in the dark of that tiny closet, and I traveled to distant lands, communicating with beings only I saw. Some of these beings continue to populate my dreamscapes today. Some of the landscapes turned out to be real places far removed from my little world, a reality I discovered only decades after my experiences. So, I was not traveling solely to some parallel world but doing something that stretched my consciousness to see beyond the limits of my waking reality world in what can be seen as akin to remote viewing or out-of-body experiences. For me there is a common thread here, since they all take place with my entering the imaginal. They are forms of what I can call dreaming, an altered state where seeing is not accomplished by eyes that look out at our proximal location.

As I studied for my doctorate in transpersonal psychology, the opportunity arose for me to learn more about shamanism. I began by attending Michael Harner's Way of the Shaman workshop and spent years in his advanced shamanic-studies course. Michael Harner was a respected anthropologist who studied shamanism and brought it to the West, creating the Foundation for Shamanic Studies. Michael's teachings focused on what he called "core shamanism." Thus, while he studied and witnessed a great variety of rituals and shamanic ceremonies, core shamanism focused mainly on the shamanic journey, seeking healing, information, and understanding by traveling— journeying to the non-ordinary-reality landscape by altering of consciousness in accompaniment to drumming. Here was the imaginal experience I sought to explore.

My initial experience was joining fifty people in a workshop held in a school building in downtown Manhattan. I was excited to see if what I experienced entering the imaginal quite naturally since childhood was in any way like shamanic journeying. Michael walked us through finding our safe place of transit, our "airport" from which we would travel from our waking environment onto the shamanic landscape. This process is called "journeying." We would begin and end at our airport, which could be any favorite place where we felt comfortable: perhaps a tree where we imagine ourselves moving into, up, and down branches and roots, or perhaps a body of water where we descend and ascend from the depths. Drumming for us, Michael led us on our first shamanic journey. For me it began before he drummed. It was merely a confirmation of what I had been doing all my life, minus the drum. Once we experienced our shamanic journey, he suggested we pair off and journey on behalf of a partner, a stranger. Naturally, I knew no one, so it was easy.

The lovely woman who sat next to me was a perfect partner. We introduced ourselves. She was a formidable lady of middle age, a psychologist who lived in the city. I found her dress, ultraconservative and professionally severe, far from what one would expect to find at this type of workshop. I, with my waist-long hair and long skirt, fit in more easily with the freer, more-spirited seekers. Yet, we were compatible partners and thus we began. Our task was to journey on behalf of one another in order to discover our partner's power animal, another name for what many identify as a guardian angel. I went first. I always journey from a bridge that stands in the center of what is like a medicine wheel. There are roads going in four directions. There is a tree towering into the heavens. And beneath the bridge there is water flowing from west to east. I seemed to have the perfect place to begin, having all directions open to me. The journey began quite easily. I quickly found myself on that bridge, and walking alongside the shore that lined the water beneath the bridge, I saw a creature appear from out of nowhere. It was a young, mischievous monkey! All black with white markings around her eyes, she was simply adorable. She leaped onto my shoulder. Our eyes met, and she presented me with a huge mocking grin. Cute as she was, I felt she was definitely not appropriate to bring back to my conservative partner. I imagined something grander, a lioness or an eagle perhaps, not a silly young monkey. With a flick of my hand, I pushed the monkey from my shoulder. She leaped right back up. In fact, after dismissing her more forcefully several times, I finally gave up. Monkey it was. She would not let go of me, arms growing and stretching wide around me, clinging to me while laughing, taunting me to dare try to dislodge her; I knew I had no choice. Thus, I walked back to the center of the bridge and willed myself to return to the waking reality room with the other forty-nine of the circle.

Most were continuing on in their trance, quietly journeying. Michael was still drumming while I sat up and took my pencil in hand. I immediately began to draw Monkey. All the while, my partner sat watching. She had not been able to get into the shamanic-journey space, and thus, giving up, she merely returned to the room without seeing anything. She watched as I drew. Tears etched their way down her cheeks. I did not know what to do, sorry I did not have something more powerful to present to her yet truly surprised at her emotional reaction. The drumming gave the callback for the rest of the group, and soon everyone was out of their shamanic trance. The lights were on. We were told to share. My partner immediately shared her story. Her significant other had died recently. She was the lighthearted comedian of the pair, bringing joy and comedy into their relationship. My partner said she was looking for her, hoping to connect today since that was the reason for her presence in this class. Her partner had found a way to communicate. Monkey. In fact, I found out that her partner's nickname was Monkey. And here it was, my image of the young female monkey. The tears were tears of joy. I was so pleased on her behalf. We broke for lunch, and my partner did not return back for the afternoon sessions. I never saw her again. She had received what she sought. Her deceased partner had sent a sign of her continuation in the afterlife. The nonordinary reality of the shamanic dream space was the domain of the mediumistic communication. Imagery, the language of transcendence, communicated the presence. The deceased had appeared as a monkey in response to her partner's call. Monkey had manifested within the shamanic-journey dream.

I often think of this lovely lady, wondering if she returned to seek more deeply the shamanic connections in another class. After all, would it not have been more satisfying if she had connected personally? It might take time, but I certainly believe every minute would be worth such an experience. It is what I hope to demonstrate in the following pages, the value and joy in personally retrieving, and understanding, the contents of a dream, waking or sleep initiated.

The shamanic journey shared above, the altering of consciousness to accept input from beyond the limitations of physical reality, very much matched my imaginal experiences. Studying the shamanic journey was key to what I sought (as opposed to the entire history and full significance of belief systems that accompany a serious study of the entire range of phenomena of shamanism). In order to enter nonordinary reality, we need to shift our consciousness and embrace our imaginal faculties. My lifelong commitment to what I call "entering the imaginal," shifting consciousness to attend a waking dream, matched the shamanic-journey experience. Thousands learn to journey shamanically. And while my lovely shamanic partner who received communication with her deceased significant other via the monkey power animal experience at the workshop, now over thirty years ago, seemed satisfied with her one connection, leaving that workshop and possibly never pursuing further, I am suggesting that no one give up so easily without truly giving time to explore a gift we all possess. I admit I was born surrounded by encouraging support, but I have seen many develop their abilities much later in life. It is real, a connection that empowers us to see beyond the limits of time and space. While embracing a tribal belief system to learn the process is certainly more problematic for most, learning the journeying technique and honoring it with respect is accessible to all in spite of our differences in spiritual and religious beliefs. The process connects us beyond what we access by our physical senses alone. We are more than what waking consciousness perceives. Learning to shift our consciousness helps awaken this knowledge, enriching each of us. I use this example because it is quite simple. The shamanic-journey process alone is a waking dream, much like the lucid dream, since we experience something imaginal while remaining aware instead of being asleep.

The waking dream, entering the imaginal outside dogmatic restraints, merely teaches us to shift consciousness, go within, and freely observe, retrieving information that in the end offers comfort, guidance, and healing. We can teach ourselves to do this in the waking dream. And I emphasize, we, *all* of us, can personally experience the satisfaction of knowing we are all connected to this great communication network I call dreaming, entering the imaginal.

While I retrieved a simple piece of information on behalf of one individual in the above waking dream or shamanic journey during the Michael Harner workshop, there are many other gifts from dreams that have wider fields of influence, benefiting all of us. Elias Howe, the inventor of the sewing machine, entered a dream where he was being attacked by natives thrusting spears at him. He noticed that the spears had holes on the tips, and, upon waking, realized that was what he needed to make his new machine work. Hence the birth of the sewing machine upon the creativity that rose in dream.

Auguste Kekulé, father of organic chemistry, gave up on attempting to solve the puzzle of the chemical configuration of the benzene molecule, and, slipping into a dreamy state, he saw an Ouroboros, a mythical serpent wrapped around itself with its tail in its mouth. It gave him a "eureka" moment. He roused and realized benzene was a ringed structure, thus opening the entire world of organic chemistry. The periodic table was discovered in a similar manner, with the elements all sitting on a table in the dream. Upon waking, the dreamer, Dmitri Mendeleev, arranged them on what we are all familiar with: the periodic table of elements.

The Red Book, the creative work of Carl Gustav Jung, was generated by his actively entering the waking dream, journeying like the ancient shaman. His work forms the foundation of Jungian dream analysis, comforting and assisting thousands of individuals in seeking dreams as a means of self-individuation and healing. Edgar Allan Poe, John Lennon, Mary Shelley, and others all credited some of their artistic endeavors to the inspiration received in dreams, gifting us with poetry, music, and story. There is simply no end to the value of dreams.

Finally, dreams have a long history connecting them to healing. The shaman often enters the dreaming state to obtain healing for his clients. Sometimes in the dream state, information is given on herbal formulas as well as specific therapies. Other times the shaman performs the healing while in the altered state of consciousness. In antiquity we discover texts describing the actual practice of seeking healing during what is called dream incubation. Historical documents demonstrate the widespread acceptance of dream incubation during this period. In specially designated places, Asklepion, temples in honor of Asclepius, the god of dreams and healing, an entire priesthood dedicated themselves to this practice. Pilgrims traveled great distances to sanctuaries in search of communication, guidance, and healing compliments of the deity.

Dream healings from antiquity fill volumes, awakening us to the power of mind/body healing. There are ancient tablets that speak of specific healings received at these places. Sometimes individuals received the healing along with a personal-healing dream. Other times a special sanctuary dreamer sought the dream on the seeker's behalf. Either way, the ancient world was filled with stories of pilgrims who received healing through dreams.

The ancient Upanishads speak of dream incubation healing as well. Interestingly, the Upanishads instructed the seeker through a ritual that took place in their own homes. Through suggested rituals, the petitioners lit fires and drank special elixirs before asking the deity to come in dream to aid, comfort, and heal them. I love this particular manner of dream incubation since it illustrates how the true dream sanctuary lies within everyone, merely waiting for us to access it. We need not travel thousands of miles to special sanctuaries, which, while exciting and rewarding, are not essential in accessing what we need. I think of the saying on a stone at the ancient oracular site of Delphi in Greece: "Know thyself." The pilgrims traveled over vast territories seeking their answers, yet in the end the Pythia, priestess of Delphi, presented each with a riddle. The pilgrims needed to go inside themselves to access the hidden message in the priestess's words. "Know thyself" was truly the key to their answer. They traveled miles, and yet in the end, they only needed to go inside themselves to source the very answer they sought. Inside is the territory of the dream; inside is entering the imaginal by way of the Gate of Dream.

Each of us carries this ability. We dream at night even if we do not remember our dreams. During the day we can enter the waking dream when we focus inwardly. We have all we need. We merely must tune our abilities and focus our attention. Dream wisdom awaits, awakening creativity and offering guidance, healing, and insights often missing from waking reality. Dreams . . . should we not pay more attention? Do we not wish to expand our understanding of ourselves? Indeed, let us begin our journey to better comprehend and work with our own inner treasury. While it is lovely to be born into a culture and a family where dreams have an honored place, there is no reason why we cannot begin our own tradition so we and the generations that follow may benefit from this hidden side of consciousness.

CHAPTER TWO

Dreaming: It Is Not Just Something That Happens When We Are Asleep!

Having established the value of dreaming as a worthy pursuit, let us move on to discuss the actual territory we shall embrace—dreaming. I wish to remove the notion that it is just about having dreams, visions, while sleeping. While the sleep dream is certainly something we will consider here, I wish to expand it to include all altered-state experiences: visions, shamanic journeying, trance states, active imagination, and hypnotic encounters. I am doing this for a reason that I feel is important. Increasing our attention to the altered states beyond waking increases our nighttime dreaming. I feel this will welcome all of you, whether or not you have a battery of nighttime dreams to explore or not. By including the waking dream we truly open the Dream Gate to everyone interested in dreams, even if some do not remember sleep-generated dreams. I wish to tell you that paying attention to the wider territory, which includes all these waking dream experiences, shall allow you entrance through the Dream Gate, actually helping increase the number of remembered sleep-generated dreams. After all, we each dream every night. We merely do not always remember them. So, in this chapter I will explain more clearly the many types of what I shall call imaginal experiences or waking dreams, sharing with you my experiences along with hints at experiencing your own personal waking dreams. This is, after all, about each of us having the experiences, remembering them, and working with them to better understand our lives. Once we begin this process, the Dream Gate opens wide to welcome us.

The implication is that fantasy and dreams are part of a single continuing fantasy process that is subject to certain transformations imposed by physiological and stimulus events. It is unnecessary to sleep in order to generate dreamlike ideation (Klinger 1971).

My decision to look at our altered state of consciousness/mind adventures as forms of dreaming is not so strange. Whereas some might refer to the imagery generated in a dream state as "fantasy," this does not mean it is merely escapist nonsense. Rather, the word "fantasy," which points to awareness of that which is not physically tangibly perceived, better describes the dream experience. When Carl Gustav Jung investigated his waking dream experiences, he spoke about giving free reign to his fantasy thinking, something he carefully noted in what is known today as the *Black Books*. Meticulously journaling and painting alive these experiences, he birthed his cherished *Red Book* (Jung 2009). These investigations, dialogues, and communication with beings he experienced in the imaginal were in the end what he referred to as work with active imagination. In other words, he intentionally entered the waking altered-state experience as he turned his focus on that which rose on the mental landscape.

Often considered a modern shaman, Jung journeyed beyond the limits of the physical waking reality to engage in what he met on the imaginal domain. "Fantasy" thus refers to what is perceived on the mental landscape as opposed to proximal physical environment. Fantasy is experienced on the internal nonphysical domain, involving what is perceived in the imaginal. It does not necessitate the notion of impossible, escapist nonsense. Naturally, some fantasies are merely mind candy as we imagine some wonderful situation that is absent in waking reality. An example would be creating a mental scenario in which we believe we can turn back the clock and chose a different life than the one we live. We can move ahead and shift things, yet unfortunately we must accept that our past choices cannot be changed. That is an impossible fantasy. On the other hand, we may fantasize electricity and, in the end, create it. Edison's imaginal waking dreams were fantasies, seeing things in the imaginal that did not exist in waking reality, or should we say did not *yet* exist? So, a fantasy can yield discovery and invention. Let us establish here that we understand the word "fantasy" refers to what we imagine. The product of the fantasy can be pure brain candy or something else, quite productive.

In an original research article published in July 2013, a group of researchers investigated what they labeled "mind wandering," brief interludes of dreaming consciousness that occurred during our waking with the dream state that rises during sleep (Fox et al. 2013). The authors presented thoughts that pointed to the positive effects that both mind-wandering and nighttime dreaming shared, such as playing adaptive roles in goal-directed planning, deliberation on current concerns, creative insight, individual growth and inspiration, insight, emotional adaptation, and problem-solving (Fox et al. 2013:2). Their work investigating underlying neural processes did confirm strong evidence supporting similar activities both in sleep-dreaming and mind-wandering processes. We can see how paying attention both to our sleep-induced and awake dream experiences can be beneficial. If we do not remember our nighttime dreaming, we can begin by understanding the opportunities that rise during waking dreams. There are many portals leading to this fertile space. Below are a few examples. The names given for each are not important. What is important is opening our awareness to their presence in our lives. Some are quite spontaneous. Others are doorways that open if we wish to study and to investigate them. Knowledge frees us. The information is here. The choice is ours to make. The benefits come along with our efforts to learn more.

Dreaming does open us to a world beyond our physical limitations. Most admit a desire to experience more fully its fruits. Let us investigate the many different opportunities that rise as dreaming.

1. THE ULTRADIAN NAP DREAMING

In view of those of us who may yearn to have more dream experiences, I will begin simply with something that happens to everyone of us every day. Most of us wake at dawn, working during the daylight hours before relaxing and seeking our beds and sleep at the darkness of night. We follow a regular circadian rhythm. We think of being awake during the day and asleep at night. What we might not notice is we are also involved in ultradian rhythms. These are cycles that run several times a day. I like to think we inherited this rollercoaster of energy from our prehistoric ancestors, who took little naps during the day, short periods of time when they could feel safe in their uncertain environment. Unlike their modern successors, there were no homes with thick walls and locks to keep out wild animals and unfriendly neighbors. Thus, short napping periods helped keep our prehistoric ancestors' energy reserves going, while the short durations minimized their exposure to dangers. For us, today, we still have these ultradian rhythms that cycle throughout the day from about ninety minutes in length or more. We get a blast of energy during which we can run through our work before the energy falls, and we find ourselves dragging. Generally, these moments are the reason for coffee breaks. We need to clear our head and to reboot with more ATP (adenosine triphosphate), our energy packets.

Sugar and caffeine are our go-to energy sources to reboot our lagging machinery. The body quickly breaks them down into the energy packets of ATP that refuel the depleted system. Too often we ignore our needs and push on, trying desperately to clear our head while our mind goes off on its own. We struggle to concentrate as thoughts scatter our focus, disrupting the flow of the desired work plan. Often we actually "nap." Yes, spontaneously we snap out of it for a moment or two before catching ourselves, one hopes before our superior notices. It is these moments when a dreaming, short as it might be, occurs. Thus, the number one moment of dreaming that all of us experience is this ultradian nap. While a lazy, tired mind might just max out on worrying about waking-reality problems, the actual nap is generally far more generous in offering imagery and scenarios that arise to comfort, guide, and help us see current conditions more clearly. The trick is to pay attention to these spontaneous little-nap visits. The imagery that arises is important, and if some of us forget our dreams, here is one place we can begin to pay attention. Remember, the more attention we give our altered-state experiences, the more they manifest. If we wish to study our dreams in service of understanding more about them, we first must work to access them through whatever door they choose to appear.

Example: I recently held a Dream Chat session where individuals presented their dreams for discussion. At this specific session I invited each to participate in a waking dream. I suggested that each of our group think of something they wished to dream on, something they were unsuccessful in manifesting or something they had manifested in dream but wished to reenter for more information. I led the Waking Dream process by chanting along the face of my drum, gently relaxing and leading each to see a door through which they would reenter the dream territory. The door opened into a glass elevator, which took them through the starry night, where each entered an ancient dreaming temple. I reminded them to bring to mind their intentions. Chanting their way in, I left them to their experience while I softly drummed. The drumming helps keep each person relaxed and comfortable in the visionary experience.

While many may think of using a drum solely for placing a beater on it to hear the heart-like steady thumping, the drum has the extraordinary ability to add depth to the voice that whispers along its surface. I found this quite by accident when I came into the presence of my first drum. I was seeking a bodrum, a Celtic drum favored by the bards in storytelling. To this end, my beloved husband drove several hours to a small artisan who sold handmade drums at a market outside Washington, DC. The drum maker displayed a large selection of beautifully crafted bodrums, and yet, one Native American drum called out to me, catching and holding my attention. Strangely, it was unadorned and quite unremarkable physically, yet I could not keep my eyes from it. While I fidgeted with the bodrums I kept returning my gaze in its direction. Finally, I picked it up, and instead of asking for a beater to create the "thump, thump, thump" rhythm, I brought its face close to mine and I began to whisper and then to sing. My song expanded and filled the space and me. I literally floated above the room, effortlessly journeying beyond the seen. Slowly I moved my lips from the drum's tightly fitted skin. Slowly my eyes opened wide as I landed back into the room. I laughed with joy. My husband smiled and uttered, "That was quite something. May I assume you have found your drum?" Indeed I had. In those few moments I felt an immediate connection. My lips breathing upon the stretched skin of its face, and it breathing with me, creating a duet powerfully enriching the sound, upon which I knew I could travel imaginally into the extraordinary nonordinary reality of dream. The long journey to source a bodrum had resulted in my finding my soul drum, one that remains my favorite today. Thus, my Waking Dream presentation includes this process of often singing across the face of the drum, which deepens and empowers the experience, gently relaxing and leading each listener to see a door through which they would reenter the dream territory.

After twenty minutes I chanted everyone back into their waking rooms and our collective experience. One woman shared how she had for several weeks attempted to experience a specific dream without success. She was thrilled that she had actually remembered the particular dream, since she shared that she rarely remembered her dreams. Yet, in excitement she told of her waking dream experience. She followed all the instructions and saw herself arriving at the temple. Up to this point she was experiencing the waking dream, much like a shamanic journey. Yet, what happened next was significant. She no longer heard my voice or the drum. She was amazed at her experience as she realized she was dreaming; indeed, like a lucid dream, she was aware of the experience. She was pleased to report the dreaming had manifested what she requested. She had spent a day pushing herself to complete a set of complex issues and thus was ready for her nap. Pushed to our session, she was in the right mindset to allow it to manifest her vision. This "nap" dream was initiated in the right place for immediate gratification and discussion. Each of us can catch our napping thoughts and record them.

Experiential: In order to make the most of the ultradian napping period, I suggest paying attention to energy levels during work. When the bright flow seems to get sluggish, we need to take a short break, even ten minutes. We can close our eyes and relax. If there is something that is particularly high on our priority list, something we wish to investigate more closely, it will probably circle around us as we take our break. Often it is the time when images rise like bubbles in champagne, helping us see a different angle than what is presented by our waking mind. In order to keep ourselves from falling into a deep sleep, after which we might more easily forget our little-nap suggestions, we might do what Thomas Edison did to catch his napping dream material. He would hold little balls in the palms of his hands. As he relaxed, the hands would loosen around the balls, letting them drop and wake him. He would then successfully remember his experiences and their creative ideas.

Example: A big beetle appears at your doorway in your napping vision. You have no liking for bugs. Neither are you interested in one by your door. So, move beyond the manifested initial image to what it might represent. Any past history with beetles? Is there someone you might think of in a negative manner represented by this black beetle? Is there a problem you might wish to squish beneath your feet? Or is a beetle significant as a representative of some ideological or mythological system? In this manner the nap image can bring a message.

2. AUTOMATIC HYPNOSIS

Most may immediately think of hypnosis as the state of mind induced in a professional session with a certified hypnotherapist. This is not what I am referring to here. Imagine standing in a line waiting to pay for groceries. You are bored, and after looking at magazines near the checkout you merely stand by your grocery cart, just waiting. Boredom is not something the mind likes. Slowly, without your conscious consent, you are no longer attentive to your surroundings. Like the ultradian nap, this time boredom has propelled you into an alternate fertile dreamscape. You may think of a person you have not seen for months or years. You might remember some event that just rises to consciousness without an immediate reason. Yet, this hypnotic moment is retrieving information that does have meaning. The altered state of mind that is directing your attention beyond your immediate waking environment is now center stage. In fact, so absorbed in your reverie you may for a moment not even realize what is happening around you. A voice might call to you to move forward, that your turn has now manifested. You suddenly snap back to the proximal environment. Yet, you have a period of dreaming. It should be noted. It is an opportunity to discover what is hidden beneath what is seen in order to clarify issues.

Experiential: Next time you find yourself needing to wait for an appointment, pay attention to the drift of your thoughts. You may find yourself surprised at what rises to awareness. Do not let it escape your lens. Think about it and walk with it until it reveals its message.

Example: You are in an office awaiting your appointment with an accountant. This is about business, taxes. You are worried about these financial drains on your limited income. You wait, and for no apparent reason you are remembering a childhood scene where you are swinging on an old rubber tire from an old oak tree. Your father is pushing you, and you remember how it filled your heart, knowing he was protecting you from falling. The scene is retrieved from memory, one possibly decades long past. If this were your experience, what do you think it might mean? You are worried, and this scene manifests. A lovely father's support is brought forward. Do you think this is a random pick of a tired brain, or does this give rise to a message? If we look for the message in this, we can see a supporting hug coming our way. The scene brings momentary joy. It raises our immunoglobulins, the fighters in our immune system, by giving us comfort. At a moment of stress, it is relaxing us. Depending on the strength of our momentary vision, it could even represent an afterlife communication where we are receiving a message not to worry, to have hope in believing someone has our back just like in this long-ago memory. They shall push us up and see we do not fall. Thus, the message here is to remind us that even during boring moments, we can experience a dreaming that brings comfort and healing. The memory, the thoughts, and the inner vision are a message from the dream reality.

3. SHAMANIC JOURNEYING

As explained above with the work of anthropologist Michael Harner and the Center for Shamanic Studies, shamanic journeying has been embraced by the Western world. Because the tribal shaman was the medicine person of a tribal community who altered consciousness, seeking a vision in service of his or her community, this process of shamanic journeying is now widely practiced today by ordinary people in cities and small communities alike. The process of shamanic journeying is one of turning one's focus inwardly with the help of chanting or drumming or a similar monotonous beat. A person is trained to formulate a question, intention, or petition for healing before closing waking eyes to seek an inner vision. Listening either to a drumming tape or similar accompaniment, they usually spend around twenty to thirty minutes seeking information in this manner. The seeker then visualizes a doorway through which they move from the waking reality onto the shamanic visionary landscape. The rest of the experience opens to vistas often beyond any waking reality memory. In the end, after experiencing the nonreality vision, each writes their thoughts, attempting to work out the meaning, much the same as we do with nighttime dreams. Thus, I consider this shamanic journey a form of waking dream, interacting with the inner realm of the imaginal while in the waking state, with focus directed inwardly away from the external proximal environment. It is close to a lucid dream, where the dreamer is aware of the dream state while experiencing it. The benefit of the waking dream or shamanic journey is that there is less chance of forgetting what is experienced. I must emphasize that I am focusing on the shamanic-journey experience, just one aspect in the vast territory of shamanism, much as it is taught in core shamanism. A full discussion of shamanism involves far more than the journey experience.

A less familiar word that was used in antiquity likewise referred to special priests, physician seers who went into ecstatic trance or dream to access healing. They were called *iatromantis*, what is believed to be the Greek name for shaman. A separate chapter shall be devoted to the entire process of dream incubation, since our knowledge of this once highly respected ritual can be of great assistance in our dreamwork today. Yet, for now we merely note that while names vary with time, and place may change as well as our perception and acceptance of what they represent, the basic connector between what we see is dreaming, the altered state of focusing within on the imaginal plain. The actual rituals vary, yet each is directed to gain access through the Dream Gate. The experiences may take on varied spiritual and religious significance, yet the fact that the experiences are respected and eagerly sought tells us of their importance. The iatromantis, shaman, seer, or medicine person represents a tradition of forming an intention and seeking it through the altered dreaming state, awake or asleep. The territory sought was in the beyond, each with rituals that aimed toward the altering of consciousness, the drive from the waking environment into the mysterious terrain of dream. Healing and wisdom, communication, and resolution of waking issues drove the process. The dreaming state was considered sacred territory beyond the physical. Its navigators were technicians of the sacred.

Since each shamanic experience is led by an intention, the healing or information received through the experience is valuable in assisting with a waking-reality situation. History records that shamans were experts at attaining a successful shamanic journey, being honored members of their communities where they served as healers. There are volumes written on their experiences and the wisdom received during their shamanic journeys. In communities where their lineage continues, the process continues as modern tribal shamans manifest healing while in trance, as well as retrieving information on successful therapies for individuals who seek their advice. Like the prophets and seers who contributed to the religious literature of the Western world, the shaman influenced and continues to have an impact on spiritual beliefs of individual tribal communities.

Introducing the shamanic journey as a form of dreaming brings up the entire notion of the intention, petition, questions, or such that prompt the entire shamanic experience. Forming this initial quest intent helps place focus on the process. This is true in dreaming as well. As I will explain later in this text, dream incubation, putting an intention in mind prior to setting off to sleep, helps one focus on the meaning of what rises. The shamanic journey never moves ahead without the intention well set.

One who practices shamanic journeying, altering consciousness to enter the nonordinary state of consciousness, becomes familiar with the imaginal territory and its offerings. Communication with the beings, spirits, that arise brings understanding.

Like explorers, the more one visits, the more one knows where to source what one needs. I compare this with dreaming. My diaries are filled with visits to landscapes that have become familiar. They are not places I know in waking reality. They remain important dreamscapes, sometimes holy places, lyceums or schools, or libraries where I often find information and healing. Like the shaman who knows the territory of the altered imaginal space of the journeys, we can become familiar with our dream domain. We may use different vocabulary to describe what we see, whom we speak to, and how we understand the spiritual or nonspiritual nature of our experience. We are free to interpret as our hearts lead us. No dogma need inhibit our journey. We listen to the teachings of others, yet we make our own conclusions. Our experiences arise from our personal domain, and thus in the end the dream language is specific to us.

Example: My formal shamanic practice began over thirty years ago. I journey on behalf of others as well as for my own individual advancement. I often use a drum, my cherished friend, as the driving vehicle upon which I travel beyond my waking environment. I share one experience I had on behalf of another.

I once had an individual request that I journey on her behalf. She was suffering from a condition that gave her great pain. To the accompaniment of my drum, I moved my consciousness to the inner plain. A doorway opened and I found myself inside her body, looking at the troublesome bone articulation. I have a teacher who always accompanies me on these shamanic journeys, and I watched as he removed the bone in question and applied a paste of a particular herb upon it. I inquired as to why this particular herb, since I had no waking knowledge of its use in this disorder. I was given no response. The process continued and the shamanic journey soon ended. The seeker was unaware of the particulars of my vision. Yet, she sat up and reported a definite softening of the pain. Demonstrating movement, turning her body in such a manner in which she had been unable to do for several years, she attributed it to something that shifted during my shamanic journey, since she merely relaxed during the healing inner ritual. I shared what I witnessed, and she was off. A week later, she called to communicate the results of her visit to her pain management physician. The doctor noted an improvement in the range of movement of that particular articulation. The shamanic journey had produced a physical change, which continued. It was not until months later that I discovered that particular herb was used by Indigenous people for just that condition, yet at the time of the shamanic journey I had no knowledge of this. The shamanic dreaming not only had given the woman pain relief but had awarded me with herbal information for my personal herbal *Materia medica*.

What I witnessed in the shamanic dreaming was not unlike what was sought in dream incubation for centuries. Centuries of pilgrims sought healing through dream by visiting special dream incubation temples. It was highly regarded. The deity of healing and dreaming, Asclepius, was held in such great esteem by the philosopher Socrates that his last wish before drinking his death potion of hemlock was to ask his followers to make an offering to this very god. I mention shamanic journeying because it is yet another form of dreaming while awake. My years practicing shamanic journeying have given me a powerful way of getting in touch with the dreamworld, which offers great healing to the physical. Thus, for those who forget their nighttime communications, it is the perfect manner of seeking to remedy what they are missing.

Experiential: While this is not a book on shamanic journeying, I can offer a simple method of entering the shamanic state. First, I would suggest going online to source a twenty-minute audio recording of shamanic drumming with a callback. This means the drumming signals a change in beat announcing the coming end of the journey. Second, once you have the tape, find time—a half hour at least—to close doors, shut off phones, and be in a space where you can have uninterrupted privacy. Make an intention; form a question of what you wish to accomplish. Examples are the following: I wish to know more about (such and such) . . . I would like to communicate with a deceased friend or loved one . . . I would like more information on a contract I am offered (or a job offer, a new home, new relationship) . . . and such. Do not formulate a "yes" or "no" question but one that demands a deeper response. Once the intention is formed, imagine a candle before you. It is the light you seek inside yourself. Ask that you are protected in this journey by the Unseen, a guardian, an angelic creature or teacher, or power animal. You need not see this being, but asking for their presence confirms your knowledge that no journey manifests without this help. Then lie down and put on the audio recording. Imagine yourself before a doorway. Beyond that door is nonordinary reality, the world of dreaming. Step beyond the dream portal, the Dream Gate. Keep your intention in mind. Be alert to the thoughts, the images, the feelings that arise. Do not dismiss anything. Just accept and let the experience manifest. When the callback comes with the change of the drumming beat, say a quiet prayer of thanksgiving for all that you experienced, and gently allow yourself to see your doorway back into your waking-reality room. Honor the ceiling above, the floor beneath, and the air around you. Give thanks for the safe return to your waking-reality room, your temenos or sacred space. Give yourself a few moments to settle back, feeling the room around you. Then open your eyes and rise. Blow out the imagined candle, remembering that the light represented the light within. Pay attention to how you feel. Write down your experiences. What do these experiences bring to mind beyond what you experienced during the shamanic journey? Try to determine if what you experienced mirrors your waking-reality situation and intention. For now, just keep a record. Later we shall explore all the ways we can interpret the images that arise in dreaming.

4. MEDITATION

Meditation, like shamanic traditions, involves the altering of consciousness involving certain rituals influencing perception, attention, and shifting consciousness, many flowed with religious movements. Sects of Hare Krishna, Buddhism, and Hinduism are noted for the chanting and postural yoga, which are sought by followers who embrace these mind-altering/meditative techniques in order to delve beyond what is seen as the illusionary nature of waking reality. If we look at the stages of meditation as presented in the Yoga Sutras of Patanjali, we see how they deal with the reduction of psychophysical distraction, quieting the emotions and desires and, in the end, reducing or eliminating external noise as fully as possible. One brings one's attention inwardly to reach *samadhi*, the state transcending space-time. Patanjali referred to this as attainment of *siddhis* or paranormal powers (Mishra 1967).

Thus, like the shamanic rituals, meditative techniques sought attainment of alterations in consciousness ushering in the dreaming, or imaginal, state. Interestingly, Michael Harner suggested that the silent yoga meditative practices allowed for altered-state-of-consciousness experiences to continue when shamanism suffered oppression from state-sanctioned religions (Harner 1982). The quiet of the practice allowed the altered-state activities without bringing attention to themselves with the banned drumming. Again, here is not the place to delve into the spiritual or philosophical beliefs of individual meditative communities. We are seeking only to make a connection to altered-state experiences, dreaming, which is sought through many different venues. It is the ability to alter the consciousness, opening the Dream Gate to the imaginal experience, that concerns us here. The cross-cultural interest only confirms our belief in the importance of such achievements. Attaining the imaginal experience is worthy of our attention. As we look at meditative traditions, we see how some speak of the value of developing consciousness during sleep dreaming, thus pointing to the lucid dream where the dreamer knows they are in a dream state. Called dream yoga in the Tibetan Buddhist tradition, this is considered an important and highly respected state.

"People who have practiced dream yoga have been able to visit teachers they missed and travel to lands they never managed to get to in the waking state. The dream state is a very pure state of mind. . . . When a person knows the nature of the mind, he or she can transform anything. . . . We can transform our perceptions" (Yuthok 1997:230).

The one who practices dream yoga learns to recognize the dream state, working with the dreams, something we in the West refer to as lucid dreaming. The dreamer is aware of the imaginal experience while the physical body is sleeping. The shaman who intentionally alters consciousness to enter this imaginal or dreaming state is aware of the experience while his or her physical body is awake. The imaginal state and its openness to experience beyond the physical remains the significant meaningful event. Naturally, when we seek to enter the waking dream, we are awake and conscious of the dreaming. The experience sought in the various meditative traditions is honored just as it is in shamanic traditions. Individuals seeking to practice meditation yearn for a mystical experience, what is labeled the "absolute unitary being" state, where they experience a feeling of bliss, of oneness with the cosmos, self-blending into others with time and space suspended (Winkelman 2010).

In reviewing several texts on dream yoga, one in particular caught my attention. The very preface speaks to this work:

A well-known saying in Tibetan states "One should explain the lineage and the history in order to cut doubt about the authenticity of the teaching and the transmission." Therefore, I begin this book with a short story of my life. (Wangyai 1998)

The text continues a few paragraphs along:

"The best approach to receiving oral and written spiritual teachings is to hear, conclude, and experience," that is intellectually understand what is said, conclude what is meant, and apply it in practice. If learning is approached this way, the process of learning is continuous and unceasing, but if it stops at the level of the intellect, it can become a barrier to practice.

It confirms the very approach we take here. My initial presentation of my life, the ground upon which I began my journey, marks my deep devotion and lifelong dedication as a dreamer. I share my story and others to help demonstrate the importance of dreams. It is not just about understanding one confusing dream. It is about a lifetime that is filled with dreams arising to stir our thoughts to contemplate more deeply our existence. Our brief visit through different traditions and different doorways of experience, along with the deep respect others place on the dreaming, calls us to notice and to draw our own conclusions, on which we must move ahead in developing our own personal experiences. The knowledge awaits us. We can read, yet without our own experiences we remain outsiders, mere observers. As Andrew Holecek, the author of *Dream Yoga: Illuminating Your Life through Lucid Dreaming and the Tibetan Yogas of Sleep*, proposes, we must embrace the practice (Holecek 2016). I have always enjoyed sharing my dreams, yet in the end my excitement grows as I bring others along to this extraordinary territory. It is the very purpose that guides my fingers in writing this text. I wish to share this knowledge and open each of us to the amazing depth of dreaming experiences. Yet, we must experience in order to seek. We must pass the Dream Gate, above which sit the words "Know thyself."

Examples: As noted above, different spiritual groups represent the variety of meditative techniques available to seekers of meditation. Yoga is widely offered worldwide. Ashrams offer online sessions, and individuals may seek to practice in the quiet of their homes.

I can personally attest to the meditative experience as accessed through yoga. While I never took formal yoga classes, I did study modern dance for years. We always began with yoga exercises for warm-ups. I so loved the exercises that I incorporated the practice in my morning rituals, rising around 4:00 a.m. to do a round of warm-ups—yes, yoga (I naturally wake at 4:00 a.m. just about every morning, so it is no huge task for me to rise). The morning is quiet, and once up, the body welcomes the stretches. I am reminded of the ancient Egyptian goddess Meretseger: "She who loves silence." In silence the inner voice rises to speak. In silence there is communication. As a young woman I was interested in joining a religious contemplative order, a cloister where silence ruled. Silence always held an appeal for me. Modern dance brought moments of inner silence ushered in by well-chosen music; not unlike the drumming of the shaman or the chanting of meditative groups, dance warm-ups were accompanied by the mysterious *Trois Gymnopédies* by Erik Satie. I do believe the music alone would have taken me into the imaginal. Yet, at home at four in the morning, without music, I would lean into my stretches as the sun lay lazily upon the horizon. Without effort, I would "go" somewhere far from my stretches. Images would arise and disappear before my eyes. I felt as though I were looking down upon that stretching form on the floor beneath my consciousness. The feeling was what mattered and is most memorable. The mystical experience of feeling at one with the cosmos filled me. It is as though the body was extraneous, and all that mattered was being a part of everything. In this state I know I can endure anything, since the "whatever" is insignificant. I must admit that in my life, where a large peppering of tragedy fell at my door, it is these moments of what I call "mystical union," the state of absolute unitary being, that hold me secure and stable when storms erupt and all that is familiar and safe is stripped away. I remember. I am remembered, put together. I hold dear these experiences, which reveal to me something powerful. I remember how nothing transient really matters, since in the end, all waking phenomena come and pass. Some might say these experiences are out-of-body experiences. I say they are times when consciousness expands beyond physical form. I need not study it scientifically. What remains is the experience, and how it empowered me. The altered state, the dreaming, expanded my consciousness. That is what the dreaming is about. It helps us become whole. It puts us together, aiding us to navigate through all storms, to best carry our burdens, and in the end to better understand our journey. The altered state, entering the imaginal, opens one through many different routes. This example is just one, and for me a memorable one that I shall carry with me like a sacred amulet. It is an example of the waking dream, entering the imaginal. It is where we go as we investigate ourselves. Dreaming holds so many answers.

Experiential: Years ago I fell quite accidently into meditating as I worked my way around a traditional rosary, a circular ring of smooth, rounded prayer beads. Dismissing the conventional manner of alternating certain prayers, I settled on one prayer, repeating it over and again. Somewhere along the umpteenth prayer, I "went somewhere," much like my experience with the modern dance warm-ups or yoga. It was a place of calm, of peace. The feeling of the experience filled me as I experienced that same out-of-body freedom of the yoga stretching. I shared my experience with many friends, and I share this same directive here. Find a pair of prayer beads. Mala beads, small elastic wrist bracelets with a series of rounded prayer beads, are found everywhere. The trick is to repeat a simple prayer while touching a bead, over and over again. A short, simple prayer works. The idea of a mantra, one word, repeated over and over again quiets the mind, brings one into a relaxed state, and, if continuous, produces the altered state where the Dream Gate opens to the expansion of consciousness. All that is needed is a safe, quiet space where, uninterrupted, we can take a comfortable position as we touch the beads, repeating a mantra, single word, or prayer of our choice or making. At the very least, the practice is relaxing.

5. ACTIVE IMAGINATION

Active imagination is a phrase coined by the great psychologist Carl Gustav Jung. Perhaps the simplest manner of explaining it is to say it is a conversation—a dialogue between our waking persona, the "I" we identify with, and a more hidden part of our personality. I love the story Jean Houston tells of such a conversation she witnessed when one day she and her father visited the famous ventriloquist Edgar Bergen. Coming upon him unannounced, they stopped when they heard him deep in conversation. They listened as Bergen rehearsed with his dummy Charlie McCarthy. Bergen was asking deep questions, such as "What is the nature of life? What is the meaning of a life well lived? What really comprises the good, the true, and the beautiful?" Jean and her father were amazed at Charlie McCarthy's answers, which showed a wisdom far beyond what one would expect of a wooden dummy. They joined Bergen and shared their admiration for his practiced performance. Edgar Bergen quietly explained that Charlie was indeed wise, while Jean's father remarked that it was Bergen who was the true wise one, for Charlie merely represented a more hidden part of Edgar. Such are the workings of active imagination. Since Bergen had been in Jungian analysis, the conversation would have been looked upon as the opening of a session of active imagination. While in such a conversation, the boundaries of waking reality relax. Charlie McCarthy, a wooden dummy as perceived by the waking rational consciousness, becomes a communicator of the hidden when the more relaxed intuitive mind interacts with him. Such an experience may be considered a waking dream, a lucid one, in which we interact and communicate beyond physical boundaries. We may use this technique to reenter a nighttime dreamscape in order to see more and to investigate parts of a dream we might wish to better comprehend. If we compare this method with the above shamanic journeying, we can see that the common feature is moving into the altered state. In the intense conservation with Charlie McCarthy, Edgar Bergen was beyond physical limitations. He was awake. Yet, he was not focused on his proximal environment. His attention was on the conversation and what rose to him, as though it indeed came from Charlie. It came from another part of his self. And it reveals a depth his waking self was unacquainted with. The experience, the conversation, revealed something of value. In a formal therapeutic atmosphere, the practitioner is the companion to the individual who enters the active-imagination dreaming. Likewise, it is the practitioner who in the end assists in the interpretation. Yet, the very process of active imagination is a turning within, with intention to increase understanding of self and one's relationship to life. The experience takes place while the seeker is fully awake yet focused on the mental imagery and conversation that arise.

Example: My work with a dreaming circle on Dream Chats brought several instances of this waking dream / active imagination. In the waking-dream experience, we revisit a dream in order to resolve issues that were left hanging in the night version. In these groups we never choose something that is traumatic or terrifying. That is left for private therapy. We merely seek more information on a past dream in order to better understand it. As the practitioner, I am present to lead my group via my voice. I may use a drum or singing bowl to aid in safely shifting consciousness. Afterward, individuals share their experiences, and as practitioner I help them in interpreting what they see. So in active imagination, the process is carried on with the psychologist / dream analyst aiding the entire process.

Experiential: If this is something a person wishes to explore, it is best to seek a professional who works with active imagination. Jungian analysts follow the teaching and offer this as part of therapeutic analysis. Edgar Bergen was a well-balanced individual who had spent time working with active imagination in a healing therapeutic setting. Thus, he could safely communicate with his "other" hidden personality via Charlie McCarthy to great advantage. The groundwork was laid for stability. We each first need to work out our hidden, less pleasant shadow persona personalities before we attempt this work alone. What arises in the active-imagination communication must be met and studied under the lens of waking rational consciousness. The contents of the imaginal must never be blindly followed. That is the reason for serious professional guidance in the process. I mention active imagination merely to widen the field of what is available in the hidden depths of consciousness, shining light on the dreaming state, that which is usually unconscious and unavailable to waking consciousness. As we seek to understand more about our nighttime dreams, it helps to understand that the territory of the domain of what I consider the imaginal is not limited to nighttime dreaming.

6. HYPNAGOGIA

Hypnagogia is defined as the state of consciousness between wakefulness and sleep. The term comes from the Greek: *hypnos* (sleep) and *gogia* (leading into). It is a period when visual and auditory phenomena arise just as we are preparing to fall asleep. We are in our bed with our head upon a pillow. We relax and begin to drift into the in-between state when the exterior is fading and an interior world is arising. Thoughts just arise, as though with no conscious effort. They may reflect the recent day or something else, perhaps an old memory, or unexpected or even creative thoughts. Hypnagogia is often compared to the lucid dream state, since one may be aware of the inner experience while not quite asleep. As we all fall to sleep each night, consciousness falling into the abyss of unconsciousness, we all must pass through this gate called hypnagogia. Thus we have this opportunity to experience an expansion of the visionary state. When fully conscious and awake to our external environment, we experience beta consciousness. As we drift to the in-between state of hypnagogia, we enter the alpha and then the theta state of visionary consciousness, where dreaming begins. We fluctuate among alpha, theta, and the deep, dreamless sleep in delta. During the night we cycle every ninety minutes or so, experiencing dream and dreamlessness. Unfortunately, we do not always remember each period of dreaming, so we lose most of what arises. This rich period between waking and sleep provides another space for us to explore.

Example: In the world of fiction, perhaps one of the most famous plots is credited with its stirrings in the midst of hypnagogia. Mary Shelley and the poet Percy Shelley were spending a rainy weekend in the home of another illustrious poet, Lord Byron, when, due to boredom and poor weather, Byron suggested the group enter a contest to see who could create the most captivating ghost story. Against the prejudice that would have her work first published anonymously, with the hinted allusion that Percy Shelley was the true author, it was Mary Shelley who came up with the winning tale of Frankenstein, which still captivates us today. Percy publicly attributed the work to Mary to dispel all doubts about the authorship, and thus Mary, a woman, was accepted into a mostly male-dominated field, introducing a new genre of science fiction writing. Mary experienced the Frankenstein scenario in a hypnagogic trance. She was moved to write the story that still fills our imagination. Writing in the voice of the work's protagonist, she maintained that "my dreams were all my own; I accounted for them to nobody; they were my refuge when annoyed—my dearest pleasure when free." In 1910, a little less than a hundred years later, Mary Shelley's 1818 novel became a film when the Thomas Edison Studios produced the first *Frankenstein* movie. In 2018, another hundred years forward, *Mary Shelley*, a movie directed by Haifaa al-Mansour, brought the life of Mary Shelley to the big screen, keeping her voice alive for a new generation. From the territory of dream hypnagogia came a story that blazed a trail far beyond its author. From the domain of the imaginal realm, her story invites us today to expand our consciousness, to enter and imagine the world of her dream, and, perchance, to wonder and to investigate the territory of our very own dreamscape.

Experiential: I often recommend people take the opportunity to catch their hypnagogic moments by doing something that will awaken them before they enter deep sleep. At night, placing their arm straight upward often helps. If they try to catch the imagery of the ultradian nap, they might follow Edison's lead. As they begin to drift off to hypnagogia, their arm will fall and they will wake, catching, it is hoped, the momentary imagery that arose in the in-between state. Note that hypnagogia is the point of going into sleep mode. It may be during the day at an ultradian rhythm moment or at night during the going-into-nighttime sleep. Hypnagogia thus always accompanies the shift of consciousness away from waking beta consciousness, where one is aware and alert to the waking environment, and into the alpha/theta altered state of dream that precedes falling into a deep sleep and goes through phases of dream and dreamlessness. The example with Edison demonstrates the brilliance of an individual who recognized the need to follow his ultradian recharge cues to take a short nap. His use of the balls is likewise brilliant, realizing that if he wished to catch new ideas he needed to be aware of them. Falling into a deeper sleep would banish them from memory, and thus he learned to wake in the hypnagogic moment, when the visions were fresh.

7. HYPNOPOMPIA

Here we have the Greek *hypnos* (sleep) and *pompia* (leading out of), referring to the process of returning to wakefulness from sleep. This is the reverse of hypnagogia. One exits the Dream Gate, moving through theta and alpha back to beta or waking consciousness. In the morning upon waking, thoughts and imagery arise in much the same manner as the presleep period. The problem is the alarm clock and the rapid rush to shower, drink coffee, and run to work. It is thus more difficult to catch this phase naturally. While I recommend people rise slowly, allowing themselves to quietly remember any dream material, the very waking process presents challenges for most.

Example: I can say that many report the morning awakening as a time when strange appearances seem to occupy their waking space. I have experienced this as well, certain I experienced someone in my room speaking to me as I awoke, only to rouse to the disappointment that no one is present. Yet, for me I wonder if my experience is part of the last of the nighttime dreaming or actually part of the prewake hypnopompia. I cannot say for certain. After all, the most remembered dream material often does come right before we wake in the morning. Yet, some individuals actually say they open their eyes to their waking environment and are so certain of what is before their eyes, only to watch as their apparition disappears. Hypnopompia? Are they in the altered state with eyes wide open, not quite fully returned into waking consciousness? Such experiences remain mysterious, seen either as hallucinations, fantasies, or possibly paranormal episodes or simply an altered state of being caught between sleep and waking. Note that both hypnagogia and hypnopompia are the in-between times, not quite awake and not quite asleep. This period of the in-between in both cases is fertile, filled with the imaginal thoughts.

One of my most powerful dream experiences arose while I was in the hypnopompic state. It was years ago, about twenty years after the passing of my daughter Janette, who predeceased me at the young age of ten, losing her battle with acute lymphoblastic leukemia. My son Ignatius had by this time also passed away, his fatality due to aortic stenosis. While to this day I sorely miss them both, the grief was not fresh at the time of this hypnopompic experience. Thus, the hypnopompic encounter did not arise from wishful expectation. It was in the month of March, while my beloved husband, Ignazio, was busy at his work with the income tax season heavy upon him. I well remember that night. I arose often from my bed to go into his home office, urging him to join me, to quit working so late. Several times I attempted to have him get his proper rest. Each time he would tell me he was almost finished, yet he continued to work. Thus I was pleased that upon waking around 4:00 a.m., I saw him standing by the bay window in our bedroom. I sat up in the bed, and as I was about to call him to me, I realized it was not he but my daughter Janette. I gasped, knowing she had passed, aware that this experience would not last long. As I placed my legs over the side of the bed and began to move toward her, Janette crossed the room, coming to me. She embraced me and I wrapped my arms around her, my child, warm, solid, and very alive. I was excited and

I called to my husband to come from the office. He came quickly, responding to my request. Janette lifted her head from my shoulder and spoke to him. "Thank you, Daddy, for saving my stable," she whispered. And then she turned and looked at me. "Do not forget me, Mommy. Do not forget me." I responded, "I shall not forget you. Of course, I shall not forget you, my darling." And then Janette disappeared from my arms. She was gone.

The next I knew, I was sitting up in the bed with my beloved Ignazio sleeping by my side. It was dawn. I knew the experience was real, and yet I wondered if Ignazio would remember it. In the vision, I called to him, yet had I merely connected with his inner self psychically? Would he remember anything? When he woke I shared the vision with him. He remembered nothing. He was silent for a moment, deep in thought. Then he spoke, telling me that recently when we had thrown out old boxes from our basement, he had opened some in which he found two items he saved, things he thought to keep since they reminded him of sweet Janette. I asked him what they were. He could not say, since he really did not know. They were merely two things that he remembered Janette carrying around with her on her many hospital visits. He could not bear to throw them out and wished to keep them. He had placed them in the garage, not telling me, because he believed it would make me sad. This was the first I was hearing about this. Obviously, I knew nothing concerning what he had done or saved. I sent him to the garage to bring the toys inside. One was an antique metal doll-carrying case we had purchased for her. She loved it and carried all her little precious items in it, using it like a treasure box. The other was a small, slender carry case with a little handle and images of ponies on it. It was a carry case called My Little Pony Stable.

"Thank you, Daddy, for saving my stable," Janette had whispered to her father in that vision. Janette had shared information that was outside my waking knowledge, giving me confirmation of her presence, knowing this was something I would not easily dismiss. The hypnopompic experience had opened the dreamscape to an afterlife communication with our child. In that hypnopompic vision, our daughter, warm and very alive, shared information that confirmed the truth of the communion. The little stable and the antique doll case remain now upon her dresser, forever connecting me with my child and with the amazing afterlife communication that came during a hypnopompic vision. Hypnopompia, coming out of the dream space, floating in the liminal space between sleep and waking, presenting the powerful place of expanding consciousness. It is a very special time, not to be ignored.

Experiential: If we wish to take advantage of this powerful shift of consciousness from sleep to waking, we must open the space to it. Thus, if we have a schedule that demands we arise at a certain time and get ourselves dressed and ready to leap to work, we need to shift things to pay attention to the liminal morning hypnopompic time. One way is to use an alarm clock to wake up at least twenty minutes prior to the actual time we usually rise. This is also helpful in paying attention to night dreams, which evaporate quickly in the morning. The alarm should be a gentle, soothing wake-up sound, a chime or something similar that does not jolt one out of sleep with a startle.

Waking gently shall assist in slowly adjusting consciousness to be more aware of subtle experiences. Staying still, keeping eyes closed or open, yet not focused on the waking world but that which seems just out of focus. Taking inventory of what wishes to come, thoughts arise, and perhaps out of the frame of what is seen is something that wishes to be noticed yet seems elusive. Ask what it is. Shapes may form, music may come to mind, and yes, for a moment, awareness expands and the feeling arises that something or someone unseen is present. Something may move as though a gentle breeze passes through. If we are fortunate enough to have time, we write down our experiences and revisit them, allowing them to blossom into other thoughts, each like small bread crumbs leading us to that something that wishes to get our attention.

8. TRANCE

With its Latin roots coming from *transire*, to cross or to pass over, it is no wonder that this term may extend to include trance mediums who go into this altered state to seek to communicate with individuals who have crossed over to the afterlife. Yet, trance may be viewed in a much-wider context to include meditation, hypnosis, and other waking dream states of altered states of consciousness, including drug or electronic mind-control-technique inductions.

Trance may be loosely looked at as a state of consciousness where an individual is semiaware of their waking consciousness, truly in the in-between state, much like hypnagogia. A deeper trance state is rarer and is described as a plunge into a state of unresponsiveness to external waking stimuli or perhaps narrowly limited to suggestion of a singular source of command. The latter would refer to a hypnotic trance induced by a hypnotist, who gives the command that no other stimuli will interfere with the hypnotist's voice. Most of the time, trance is taken in the more loosely altered consciousness, where a critical observer in oneself is aware of the waking environment, mindful of the body location, while consciousness is stretched elsewhere, retrieving information, healing, or, in the case of a medium, connecting with a personality absent from the waking room, often a deceased individual. Trance is scary for many people, who believe it places them at risk of stripping them of their self-control. The trance I discuss here is the safer, lighter version, which includes meditation, hypnosis, and the waking dream state. There is nothing to fear in any of the waking dream states I discuss, since we exist between the worlds, always with the freedom to end our experience as we wish. There is usually a feeling of safety along with 1 percent of consciousness that understands we can exit at will, like a lucid dream.

Example: Years ago I had the pleasure of making acquaintance with trance medium Ethyl Johnson Myers. As a student of the dean's honors seminar, I was studying parapsychology, and Stanley Krippner, my external mentor, arranged this visit. Ethyl Johnson Myers was a respected medium often called to communicate with Hollywood stars, so I was elated, feeling honored to have this meeting set up as part of my studies. I certainly believed in afterlife communication, since I had already had personal experience in my early childhood with my deceased grandfather visiting me. I just did not know how séances worked, with strangers bringing through beloved relatives. I cherish the memory of the first séance with Ethyl. Operatic music streamed in through an open window as dusk settled in, and we sat in comfortable chairs in her lovely music studio. Ethyl was a former opera singer and lived in a music conservatory building. We did not sit around a table holding hands, as I might have expected due to the movies. We merely sat as friends captivated by Ethyl, who shared the story of her life. Around her neck was a silver chain with a dangling teardrop crystal. She held it and moved it to and fro all during her talk. We listened, hanging on each word. She had lived a normal life until her husband, Albert, passed from a tragic error in medication. Distraught, Ethyl was ready to commit suicide when Albert appeared, warning her that suicide would keep them apart. She needed to complete her life. She interpreted this to mean studying mediumship. Ethyl began her work and embraced mediumship. Albert was her connection with the afterlife. When she entered deep trance, she never remembered her experiences.

The evening of our séance, Ethyl entered a light trance. The dangling crystal seemed to act to hypnotize her, much like drumming can usher in an altered-state experience. She began to speak about seeing visitors in the room. None of us witnessed any physical manifestation. Neither were we in an altered state. As she continued she gave a full description of our visitors and asked for their names. It was quite amazing, since the two visitors were my grandparents, Rocco and Georgiana, not common names for sure. Ethyl continued, going more deeply into trance, and suddenly her voice changed completely. It was a male voice with a really distinct accent. The student who accompanied me rose and shouted. She knew that accent; it was her grandfather. The séance was totally different from what I had imagined; *Séance on a Wet Afternoon*, which filled theater movie screens at the time, was all wrong.

I visited Ethyl Johnson Myers on several occasions and witnessed her incredible abilities to shift consciousness. She was a warm, loving individual. She was taught to develop her abilities, she shared with me, telling me I should learn as well. Anyone so interested, so enthusiastic, and so set on investigating our truth should take this path, she instructed. My path was certainly set to study and broaden my experiences with the hidden world of our consciousness. I would not settle on one aspect but embrace the wide territory of what I saw as dreaming, altered states of consciousness. Trance may be defined in so many ways in science, psychology, and parapsychology, yet in the end it is altering the state of consciousness. Ethyl demonstrated the spectrum of its depth from light to deep when indeed she entered the space. Sadly, she never remembered her deep-trance experiences, which manifested her beloved Albert. The famous ghost hunter Hans Holtzer, whom I likewise had the pleasure of meeting at the Rhine Institute for the Study on the Nature of Man, spent a great deal of time with Ethyl when she was in the deep trance state, and thus he, not Ethyl, got to experience her beloved husband and guide, Albert, as he communicated from the other side. My time with Ethyl reinforced my belief in the wide expanse of the altered state and its mysterious abilities, which defy scientific explanation. It taught me respect for all we are and all we need to learn. The world before our eyes shows us only a small part of our truth. Indeed, the altered state expands our consciousness and gives meaning to existence. I was convinced that waking and dream consciousness needed to be joined so that each of us becomes whole, becomes remembered. Without the dream consciousness, in my mind, we are dismembered, only partly conscious.

Experiential: I give no experiential here, because that would be unprofessional of me. I do take people within through hypnosis, which takes them into a trance state. I witness a spectrum of depth from light to pretty deep. Only once have I experienced a deep amnesiac type of trance where I needed to depend on others to explain my words and presentation. I am no expert on experiencing the deep trance state. I seem always grounded in a light trance state with my critical observer at hand. I like it that way. Yet, for those interested in the trance experience, it should be attempted only with guidance of a professional, until one is taught to safely cross the boundaries and move confidently in the shifting world of consciousness. Shifting consciousness does not always yield truth and wisdom. Folly and fantasy dwell in the in-between as well. We must be aware. I mention trance here to include it within the framework of altered state of conscious, the imaginal state that I like to call "dreaming."

9. THE NIGHTTIME DREAM

Finally, you may say! The dream we all seek as *the* dream, compliments of the night, of sleep! We often have more than one dream a night, typically cycling every ninety minutes or so between dreamlessness and dreaming. We all recognize the dream as a series of episodes that arise like scenes of a play. We may have images that appear and disappear along with emotions that fill us. We may experience the dream as an observer or as a participant interacting with friends, family, strangers, or otherworldly creatures. Dreams simply have no rules. People fly and plants speak. Ordinary reality pales against the drama of the dream. We may or may not pay attention to dreams. While our culture plays a great part in our dismissal, our family attitudes toward dreaming greatly influence our attitudes.

In the beginning pages I presented my story, the terrain where my seeds of interest had their beginnings. I look at that as playing an enormous role in my life as a confirmed dreamer. It is not so much a belief that I come from a long line of some genetically appointed dreamers; rather, I was fortunate enough to come into a family where generations placed great importance in dreaming. This support continued even within the wider view of modernity. I can compare my family to the continuation of the ancient tribal community where each day began with the sharing and interpretation of dreams. Young and old alike contributed. Dreams were simply part of the flow of life, the communication and discussion all paramount in the understanding. The childish nightmare would not be dismissed but would be turned into some wisdom teaching to help the young see beyond the appearance of a danger. The elders would nurture interest and continued respect for the mysteries of the night, which needed the light of day to shed their skins, revealing what lay hidden. Such was my childhood home. Like the seed that falls upon good ground, I blossomed and grew in my respect for the entire experience of dreaming, complementing it with continual studies to aid my waking mind in understanding them.

As we move ahead to invite and reflect upon dreams, I wish to acknowledge my good fortune in my childhood support, directing each of us to think back on the terrain that welcomed or dismissed dreams. Each one of us is a born dreamer. Yet, like the seed that needs nurturing, we each need to prepare the ground for our dreamwork. If there was no support right from the beginning, then it is no wonder that some of us have never given more attention to the importance of our dreams. Either we see them as chaotic nonsense or we simply do not remember them. Dreaming does not belong to a select few who are somehow gifted with special dreaming skills. It is our common heritage. When we accept this heritage, we have the opportunity to realize we are all dreamers. Looking back on how our ancestors of long ago accepted dreaming as an integral part of life, we can begin to understand just how important dreaming is.

We look to the literature left behind from ancient civilizations to better understand the importance of dreams. From antiquity we have a book of dream interpretation that dates back to the ancient Sumerians (ca. 2000 BCE). They looked toward dreams as a source of divine communication. Dreams acted as a bridge to another world. There are stories of their kings seeking dream interpretation, with the resultant obedience to the messages believed given by the gods in the dreaming. Gudea, the king of the Sumerian city-state of Lagash ca. 2130 BCE, dreamed of rebuilding the great temple of Ninurta, the god of farming, healing, hunting, law, scribes, and war. In response to his dream, Gudea accomplished the task accordingly, feeling that the request came directly from Ninurta.

Even Sumerian stories demonstrate the power of dreaming. In the Epic of Gilgamesh, the hero experiences several prophetic dreams, demonstrating the power of belief in this ancient community. The shamanic view of dreaming as a means of seeing and communicating with deities and spirits of other worlds was prevalent with these ancients, who believed that the soul was capable of flying from the sleeping body, visiting distant places and persons the dreamer experienced during dreaming.

Dreams were divided into both good and bad dreams by the Babylonians and Assyrians, since both protective and destructive otherworldly beings were cited sending each. This idea of true and false dreams comes to warn us today that we must beware, working to better understand our altered-state visions. Both waking and dream consciousness must communicate with one another that the union of the two halves increases our understanding of ourselves and our place in the cosmic plan. We must plummet the depths of dream to pluck the hidden gems that must be brought to waking, where they shine light to expand our waking knowledge. Babylonian dream interpretation may date as early as 3100 BCE. An interesting collection of dreams called the Iškar Zaqīqu—the core text of the god Zaqīqu—consists of eleven tablets of dream study or interpretations. It shares thoughts on dream divination as well as various dream scenarios and possible outcomes based on similar dream experiences. We see wisdom here in working with dreams as good and bad, paramount in our true understanding. Homer talked about the Gate of Horn producing honest true dreams, and the Gate of Ivory yielding dreams of deceit. It remains a warning for us today. We may go off on daydreams with flights of fancy, unrealism, and nonsense. Likewise, we may—like visitors to the ancient oracles—simply misinterpret dream material, leading to disasters. The fact that ancestral dreams were not simply taken for their manifest perceptual meaning but that they were studied for interpretation, often by professional dream interpreters, is important. It remains solid advice for us today.

Dreaming in ancient Egypt unfortunately suffers from a paucity of actual dreaming material until the Ptolemaic period onward. It is no wonder, since a very small number of the population was literate. Also, we do know there was a strong belief in the power of the word to make manifest, to create what was spoken or written or even drawn. Images of enemies are always displayed either bound or beneath the victorious. Egyptians never displayed defeat, since that meant they were creating it, opening the portal for the image to become reality. Thus, if most dreams portrayed fearful, disturbing events, it would be reasonable that such would not be recorded. Yet, in the later periods, dream incubation during the Ptolemaic period of around 332 BCE, there was more written about dreams and even dream interpretation. Special temples were set up where people went to seek out dreams through priests who doubled as specialists, dreamers, and dream interpreters. The ancient Egyptian word for dream can be roughly translated to mean "awakening." There was the image of an open eye that accompanied the hieroglyph. Centuries later, Carl Gustav Jung would make his famous comment that one who looks inside oneself awakens, thus bridging time with the notion that what we see inside through our imaginal faculties is worthy of notice—indeed, it awakens us.

Dream incubation, seeking healing and guidance through dreams in special dream temples, flourished in ancient Greece. Special healer priests, the *iatromantis*, were physician seers who entered the dream space during special incubation rituals. Compared above to shamans, these priests penetrated the dreaming space, seeking communion with the divine in service of healing, wisdom, and greater understanding.

What is important here is the general attitude of the ancients toward dreams, which birthed the idea of creating the proper environment for the dreams to manifest. The belief that the dream was a real event where real healing manifested arose from the idea that disease was a spiritual attack on the soul and thus was cured by spiritual means.

While it is not our purpose to follow the history of dreaming, it does help us appreciate the lineage of respect in ancient societies who sought them for healing, guidance, and wisdom. In our current era, dreams continue to seduce us with their mystery, since they invite us to see more of what life really means beyond what the eyes see.

We all like to hear of the extraordinary dreams of divination, of afterlife communication, of discovery and creation. And the world of dreams does not fail to amaze us with its scientific, artistic, and spiritual yields.

In truth, most of our dreams may not have such dramatic results producing great literature or spectacular discoveries, yet dreams do serve the purpose of helping us clarify our world, guiding us toward solutions that are simply missing during our waking hours. They shuffle the way we look at situations, to give us new perspective, often warning us of coming dangers, and in the end help us better see our role in our world. In a way they turn us upside down, like the Hanged Man on the Tarot card, helping us readjust our view to see things differently.

Thus dreaming . . . not just a nighttime experience, but expanded to include all our altered-state encounters. When we become aware, we awaken to the hidden and expand our knowing. Our object shall be to pay attention, record, and be aware so we may enter into the process of working with our interpretations. After all, dreams often come in riddles, like the great prophecies of the famous oracles. It is left to us to interpret them. In the end this is our quest: that we awaken the dreaming experiences, remembering and recording them so that we may interpret them in service of expanding consciousness.

We have taken a journey through some extraordinary dream experiences and visited different dreaming types, and now we are ready to do the real work.

CHAPTER THREE

Dreams Elusive, Dismembered
from the Dream upon Waking:
How to Capture Dreams

A remembered dream is an invitation to an emotionally healing experience. We become more "whole" as we learn how to read the messages to ourselves contained in our dreams—when we are about to cut through the personal myths, the self-deception, and just plain ignorance that have obscured the real nature of an issue of importance to us. We grow emotionally as we allow ourselves to face the truth of the matter (Ullman and Zimmerman 1979).

Before we can learn how to interpret our dreams, we need to actually remember them. For some it is quite natural. I am simply one of these people. My oldest memories are dreams, and I remember some as vividly as though I dreamed them last night. I admit I am one of the fortunate ones. Many are not so fortunate. Why? You may wonder.

Research on dreaming seems to suggest that the more emotional we are about things, the more easily those things are planted in our memory, something scientists believe is facilitated by a specific brain region in our prefrontal cortex and hippocampus. While most of our dreams may present events lacking in heavy emotion, the thought is these dreams easily disappear. The more unusual, emotionally charged, serious, frightening, or bizarre, the more probable the thoughts are placed in our memory. This appears to be an economical manner of dismissing what seems pretty dull while securely keeping in memory what appears important. That frightening dream often wakes us, with the complete scenario not only clearly remembered immediately afterward but held in memory for years. I often have analysands tell of frightening dreams of childhood that they experience as clearly as they did decades beforehand. Without emotion we can easily lose the dreaming material. If we think about the dreams we do remember, we will probably all agree they were anything but dull.

1. Intention. First and foremost, if we wish to dream about something, seeking guidance on an issue that is troubling us, we need to get involved prior to going to sleep. Emotion will help us remember, and emotion is going to help us enter the Dream Gate as well. I often suggest that people who wish to dream of a beloved person who recently passed away begin by having a lovely cry before going to sleep, thinking of that individual and presenting their issues during a heavy emotional bout. If there is a problem at work, a relationship conflict, a difficult court case, a divorce, or such, getting involved emotionally helps manifest the dreaming with a good chance of remembering it upon waking. If you seek an answer to a creative problem, get passionate about your need; give it a major thinking prior to getting into bed. Remember, emotional input shall yield the necessary push to get things going and, one hopes, to signal the frontal cortex that your need is important enough to be marked for memory!

We must be sincere, motivated, and dedicated in our desire to work with dreams. We need to get the energy rolling. We begin by telling ourselves that we are going to remember our dreams. We can put a notebook by the bed and clearly write our intention to remember at least one dream we have. We must commit to waking in the middle of the night to write anything we remember. We must be firm about this. We, I included, often wake and wish to ignore this command. I attempt to convince myself that I shall remember the dream upon waking—after all, it seems quite simple—and I am clearly remembering it in the middle of the night, so why should I not remember it when I wake a few hours later? Important alert: *This never works!* After decades of dream journaling, the seduction remains quite real. The same lure presents itself: either the belief that such a dream will be remembered, or such a dream is not worth remembering. *Neither is valid.* Do not be seduced. Remember, in our lazy wish to return to sleep mode, we simply deceive ourselves so we might return comfortably back to sleep. Thus, prior to sleeping we make the intention not only to remember a dream, but to record it if we are fortunate enough to remember something upon waking in the middle of the night. We add that we shall not fall victim to the seduction that would keep us from our intention.

Anything that reflects our intention to seriously seek dreams will help in manifesting them. Thus, we can place special items in our bedroom that show our sincerity. In ancient Egypt, a bedroom might contain images of protective beings drawn or etched on their headrests, which were used as we use pillows. As a child I drew images on the pillowcases and sheets, something I continued into my adult years. Sacred writing, often in Latin, accompanied my imagery. For me it created the perfect terrain for dreaming. The Egyptians often had the god Bes, a dwarf deity with plumed feathers on his head and knives in his hands, perhaps ready to deflect the bad dreams and nightmares. Dr. Kasia Szpakowska (private correspondence), an authority on Egyptian dreams, suggests that the power of the cobra was likewise used to protect the ancients from the unfriendly forces that produced unwelcomed nightmares. She suggests that clay cobra figurines possibly sat in the four corners of the sleeping chamber, ready to protect the dreamer. The idea supports intention well demonstrated by manifesting physical items to support one's hopes. Today we can imagine a dream catcher trapping the nightmares and keeping them from manifesting on our dreamscape. Alternatively, we can place several, assigning some with the task of capturing the illusive dreams from escaping our memory. Perhaps we have amulets or icons that we like. We can place them in our bedroom as guardians of our dreams. In each case they remind us of our intention. We simply wish to remember our dreams so we can work with them. The more we reinforce our intention, the better our chance of remembering, capturing our dreams.

2. An evening drink. One of the reasons I remember so many dreams each night might have something to do with my love for tea. I drink several cups in the evening, ending up rising from sleep when the call comes to urinate. It never bothers me since I know I can easily return to sleep. Yet, it does serve the purpose in waking me with a vivid memory of a dream. Thus, I record the dream and return to sleep, only to wake perhaps ninety minutes later after another dream, with the urge to relieve my bladder once again. If you enjoy an evening beverage, then indulge. Far too many people tell me they stop drinking any liquids at six in the evening because they do not wish to interrupt sleep. Perhaps this is why they rarely remember dreaming. They never wake during the night. Here again, the waking-up period must be respected. Unless there is real urgency to leap from bed to the bathroom, give a few moments to gather all that's remembered into the dream catcher of the transition period. Rise and continue gathering and placing each item, feelings first, then general themes, characters, and setting. After you have returned to bed, write what you can in your dream journal. There shall be time enough during the following day to think more about your notes. You need not spend time during your brief wake-up period for the investigation. The most important thing is that we show our devotion to the process.

3. Remember to save time to explore the hypnagogic presleep period. One way to capture hypnagogic thoughts is to place one arm up as we seek the quiet drifting time, the relaxation before floating off to sleep. As we lie comfortable and warm beneath the sheets, pillow beneath our heads, the one raised arm will alert us as consciousness shifts fully. As we enter hypnagogia, the arm will fall and wake us, at which point we can retrieve the passing reverie, the first dream of the night. If we do not wish to write our thoughts, we can record them on our cell phones or tablets.

4. Waking gently helps the transition period of hypnopompia. I often suggest that people put on a gentle chime-like alarm to wake them. The gong "big bang" alarm is definitely not favorable in catching dream material, since it causes such a rush of adrenaline that we merely leap from the dream state into the shock of waking consciousness, without memory of anything other than stress. I also suggest setting the alarm to ring at least twenty minutes before you actually need to get up. That way you can give yourself a gentle in-between time of lying while quietly remembering the last dream. If we really wish to experiment, we can set the timer for an hour before rising, since this is about the time you experience your last dream. If you wake gently to a chime, you may be fortunate enough to catch that dream in your dream net. In any case, the important thing to remember is to wake gently, without any sudden intrusion of noise, which has the tendency to transition sleep to waking consciousness too quickly, in which case you will lose dream material as well as the rich hypnopompic experiences that linger in the liminal space between the two states, sleep and waking. If you wake naturally without an alarm and have the opportunity to linger dreamily in bed, you have the opportunity to catch the imaginal material in the safety of your inner dream catcher, all ready to record and revisit. So do not give up if you try this once or twice without success. Like any good relationship, your relationship with the elusive dreams must be nurtured and developed. Do not give up and you will be richly rewarded when you least expect it.

5. Whatever method we choose to remember dreams, our last chance to catch anything is upon waking in the morning. It is time to record whatever we remember in our dream journals, which can be a book or file on our tablet or laptop, or in a paper journal, accessible on the nightstand. We give a name to a dream, associating it with the most impressive part of the dream. Thus, if a person from long ago appeared in the dream, we may wish to place their name in our dream title, so we can easily locate the dream for additional study, accessing it easily by putting emphasis on the person, highlighting it in the title line. Likewise, if a past event, such as a graduation, a wedding, or a birth, showed up in the dream, we might place this in the dream title line. Naturally, if our dream journal is electronic, we can easily access our dreams by putting a search in the "Find" option located on the tool bar of our computer page. Yet, if we use a handwritten journal, then the dream title will make our searches easier. Additionally, in a handwritten journal we can add a title index at the very end of the journal, where a quick glance will locate dreams by their most-impressive key titles. Naturally, this title index would begin on the last page and work forward as we add dreams. Since each dream title accompanies a date when the dream occurred, it is easy to locate the dreams we wish to revisit. As the dream entries grow, we may wish to see how many times we have dreamed about a certain place or person. The dream titles help us in such a search. I find the dream titles extremely helpful, since I sometimes record several dreams a night, waking up at various intervals during the night to record on my tablet. By immediately choosing what stands out, I can easily compare sometimes four or five dreams that came in one night. The comparison helps me make connections, aiding me in seeing patterns in the different dream scenarios. The same is true for working with a week's worth of dreams. Just glancing at the dream titles helps one scan through a series of dreams, which when strung together create a powerful view of something that may be eluding us in waking. The title we place on the dreams upon waking, when we are in the liminal space between sleep and dream, becomes a powerful connector, helping to lift dream wisdom from the depths into the light of waking. The wake-up period and attention to the transition from dream to waking is a powerful time filled with potential. It is the most important part of my day and has been for decades. I will discuss my process later. Yet, for each, the recording of the dreams may take a shorter period. Most important is writing *something*.

6. Most of all, if we do not have a dream to remember, we simply must make one up! We can do this by beginning with "I had a dream in which I . . ." and moving on to relate an experience, describing people, places, and events along with feelings that arose during the experience. Whom did we meet? What did we do? Where do we see ourselves? What is the main action and the conclusion? We create our story. We can be a heroine or a superstar. It is our imagination and our plot. The entire purpose is to demonstrate our intention of experiencing a dream. The creative story we make up illustrates our ability to see on a mental landscape, using the faculty of imagination, a sort of preperformance activity. Each morning if we do not have a dream, we simply repeat this process of creating a dream story we would like to have. It is imaginal muscle stretching. Eventually we will wake and remember a nighttime dream. In my decades of dream analysis therapy, I have taken on analysands who profess to never remember dreams. Using this technique, sometimes after only a few weeks the true dream is remembered. The joy on the arrival is beyond words. It is well worth the effort taken.

7. In expanding awareness to include productive dream consciousness, we need to pay attention to the moments we drift off into our little ultradian naps or the hypnotic moments where we focus on something internal, apart from our waking environment. Each time we become aware of the imaginal, the inner landscape of mental imagery we are working with, the dreaming mind. The more opportunity for practice, the better. We are walking between the worlds of inner imagery and outer physical presence. Both have information to reveal. And the more we attend and awake to the inner, the more we receive in service of better understanding ourselves.

8. Let's be more aware of meaningful coincidences, synchronicities. If our mind drifts and we suddenly think of dragonflies in the middle of winter, let's pay attention. Are there dragonflies appearing in note cards, artwork, conversations, waking reality? We may casually pass a store window and suddenly notice that there are dragonflies on display. A friend might send an email with stationery featuring dragonflies. Someone might mention them in conversation. Such will begin a weaving, making connections between waking environment and dreaming mind. In the end, we will see meaning as we enter the process of interpretation.

9. Most of all, it is important that we remain open minded. We may have an agenda of what we would like to experience in a dream. But the dreams may produce something else that does not seem to match our desires. What we wish for and what we need may be two different things. So we must keep an open mind to seek the truth above all else. The rewards await the one who keeps going.

Perhaps one of the issues most ignored with nighttime dreaming is the environment in which we seek our rest. If someone travels a great deal, with shifting hours and time zones, dreams may be erratic. If one's bedroom is chaotic, used for other purposes, this may also interfere not only with a good night's sleep but with dream retrieval. The bedroom should present a quite safe, peaceful domain while the main function is seeking sleep and dreams. If the room is multifunctional, it may not be conductive to dreamwork. Like the ancient dreaming sanctuaries that presented dedicated dream space, so must we honor the gods of sleeping by creating a sanctuary in our bedrooms. And then perchance . . . a dream.

CHAPTER FOUR

Serious Dreamwork, Journaling

Winding down the hill, he listened inside himself as if something by an unknown composer, powerful and strange and strong, was about to be played for the first time. The theme would be stated presently but . . . he would not recognize it as the theme right away. It would come in some such guise as . . . a tattoo on the muffled drum of the moon. He strained to hear it, knowing only that music was beginning, new music that he liked, and did not understand. It was hard to react—this was new and confusing.

—F. Scott Fitzgerald, *The Last Tycoon*, 1941, p. 95

Since any journey begins with serious groundwork, preparation for successful dreaming and remembering begins with a process.

To prepare for serious dreamwork, one of the first things we need to do is create a dream journal. This can be an old-fashioned pad or notebook, or a file created on a computer or tablet that can be easily accessed during the night. Long ago I began with notepads, which I would keep by my bedside, ready for any nocturnal needs. Since I often worked in the dark, I would find scribbles in the morning that were quite difficult to read. I graduated to purchasing a tiny book light, which would give me the necessary light to write without waking my spouse. This worked quite well for years. Now I have stepped up into the age of technology. I have a tablet by the bed. I love this, since the backlight allows me to easily record my dream material, with the added benefit of emailing my dream to myself, ready for the morning transcription into my huge folder of dreams on my main computer. It streamlines the process. So, number one on the list is to determine which option might work best for you. Taking a random pad to place by the bed really does not demonstrate serious intent. The pad doubles for the grocery list and "to do" reminders of appointments and scheduling. Such a notepad suggests that you hope only that maybe, perhaps, sometimes, you might need to write something if perchance a dream appears. This is not a strong statement of confidence! When I recommend a journal, I mean a dedicated journal. Such a journal projects confidence and dedication. It is like signing up for a course in a foreign language. You do not write your homework, your vocabulary list, along with the groceries and appointments. You dedicate a place to keep all your precious notes. Stringing together the cumulative vocabulary lists helps you on your way to fluency. The dream journal is thus dedicated to one thing: dreams and dream notes only!

Begin by writing the date on the top line. Leave space to place a title after you experience a dream.

Leave your chosen journal/tablet by your bed in a safe place. When you go to bed at night, you might wish to journal a brief one or two lines about your day, your issues, your chief concerns. This helps put things in perspective in the years to come, when you visit your journal and have a look at what was happening in your life at the time of certain dreams. Plan on getting into bed a good ten to fifteen minutes before you place your head on the pillow seeking sleep.

Use this presleep time to formulate your main concerns of the day along with your wishes for a dream. By setting up a dream wish, you are directing your intentions not only to dream but to the actual dream material you are seeking. Think of this as time you are investigating a video to watch on your computer screen. You may just randomly scan a list of offerings, or you may begin by thinking of a particular genre that interests you: documentary, historical, comedy, drama, romance, and such. We will talk about dream incubation much later, but I always mention using this focusing tool to help with dreaming. It also helps in understanding your dream material, since you can review your dream alongside your dream intention to see how they relate to one another. We will get into the interpretation later, but we begin the process with the actual dream journal.

Once you have collected your thoughts and gone through your mental video library, choose the one topic most important at the moment. Formulate a statement: "I must deal with . . . ," "I would like to know more on how to . . . ," "I would like to communicate with . . . ," "I need help with . . ."

Next, in bold letters write: I AM GOING TO REMEMBER MY DREAM TONIGHT!

Slip into bed, and remember the fertile period of the drifting-into-sleep phase, altering waking beta consciousness to the hypnagogic state, the alpha/theta dreaming state. Lie on your back and get comfortable, with your pillow and bedding adjusted around you. Next, place your elbow on your mattress, with your hand straight upward. This hand is going to alert you to your falling into the hypnagogia state. Relax and let yourself drift in the comfortable scenario. The room is dark now and sleep is calling. Images begin to arise, and you are beginning to experience a bit of the mental dream landscape. Suddenly your arm falls, and you are awakened from your reverie. Do not move. Be still and try to remember. What just happened? Where were you? What did you experience? If you can remember anything, sit up and take your tablet in hand.

Begin: write "Hypnagogia." Beside this one word, write whatever thoughts or images flashed before your mind. Book. Office. A window with a bird fluttering outside it. A lightbulb bursting. A face of a stranger. Thoughts of a long-ago childhood friend. The exotic fragrance of a flower.

For the above hypnagogia, you need not make sense of anything. That is for later. Right now, you are the scribe. You merely record what you are given!

Now put the journal down. Shut the light. And this time, allow yourself to go to sleep. The routine belief is that about ninety minutes into your sleep, a period of REM, rapid eye movement, commences. The early dreaming REM periods last about five to ten minutes, after which the non-REM period of another ninety minutes dips you into deep, restorative nondream sleep. Night alternates between dream and nondream states. Sometimes we wake at the right time during the night, perhaps to rise to use the bathroom. Here is the opportunity to catch a dream as we rouse. If this happens, take the opportunity to record as best as you can whatever comes to mind. I find that upon waking, I do catch sometimes three or four dreams on some nights; I will remember only a small bit initially when I open my tablet. The amazing thing is that once I begin to write, more comes, and suddenly I am remembering an entire scenario. The longest scenario is always near morning, when a dream, REM period, can last an entire half hour, a super dreaming video in technicolor!

Each time I wake, I record on my tablet in an email to myself. In the morning I collect all my nocturnal communications and transfer them to my e-file dream journal. I have thousands of pages of dreams, all in files. I have names such as Dreams of Isis, Wisdom of Tehuti, and so forth. It helps me keep the dreams in order.

Here is a short list for your journal, with several tasks to remember.

- *Dedicate a special book for the purpose of dreaming, nothing else.*

- *Begin each entry by writing down your intention each night . . . and saying out loud, I am going to remember my dreams.*

- *Put a few words on your current life situation along with the date that begins a dream recording. This helps you mirror life and dream content.*

- *Be enthusiastic and excited about your dreamwork. Get connected emotionally just before sleep as you consider a topic you might wish to explore in dream. Write a sentence on your desire . . . "I would like this night's dream to explore . . ."*

- *Try to include hypnagogic experiences in the dream journal.*

- *If you wake up during the night, record anything you can remember about your dream. Even short sentences shall help. In the morning you will work things more completely. Remember, if you are really serious about collecting as many dreams as possible, drink plenty of fluids prior to sleep. The call to urinate usually comes at the end of a dreaming cycle, so you can easily remember the most recent dream prior to waking. If you find this annoying, where you rise to use the bathroom only to discover difficulty in returning into the sleep mode, just discontinue and count this as something that works for some but definitely not for all.*

- *Hypnopompia. As you wake in the a.m., go gently and see if you can catch any last-minute images that arise compliments of the shifting consciousness of the alpha/theta into waking beta consciousness.*

- *Have a good twenty minutes devoted to your dreamwork upon your morning wake-up period. Thus, set your alarm to wake up before you need to actually get up for work. Do not use an irritating big-clash alarm to wake, but try something such as chimes to gently rouse you. You will have a better chance of remembering your dreams.*

- *If you are pressed into a schedule for work, the first dream journaling is probably done in bed prior to waking. Leave the rest for a time during the day when you can devote yourself to more.*

- *My deepest dream journaling came when I was able to devote hours to it not long after the dream's appearance. I not only journaled but drew and painted the images into my waking reality, where they continued to interact with me. Because my doctoral work focused on dreams, I was able to combine my passion with my work, my studies. For most of us this is not the case. It may not be until after dinner when the time opens to work with the previous night's dreaming. Life does have responsibilities that must be met. The dreaming should not put any of that to the side. Yet, it is important to find a manner that works, keeping life in balance.*

Set aside time that is devoted to recording the dream more fully in the journal. For me, it is the time when I take my email recordings and place them in my dream file. As I correct any autocorrect errors of the night, my mind returns to the dream and I remember more. I add to it. Each dream comes at a particular time in my life, and I keep connected to what is going on in waking with what is appearing in dream. Since I always have waking concerns, I think of these challenges, mirroring them with the dreaming. How do they relate? Can I see a connection? Thus, first thoughts circle around dream/life mirroring. We wish to see we are recording our dream experiences and loosely looking for connections to issues of our waking-reality life. We may have a dream at a time when a new relationship is blooming into our life. The dream may arrive during a time of great chaos, when we are fretting over seriously disturbing issues, perhaps referring to our job and an important client we are working with. At first, we may not see a connection, since we may view the dream as disconnected to waking. Yet, if we look more closely, the dream reveals its message. Remember, we must learn the dream language to delve beneath the appearances to the message. The message of the inner voice is like that of the ancient oracle, a riddle needing to be solved.

At this point we have walked through a series of conditions to create the perfect dream journal. We should remember to write something in it every day, even if we cannot remember one dream. I have already suggested that if a dream does not manifest, we make one up in the morning. We can give it a name, and we can write something that lets us know this was the wish dream. This confirms our dedication. After the wished-for fantasy dream, we write: *And tonight I am going to dream, and I am going to remember the dream!* Over and over again, we are demonstrating our desire to actively do our part to manifest dreams. Writing it in the dedicated journal is confirming our commitment. Remember, we are seeking to learn the language of dreams. In order to become fluent, we must devote our time. The dedicated dream journal is like a dream contract.

The better part of the deep dream interpretation shall be discussed later on in future chapters, yet we begin simply by looking for the connections between waking and dreaming. The dreams may act in a mirrorlike fashion, adding depth to what might be missing in our waking perception. When we go into examination of the various symbols in dreams, we reach an area beyond right and wrong that delves deeply into our personal mythology. It is exciting territory, where the individual dream dictionary is one that only the dreamer may write for themselves. And it all begins with journaling, the dedicated dream journal.

EXAMPLE:

Dream Journal: Reveries 2020
January 1, 2020. Title: The Turning of the Wheel

Thoughts surrounding the general waking reality: *A new year is here, and my thoughts turn, wondering what shall manifest. Fear seems to pop its head from nowhere: 2020 . . . the number seems to be an ill omen. Nothing rational in this.*

Dream focus or intention: *A sale for the building collapsed, and now, months later, nothing, no new sale. Is something coming? Shall a new buyer appear?*

Hypnagogia: *I see Dorothy of the Wizard of Oz! Judy Garland caught in a tornado! The black cone taking her far, landing at the feet of the good witch Glenda. That's all.*

Dream 1: *I am on a sailboat without someone guiding it. The waves are huge and frightening. One rises so high I fear it shall plunge the boat into the depths. I hear a voice calling me. They are warning me against this wave, that I must move away. The boat is small, and I have nowhere to go other than to hold tightly on to the ledge.*

Dream 2: *There is a circle of people gathered around a fire. I am with them. We sit and we listen to a story told by our elder. The elder is my grandfather, handsome, respected, well loved. I am proud to be his granddaughter. He tells the story of a fisherman from the old country, where once he lived by the sea. The fisherman caught a special fish, shining, splendid with scales of gold. So beautiful was the fish that the fisherman returned him to the water. Over and over again, he was forever rewarded with nets full of fish that he could sell. Such gave him the funds for passage to this new country. I looked around at the faces of the others in the circle. Rapt with attention, they glowed. Grandfather ceased his story. He walked to me and quietly revealed that he was that fisherman. As to that fish, he removed one gold scale from his pocket and placed it in my hand.*

Hypnopompia: *Thoughts fly over a contract. I dismiss these as merely my wish to see a new sale contract.*

The Mirror; dream and waking-reality connections:
Hypnagogia: *Dorothy is in a whirlwind, taken from her safety into a tornado. Yet, she does land with the good witch. Perhaps the discord of the failed sale will in fact produce something new in the near future.*

Dream 1: *Very interesting. I worry in waking about a sale of a building, and this dream has me in a sailboat. Sale/sail. Homophones. In life the waking issue is about a sale. In the dream the sale is a sailboat. The wave comes as a dangerous threat. It may be predicting a still-dangerous ride with a future sale. My irrational gut feelings that this is not going to be a great year seems predicted by that great wave.*

Dream 2: *This dream is so comforting and relaxing. Grandfather was the sole grandparent alive for such a short few years of my life. Giving me that goldfish scale . . . reminds me of the scale—justice scale? Things might in the end work out after the trip over the water, like his story of the journey to this place of calm?*

Addendum: *February 1, 2020. Waking reality: new sale contract manifested, end of January.*

Addendum: *May 1, 2020. After unreasonable delay, new sale contract fails due to coronavirus.*

December, 20 2020. Final sale, with increased financial loss. Positive in manifestation of sale. Negative in the loss due to COVID-19 conditions and downswing of economy.

Thoughts: *Dream predicted the huge wave that threatened a sale, sailboat. Hypnagogic vision of Dorothy and her arrival at the Good Witch's feet awaits a happy ending. Huge wave with increased problems: COVID. Yet, final good end in closing.*

End of journal notes.

This example of dream journaling I hope gives a general idea of how the journal material manifests. Naturally, we will explore interpretation at a deeper level later in this work, yet the very simple manner of mirroring dream with waking reality can produce enough information to satisfy most dreamers. Not all dreams are deep and mysterious. The above is an example of something much in tune with most of us. We have waking-reality life challenges, worries, puzzles, problems, and sorrows. We seek to understand better, find clarity, and discover answers to our problems. Dreaming expands our view and presents us with some answers. By attending to our dream material, we can find support and guidance beyond our waking consciousness.

Later in this text we will talk about creating the personal dream dictionary, which keeps track of the many symbols that appear in our dreams. Yet, that discussion is for later, when we look more closely into the many ways we deepen our understanding of the many facets of dream imagery. To simply begin the above dream journal is sufficient and a good start.

CHAPTER FIVE

The Dreaming Mirror:
Dreaming Connections, Synchronicities
with Physical Reality . . .

Fill your paper with the breathings of your heart.

—William Wordsworth

We set up our dream journal to record our dreams along with our thoughts on the relationship of the dream with our waking-reality life, challenges, and desires. It is a direct approach and a good way to get started. For each journal entry we already have a sentence or two describing our main waking-reality issues. Yet, we can organize our thoughts better by additionally taking a scan of conditions both in our waking and in our dream scenario. We can ask some questions that can direct our thoughts on the dream mirror. Below are some easy yet helpful considerations.

1. As we revisit the dream, one of the first questions we ask concerns how we see ourselves in the dream. *Are we an active participant or an observer?*

We can look both ways to waking and dream. In waking do we see ourselves as one who actively interacts with our surroundings, work, and family, or do we feel we merely observe life without really participating? Do we feel that most often we are not seen or heard, that our needs are ignored? Is it possible that we do more thinking than acting?

Just by viewing our "double dream self" gives us insight on an issue we may be experiencing with our own self-worth. Do we feel we have so much we wish to say when in reality we say little or nothing? Does our position in a dream mirror reflect how we stand in life?

2. *Is our dream double [1] visible, on- or offstage, in the dream performance?*

We ask this now not in reference to being an observer or performer, but rather in reference to our knowing what we looked like in the dream. Is our dream double our current age, looking and acting like we do in our present life? Is the dream double younger or older, or even completely different from our waking self? Sometimes the dream double seems to be a different sex or nationality, wearing strange clothes, living in an exotic culture in a different time period. In these cases, indeed the stage is set very differently from the present. Yet, sometimes we are not aware of how we look.

As we take inventory of ourselves in a dream, we see ourselves differently from what appears in our bedroom mirror. If we are regressed to childhood, is the dream telling us we are acting childish in a particular situation? If we are older than our normal age, is this pointing to our attainment of wisdom with age, or with the drying up that comes with aging? There is no definite, no right or wrong, in any of these

1 Our dream double is how we appear in the dream; younger, older, or different in some way from our waking-reality physical self.

considerations. Yet, each digs deeply beneath the perceptual surface reality of who we believe ourselves to be. By showing up with a different physical appearance, the dream may be pointing to some actions prevalent in that particular age. If there is regression and we are returned to a younger age, is the dream situation along with our age trying to bring to memory a past event that shall help us shed light upon a present one?

3. Who is the main character in the dream?

We think of the dream like a movie plot. Is our dream double the main character or it is someone else? Is the main character someone we know? If the main character is a familiar person, are they acting strangely or out of character? If our dream double is the main character, is there anything notable or different in the way the dream double works from our waking self? In other words, does the main character say things totally out of character or perform functions different from waking reality? A lawyer might, for example, be a criminal in our dream. A professor might be an uncover agent.

This is all about actions. Running, working, talking, eating, hiding, celebrating, and such. What are the main actions of the main character? Mirroring waking life, how does this performance match something that is current? Is this main character bringing attention to the manner we are acting? Sometimes a dream character is merely an aspect of ourselves trying to awaken us to our hidden nature. Perhaps the main character in the dream is a hero performing great, seemingly impossible feats, while in life we are quietly hiding abilities that could open doors for our advancement and happiness. In such a dream the dream character is encouraging us to take the bushel off our heads and let the light shine! In other dreams, perhaps there is a less pleasant aspect of ourselves that comes through. The main character may be continually meddling and creating discord. Perhaps a hint that we carefully watch our criticism and wait to be asked for our opinions before giving them.

3. How do we feel in the dream? What emotions filled us?

Are we happy, sad, angry, confused, scared, amused, bored, captivated, mystified, or upset?

Once an emotion surfaces, let us think about our waking life. Does the emotion of the dream appropriately describe our reaction to something happening currently in waking life? Is it the exact opposite? Do we move through several emotions in the dream, bouncing from a high to a low? Again, does this match our waking expectations and disappointments in something hoped for yet absent?

We already know that our emotional state does enter into our dreaming. At times the dream may just be a way of trying to blow off steam from a very unpleasant hay with a series of stressful events. Frustration needs an outlet. Other times the fatigue of a weighty dose of struggles just lies heavy on us. Dreams of individuals who suffered great tragedies and are left with posttraumatic stress often report dreams where they are returned to the scene of the tragedies, with the emotions high and heavy.

Yet, those of us with the typical transient yet annoying challenges find these emotions in our dreams. Learning to recognize them helps us recognize our feelings and in the end deal with them. Perhaps we are angry about something, and our anger is getting out of control, interfering with our performance. A dream may manifest where our main character's anger destroys everything she touches. Waking and recognizing the effects of this in the dream mirrors upon our waking reality, helping us minimize the negative emotion by seeking a more peaceful approach to resolve our problems.

4. What is the major situation that stands out in the dream? Is it resolved? How?

We think about this situation and its resolution or lack of successful outcome. We ponder if we would have wished such an outcome or, if we had the opportunity, would we have manifested a different conclusion. How might we have acted or reacted and why?

Now moving to compare this situation with our waking reality, we think about current issues. Has the dream shown a novel manner of handing something? Is it a feasible solution to effect positive change? Often, we have all the necessary pieces of information in our life to successfully work out a problem. Yet, our waking consciousness thinks in a specific manner that may not be able to source the right course of action to happily solve our issue. In the dream consciousness, novel ways of looking at things result in creatively presenting us with alternatives unavailable to the waking mind. Other times the dream may present information that seems outside our waking personal experience. These later dreams present what can be looked at as sourcing some kind of collective unconsciousness, information that seems common to all humankind, having its origin in our nature rather than from our personal memory bank. In the end, sourcing a solution from a dream does help us with waking-reality problems.

5. Where does our dream take place? What is the setting?

A dream takes place somewhere. Like a play performed on a stage, it likewise can consist of several acts divided by a falling curtain that separates one act from another. There may be scenery shifts, since the first act may take place on a city street, the second may move on to an interior living room, with the third finishing in a forest far from civilization. Likewise, many of our dreams shift from one place to another. In our notes, we often see this shift by saying something like "and then everything changed, and I was somewhere else." Thus, here we take note of the "where" of the dream. If it is a short dream, we may have only one place to note. Naturally if it is like a three- or four-act play, we shall have more places. We should try to describe our dreamscape as fully as possible. We can pretend that indeed our dream is a play of several acts, one that we wish to produce. In order to do so, we need to be as descriptive as possible with the necessary settings. What do the dream places look like?

EXAMPLE:

A dreamscape description, one for each of the acts.

Act 1: *Takes place on a city street. It is Paris. I see the tall, elegant, gas streetlights, black-decorated poles with their hexagonal glass lanterns on top. The gold light diffuses into the night. I am on a side street, with the store windows lighted with mannequins displaying clothing in one. In another, a boulangerie, large crusty loaves of bread sit in the store window. There is no traffic, so I can easily see the cobblestone street. It is raining and I hear the pitter-patter creating a lovely music as the rain hits the slate roofs above. There is a bookstore, and I am standing in front of it looking at the beautiful, illuminated text, a book of hours displayed in the store window. The page is exquisitely painted with gold leaf and richly colored imagery. It is night, and the sky above is just dark with the rain, yet the gas light brings a magical golden glow into the sea of shifting shadows and dancing raindrops.*

Act 2: *Everything shifts, and I am looking at that Parisian street through a full-length, ceiling-to-floor door window. There is a small terrace beyond this window, which looks out to the city. I can see the Basilica of the Sacred Heart, the lighted white dome rising high, its beauty matching the starry sky above it. I turn to see I am in a beautiful apartment, something from a past era. The ceiling above me has elaborate plaster decoration, small cherubs at each corner of the room. In the center there is a huge medallion carrying a crystal chandelier. The floor is polished dark herringbone parquet. There is a huge bookcase occupying one entire side of the room. I hungrily devour the books with my eyes. They have leather covers, a soft coffee brown with delicate gold lettering. Opposite me is a doorway. I can smell coffee brewing, and I can hear voices speaking. There are four chairs, all deep-burgundy-colored velvet, set around a low glass coffee table, upon which sits a tray of chocolates alongside a dish of pastries. There are four small dessert plates set with four folded linen napkins. I seem to be waiting for others to join me. The room is brightly lighted, and the color, the white of the ceiling and walls, is warmed by the mahogany furniture, burgundy velvet, and polished wooden floor.*

Act 3: *I am in an ancient forest with towering trees. There is moss beneath my feet and a canopy of green above me. The sun is filtered through it all. I am making my way carrying a basket, collecting mushrooms. The mushrooms give off an earthy aroma. I have a pig as a companion. Green and brown fill my world, except for the hefty pig, who is quite large; a combination of pink and black coloring. Together we merrily make our way. The basket is of woven willow, rustic and old. I hear water running ahead and believe I am nearing a stream. Yet, I am content, in the forest, my pig and I collecting mushrooms.*

End dream scenario.

From this example we get the idea of what is meant by description. We try to remember as much as we can about "where" things take place in the dream. Pretending we are being asked to re-create our dream as a play of a few acts helps us see the details.

Now as we revisit our dreamscape, the territory on which the dream takes place, we ask ourselves why this place or these places. Does this present some significance to us? Is there some wish fulfillment? Has our mind given us the vacation we needed?

Do we see something that ties into our waking life or desires? Are we perhaps seeking a vacation and have been browsing catalogs on a particular place? The location is important since it tells us something about the place we find ourselves in.

In each of the above sample dream acts, the dream double is alone except for a pig. Whether in the city, in an apartment, or in the wild forest, the dream double is without human companionship. In comparison with life, the dreamer lived alone. Thus in examining the place we find it reveals something more, information on the dreamer and waking reality.

6. *What are the outstanding objects in the dream? In other words, what are the theatrical props on the dream stage?*

We revisit the dream, trying to remember what we encountered as the dream progressed.

In the example of the three acts staged in the previous dream, certain props found their way into the dreamer's examples. Let us revisit and **underline** the props.

Act 1: Takes place on a city street. It is Paris. I see the <u>tall, elegant, gas streetlights,</u> <u>black-decorated poles</u> with their <u>hexagonal glass lanterns</u> on top. The gold light diffuses into the night. I am on a side street, with the store windows lighted with <u>mannequins</u> displaying <u>clothing</u> in one. In another, a boulangerie, <u>large crusty loaves</u> <u>of bread</u> sit in the store window. There is no traffic, so I can easily see the cobblestone street. It is raining and I hear the pitter-patter creating a lovely music as the rain hits the slate roofs above. There is a bookstore, and I am standing in front of it looking at the <u>beautiful illuminated text</u>, a <u>book of hours</u> displayed in the store window. The <u>page</u> is <u>exquisitely painted with gold leaf and richly colored imagery</u>. It is night, and the sky above is just dark with the rain, yet the gas light brings a magical golden glow into the sea of shifting shadows and dancing raindrops.

Act 2: Everything shifts, and I am looking at that Parisian street through a full-length, ceiling-to-floor door window. There is a small terrace beyond this window, which looks out to the city. I can see the Basilica of the Sacred Heart, the lighted beautiful white dome rising high, its beauty matching the starry sky above it. I turn to see I am in a beautiful apartment, something from a past era. The ceiling above me has elaborate plaster decoration, small cherubs at each corner of the room. In the center there is a huge medallion carrying <u>a crystal chandelier</u>. The floor is polished dark herringbone parquet. There is a <u>huge bookcase</u> occupying one entire side of the room. I hungrily devour the <u>books</u> with my eyes. They have <u>leather covers, a soft</u> <u>coffee brown with delicate gold lettering</u>. Opposite me is a doorway. I can smell coffee brewing, and I can hear voices speaking. There are <u>four chairs,</u> all deep-burgundy-colored velvet, set around a <u>low glass coffee table,</u> upon which sits a <u>tray of chocolates</u> alongside a <u>dish of pastries</u>. There are <u>four small dessert plates</u> set with <u>four folded</u> <u>linen napkins</u>. I seem to be waiting for others to join me. The room is brightly lighted, and the color, the white of the ceiling and walls is warmed by the mahogany furniture, burgundy velvet, and polished wooden floor.

Act 3: I am in an ancient forest with towering trees. There is moss beneath my feet and a canopy of green above me. The sun is filtered through it all. I am making my way carrying a <u>basket</u>, collecting <u>mushrooms</u>. The mushrooms give off an earthy aroma. I have a pig as a companion. Green and brown fill my world, except for the hefty pig, who is quite large; a combination of pink and black coloring. Together we merrily make our way. I love this <u>basket, woven willow, rustic and old</u>. I hear water running ahead and believe I am nearing a stream. Yet, I am content, in the forest, my pig and I collecting mushrooms.

As we look at the underlined props, an amazing feeling comes over us (we do not consider the pig a prop, but a character, a creature in our play). Seen together, the props tell a story and evoke a feeling. Lets look:

<u>tall, elegant, gas streetlights</u>, <u>black-decorated poles</u> with their <u>hexagonal glass lanterns</u> on top; <u>mannequins</u> displaying <u>clothing</u>; <u>large crusty loaves of bread</u>; <u>beautiful, illuminated text</u>; a <u>book of hours</u>; a <u>page</u> <u>exquisitely painted with gold leaf and richly colored imagery</u>

a <u>crystal chandelier</u>; <u>books</u>; <u>leather covers, a soft coffee brown with delicate gold lettering</u>; <u>four chairs, all deep-burgundy-colored velvet</u>; a <u>low glass coffee table</u>; <u>tray of chocolates</u> alongside a <u>dish of pastries</u>; <u>four small dessert plates</u>; <u>four folded linen napkins</u>; <u>mahogany furniture, burgundy velvet</u>

<u>basket</u> collecting <u>mushrooms</u>; <u>woven willow, rustic and old</u>

Taken aside from the main text, the props tell a story of richness, warmth, comfort. While the dream persona double is alone, both in the dream and in life, the props that fill up the dreamscape are lush and beautiful. They tell a story where solitude works for the dreamer. There are comforts, joys, and beauty in the solitary existence.

7. Who are the other characters in the dream? What role do they play?

The previous example has a thin cast. There is the dream double, who is experiencing the three acts. There are offstage voices, which point to additional unseen dream cast members. There is also the companion pig. In our dreams there are often more characters interacting with us, communicating, or performing actions that help or hinder us as the dream plot moves along. We make a list of them along with their actions. We can look at them and give them positions as though they are actors in our play. Our dream plot broadens as we move from the lead character to the extras, who seem to play minor roles. In comparing our character list with our waking-life friends and acquaintances, we may notice some outstanding features that draw our attention. Are most of our characters children or infants? Are they elders? Are there childish or wise actions complementing or thwarting our every dream activity? We look at these characters and try to see how they relate to us. What might they be trying to show us? If we take their view for a moment, how do we feel? Do the dream characters present a dynamic that we recognize? Are they presenting something that is missing in our waking lives, something that may help us in our waking conflicts? Is the dream cast pointing to problems we fail to see in waking, that which we need to accept and work with instead of denying? These characters may complement or compensate for our waking actions, thus helping to highlight waking-reality strengths as well as weaknesses.

8. How is nature represented in the dream?

We spoke of setting in question 5. Setting naturally can include both indoor and outdoor scenes. Nature can be included in plants, bouquets of flowers, or insects that fly around indoors. Yet, how much of the dream includes something of a natural environment, something of the world not made by humans?

In the previous sample of the dream in three acts, only one scene takes place entirely in nature. In act 3, the mossy earth, the towering trees, and musky mushrooms were all part of a forest environment. Mushrooms were placed in a willow basket, which also is very rustic, earthy. In contrast to the first two scenes, the last seemed far from their cityscape. Yet, the first acts, although in the city, present an appreciation for the fall of rain, nature's gift upon the land, along with an awareness of the beauty in the night vista offered by the view from the window of the man-made cathedral in the setting of nature's starry night sky. It presents balance and harmony. Appreciation for nature thus presents itself in each part of the three-act dream presentation. This points to the dreamer, suggesting someone at home in both worlds.

In some dreams there are dragonflies, beautiful birds, butterflies, bees. Scenes may include lakes, oceans, mountainous terrain, or deserts. Other dreams may be quite confined to plastic furniture, artificial plants, steel modular units, and sterile inner and outer environments in city offices, cement sidewalks, and towering modern skyscrapers.

We thus look at our own dreams. Is nature missing from our dreamscape? Are we missing a connection with the earth in our waking life? Is there imbalance in our setting, too much or too little of something? Is there anything we can do to shift things to balance?

In conclusion, these are merely questions we can ask ourselves when we examine our dreams. They help us see more deeply into the dream without too much effort. And yet they reveal so much. They help us see that the dream is often a subtle way our unconscious is trying to wake us to something we might be missing in our waking day.

Below is a short list to remember. Use this checklist for a quick inventory of the dream before making a waking-reality comparison:

- *As we revisit our dream, one of the first questions we ask concerns how we see ourselves in the dream. Are we an active participant or an observer?*
- *Is our dream double visible, on- or offstage, in the dream performance?*
- *Who is the main character in the dream?*
- *How do we feel in the dream? What emotions filled us? Are we happy, sad, angry, confused, scared, amused, bored, captivated, mystified, or upset?*
- *What is the major situation that stands out in the dream? How was it resolved?*
- *Where does our dream take place? What is the setting?*
- *What are the outstanding objects in the dream? In other words, what are the props on the dream stage?*

- *Who are the other characters in the dream?*
- *How is nature represented in the dream?*

You see things, and you say, "Why?"
But I dream things that never were, and I say, "Why not?"
—George Bernard Shaw

SYNCHRONICITY

Sometimes we have a dream and, to our amazement, find ourselves experiencing "meaningful coincidences" in our waking life that directly mirror our dream events. The following is perhaps the most famous example of these very special coincidences. I would like to quote it directly from the work of Carl Gustav Jung, who coined the term "synchronicity" to refer to these "meaningful coincidences" of overlap between the imaginal dreaming experience and the waking domain. Dr. Jung begins:

> *My example concerns a young woman patient who, in spite of efforts made on both sides, proved to be psychologically inaccessible. The difficulty lay in the fact that she always knew better about everything. Her excellent education had provided her with a weapon ideally suited to this purpose, namely a highly polished Cartesian rationalism with an impeccably "geometrical" idea of reality. After several fruitless attempts to sweeten her rationalism with a somewhat more human understanding, I had to confine myself to the hope that something unexpected and irrational would turn up, something that would burst the intellectual retort into which she had sealed herself. Well, I was sitting opposite her one day, with my back to the window, listening to her flow of rhetoric. She had an impressive dream the night before, in which someone had given her a golden scarab—a costly piece of jewelry. While she was still telling me this dream, I heard something behind me gently tapping on the window. I turned round and saw that it was a fairly large flying insect that was knocking against the window-pane from outside in the obvious effort to get into the dark room. This seemed to me very strange. I opened the window immediately and caught the insect in the air as it flew in. It was a scarabaeoid beetle, or common rose-chafer (Cetonia aurata), whose gold-green color most nearly resembles that of a golden scarab. I handed the beetle to my patient with the words "Here is your scarab." This experience punctured the desired hole in her rationalism and broke the ice of her intellectual resistance. The treatment could now be continued with satisfactory results. (Jung 1969:109–110)*

While the previous example is quite stunning, our synchronicities may be more subtle. Perhaps we have dreamed of a particular special occasion. In the dream we may have enjoyed revisiting with those who once celebrated with us. Upon waking, we recorded the dream and thought it merely a lovely memory. Days might pass when suddenly, going through a drawer, we find a photo of that particular event. Since the event is one we have not thought of recently until the dream, we find it interesting. Both in the dream and in waking, the long-ago, almost forgotten event arises to engage our attention. That is synchronicity. In a dream we might find ourselves in conversation with an old friend we have not seen or thought about in years. Not long after, we may meet the friend as we go about our day. Certainly, the dream did not cause the meeting. Yet, there is a reason for the connection, which is special and meaningful. As to the "why," that question awakens our need to seek answers. Discovery. We are, after all, dream archeologists, digging beneath the layers to uncover the treasure.

In my own private therapy, an interesting example of synchronicity emerged just as I was attending to this chapter. A lovely analysand presented a dream during which Paul McCarthy appeared, singing one of her favorite songs. The song woke her up with her phone ringing in the waking-reality room. We spoke at length. I mentioned the way that life works with meaningful coincidences, dream and waking reality communicating with one another. I introduced the idea of synchronicity and related the previous story of the scarab. I consoled her as to the dream ending abruptly without conclusion, and urged her to return to it in a waking dream. Thus ended the session. I assured her more information would come. The following day brought amazing synchronicities; a series of events connected back to confirm the dream content's connection with waking reality. She emailed me the following:

> You will hardly believe this. Last Wednesday I had a minor car crash with an elderly lady. She was maneuvering to come out of a parking space, and I was driving by. This afternoon, I went into mediation and a few images and scenes popped up. Mainly around scarabs, lady bugs, and . . . beetles. And then "shabaam"; it clicked together! Actually, the phone ringing during our session was the elderly lady from the mild car crash, and her car is . . . a VW beetle of black color!!!

> And Paul McCartney is from the pop group Beatles or phonetically beetles asking me to go answer that phone, drilling. And again, the beetle coming through you in the tale of Jung and synchronicity, all wound up together.

Here we've seen a simple dream revisited in a waking dream meditation, and in the end a lovely series of synchronicities demonstrating how dream and waking reality work together to present a full picture of events, bringing them together, making them whole.

In visiting our dream material as described in this chapter, we begin uncovering the hidden messages of dreams, seeking to see and to better understand how dreams and waking relate. The dream is not something that dwells in isolation, but it lives alongside waking reality. Whereas waking consciousness is like the brilliant sun that shines upon the physical work, dream consciousness is the moon that lights our way through the darkness of night. Our awareness is the bridge between the two. We see our own wholeness, and by accepting our experiences both in the realm of dream and in waking, we can approach the task presented at the ancient temple of Delphi: "Know thyself."

CHAPTER SIX

Special Attention: The Characters in Dreams
Who or what do they represent?

Subjective or Objective?

The interpretation of dreams is a great art.
——Paracelsus

We already talked about looking at a dream as a play with several acts in which different characters play roles. What we did not discuss is the variety of appearances and the possible meanings beneath the manifest appearance of the characters. As in waking life, things are often not as simple as they appear. What is presented as something may in the end be something far different. Thus the question arises with reference to the individual characters who appear on the dreamscape. Are they who they seem to be?

Sometimes there are characters in the dream that we can recognize easily: people from our lives, present or past; individuals who play or played important or less significant roles in our personal or professional lives. They may or may not appear as they did in waking life. Sometimes these familiar dream characters—husbands, wives, friends, and colleagues—may act quite strangely, often contrary to their waking-reality counterparts. We need to ask, "Why?" What is the message in someone appearing and acting contrary to their waking-reality counterpart? Who are these dream characters in reality? Do they really represent what is manifest in the dream, or are they hiding something? Are they other than what we initially perceive?

Characters may be divided into the following categories:

1. Family, friends, or associates who are present, alive, and playing an active role in the current everyday flow of events. An example would be a spouse whom we see every day.

2. Persons who are absent from current life but who previously played an active role as family, friend, or career associate. This may refer to an old teacher, colleague, or family member who is still alive but not currently involved in the workings of our everyday life. We may not even speak to these people on a regular basis, or at all. A childhood playmate could fit into this category. For no reason other than time and distance, we are separated from the once-upon-a-time schoolmate.

3. Individuals who never interacted in our life but who were known to us through stories, through family history, or even on the more collective level, historically prominent people. Here we may have a visit from a grandparent we never met in life. Likewise, Mark Twain or Cleopatra may show up in our dream!

4. Characters who are strangers, not related to anyone we know in our waking lives. In dream they can appear as strangers or acquaintances we are comfortable with, or they may appear in relationships with us. These strangers do not bring up any type of waking connection to known characters from history, reading, or media.

5. Characters may appear as mythical beings, deities, angels, or archetypal figures such as the wise man or the hierophant.

Thus, the dream characters may be easily identified as mirroring either current players in our waking life, players now absent in our present but once part of our personal history, or merely individuals we know of but never actually crossed paths with in waking life. Yet, all we know from these three categories is the manifest appearance.

1. Let us examine the first category: present players in our waking life appearing in our dream.

Do these familiar dream characters merely represent themselves? Or do they—their images—arise in dream to catch our attention, to awaken us to something we are missing in our waking-reality perception?

DREAM EXAMPLE:
The dreamer is a woman in her midfifties.

I find myself in a large hallway in an old mansion. It feels familiar, yet I cannot place it. I know I have been here before and have a memory of standing outside admiring the flowers that line the road leading up to it. Strange, for I am inside, just remembering all this as I look at the splendor all around me in this wide foyer that runs the length of the house. The front door leads into it, with a rear garden door leading outside to the back. There is very dark paneling and mahogany floors. A grand staircase is off to one side, with an elaborate carved, polished wooden banister. There are boughs of white flowers draped around the balusters. High above me are huge chandeliers. They are on and they send rainbows of light into the space. The French doors are opened to the various side rooms, and I see huge halls as though there is a reception going on here. It is all so stately, and I think this must be a historically significant hotel. Suddenly I am aware that I am beautifully dressed. I look down at my hand and see a wedding ring, golden, elaborate on my finger. I am wearing a wedding gown. This surprises me. Furthermore, I see that the groom is a young man I know! I believe I could be his mother. I am confused. As I gather my wits, wedding guests gather around me, happily chatting. The mother of the young man introduces herself to all the guests. She taps her champagne glass with a silver spoon, and everyone becomes silent. "We are happy to welcome our new daughter," she begins. "Someday we shall have a huge celebration, but for now . . . our little gathering shall be our welcome. To the union!"

The dreamer woke with very mixed feelings. She brought the dream to discuss in analysis. She had never dreamed of being with anyone other than her husband before and was confused at being joined with someone younger than herself. We focus on the characters. She knows both the young groom and his mother. She works with the mother and frequently sees the son with his mother. This fits our first category: dream characters present and active in one's waking life. Next, we focus on her dream persona. This is she at her present age. She was observant, taking in the details of this huge mansion, a house of many rooms, all familiar yet strange to her. She was likewise a participant, the center of attention, the bride. We can conclude that the dream is circling around her.

Next, we investigate the presence of the groom. He does not speak directly to her. She knows his waking-reality counterpart who, like the dream groom, is younger than she.

The fact that he is not her waking-reality husband is important. The dream is using this image to say something else. There is the internal marriage, a union of the dream voice of intuition and the waking voice of reason. This alchemical marriage is important for true balance of decision-making. Her dream persona is her intuitive inner female, what I like to call the inner bride. We can look at her dream youth as representing her inner bridegroom. While the bride brings the voice of the depths, the bridegroom brings the waking rational voice. The dream suggests that reason (bridegroom) is younger, less mature than intuition (the inner bride). Amplifying this, the dreamer agrees that her mind, her thinking aspect, is less mature than her anima. She feels her thinking overworks to run her in circles. It blocks each decision she wishes to make by indicating pitfalls, leaving her immobile. It is her gut reactions, her intuitive feelings, that help her navigate through challenges and make solid decisions. Thus, the dream character of the young groom can be interpreted as representing her thinking functions, not the waking-reality individual whose appearance shows up in the dream.

Next, we look at the mother of the groom. Here again, the manifest appearance of this person matches someone in the dreamer's present life, a fellow worker. Yet, the question arises, is that what the dream wishes to present, a mirror of the waking-reality person? The dreamer indicated she respects the groom's waking-reality mother, who is older than she and in a higher position at work. She feels the dream mother is one who is telling her something important. The dream mother uses a silver spoon to tap a champagne glass. The dreamer felt the silver spoon was referring to some financial success. Wealthy people have silver spoons. Tapping a champagne glass seemed to indicate a reason for celebration. The dreamer felt the dream mother, an intelligent fellow worker, was supporting the union of her rational and intuitive faculties, even indicating that this was a beginning, that there would be a larger celebration. Rather than representing the actual waking-reality person, the dreamer took the qualities that represented the waking person to help her interpret the dream.

Since the dream indicated her marriage, the union between thinking and intuitive functions, the dreamer felt hopeful that she would overcome the procrastination inflicted by her overthinking functions. She shared that there were several opportunities open to her that she feared taking due to her circular thinking. The dream was telling her that together, the rational and intuitive would help her succeed. Whereas she had financial worries, the silver spoon hitting the champagne glass gave her hope.

This example demonstrates how dreams may use images of people from our life to represent other than their waking-reality selves. Thus the dreamer, first confused as to why she was marrying the young son of a work colleague in a dream, came to see that the wedding was of another sort, an interior alchemical marriage that the two main characters, mirroring known waking-reality individuals, merely pointed beyond their manifest appearance to a deeper meaning.

Naturally, sometimes a dream person can represent themselves. Other time, the dream is a clearinghouse of waking-reality situations.

DREAM EXAMPLE:
Waking-reality friends appearing in a dream. This dreamer is a male.

I am in this pub, and through the mirror behind the bar I see a gorgeous woman walk in. My girlfriend comes out of the ladies room just in time to see me turn to look at the girl. Sue [girlfriend] immediately comes over and picks up my beer. Staring at me, she empties it on my head before smashing it on the floor by my feet. My friend Bob takes her by the arm to lead her out as she was ready to scratch me. I am left soaking wet, stinking of the beer. I know I shall never see Sue again, and I feel relieved. I order a round of beer for everyone seated by me.

The dreamer reported that he was having second thoughts about his current girlfriend of only two months. He felt she tended to be overly possessive and easy to anger. His friend Bob had warned him about her, yet the dreamer had dismissed Bob's opinion. The dream gives voice to his waking thoughts, concerns, and fears. His dream girlfriend magnifies the traits of the waking girlfriend. Bob had warned him that she was volatile. In the dream, Bob, his best friend, took her away before she had time to do real damage. The dreamer felt it was time to cool the relationship. He accepted the dream as a warning.

Two weeks later he reported breaking up with his waking-reality girlfriend. The dream merely opened his eyes to see more clearly that they would not fit.

2. Characters appearing in a dream who were once but not currently part of waking life.

DREAM EXAMPLE:
Dreamer is a female in her midsixties, recently separated.

Her dream is short. She is in a restaurant having dinner with John, her boss of possibly thirty years past. They are arguing about paying the bill. She is insulted that he invited her to lunch to discuss an office problem and in the end now expects her to pay for it. In anger, she rises and turns her back on him as she attempts to leave the restaurant. The problem is that the doorman is holding an umbrella at an angle, which blocks her escape. She ends up falling flat on her face, at which point she wakes.

She has not seen John in decades. He was older than she and possibly is not even alive. We conclude he must represent something that wishes to get her attention. She fondly remembers him: kind, understanding, very supportive of all his employees. He always had time for every detail, every challenge, anywhere and anytime it appeared. Thus, in the dream his dream persona is in contradiction to his true waking character. This is another hint that it is not John in the dream.

I asked the dreamer to place one defining characteristic on the waking John. The answer was patience. We conclude that John is present in the dream to represent patience.

The situation at the table reflects the opposite quality: misunderstanding The dreamer believes she was a guest at the lunch. She is not. She refuses to negotiate and attempts to leave, an act that is blocked.

The dreamer laughs at this point. She admits that in her present life, her inflexibility has led to her recent estrangement. The marital issue began with a friend reporting seeing her husband having long lunches with a female colleague. She refused to listen to what she felt would be lies, and merely asked him to leave. In the intervening weeks, she refused his calls and his attempts to present his side of the story.

The lunch mirrors the location in waking life, where the problem resided. Her refusal to listen, to attempt to leave, all mirrors her waking self. Yet, the appearance of John is significant. By seeing that John is patient, understanding, and honest, it gives her pause to think about her spouse of twenty years. Did she act too rashly in threatening her relationship on this one waking-reality event? Was this misunderstanding not something that could be resolved?

The once-part-of-her-life, now-far-removed appearance of the dream John helped the dreamer focus on "understanding." In the end she did meet with her spouse and worked things out; they listened to each other's concerns, just as her old boss John did in life. His image brought forth understanding, and she decided she was too hasty in forming her negative opinion of what she perceived was an illicit meeting. The luncheons were proved to be innocent, work related, and not at all the threatening scenario of her overactive imagination. The dream opened her to reevaluate and thus saved her marriage.

3. Individuals who never interacted in our life but who are known to us through stories, through family history, or even on the more collective level, historically prominent people.

Here we may have a visit from a grandparent we never met in life, yet there are stories about this grandparent. We are familiar with much about their life, likes, and overall life situation. On the other hand, Mark Twain or Cleopatra may show up in our dream. When this happens, it is most often not an afterlife/mediumistic visit. Depending on the dream and the circumstances, such appearances usually come to highlight an aspect of our present life that needs focus. Thus, say Mark Twain appears. It could be our life needs humor and insight. Cleopatra might indicate that there is something beautifully seductive. Because Cleopatra VII was noted for her sharp intelligence, her real seduction was her mind, not her physical beauty. Yet, since her life ended tragically, perhaps her appearance might be a warning of some sort. If a grandmother we never met appears, the actions around her would indicate the reason for her presence. If we see her in the kitchen, handing us something she just baked, it could point to something comforting and supportive. We depend on our memories to deliver us information about these dream characters.

4. Characters who are strangers, not related to anyone we know in our waking lives.

In dream they can appear as strangers, acquaintances we are comfortable with, or they may appear in relationships with us. For the most part we often have dreams populated with many strangers. They are the extras in our play. Yet they are important as we must pay attention to their appearance and their actions. If they are dressed in a certain manner their attire might point to something important. The doctors, policemen, the judges, the priests, the border patrol, and the baker all dress appropriately for their careers. Their uniforms thus announce this. The situations they are in and how they interact with one another as well as with our dream persona, give clues to meaning. The police may be in a parade or helping an elderly person cross a busy street. They may be directing traffic, or they may be apprehending a criminal, often we can look at each and ask these questions: What if I were that character? Would my life be better or worse? Can I learn from this character? Is this character mimicking me, showing me something I am missing about myself? These characters are very important for they give us deep insight beyond our waking perception of ourselves, our actions, and our present situations.

5. Characters may appear as mythical beings, deities, angels, or archetypal figures such as the wise man or the hierophant.

When we are on a spiritual journey, our dreams can take on a numinous nature, with wondrous appearances establishing themselves on our dreamscape. There are many different ways to interpret these characters, but the best is to say they, in their many different roles, are often teachers. In shamanism we have power animals and teaching spirits. In various religions we have deities and angels. And in esoteric teaching we see priests and priestesses, seers, and alchemists. There are also various archetypal figures, characters representing qualities widely displayed and typically recognized as the Innocent, Everyman, Hero, Outlaw, Explorer, Creator, Ruler, Magician, Lover, Caregiver, Jester, and Sage. Each of these images carries intrinsic meaning . . . all naturally interpreted along with a dream scenario.

Examples: The Innocent usually represents one at the beginning of a journey, enthusiastic and optimistic. Perhaps in a dream we see the Innocent as a youth wearing rose-colored glasses. The message would be to go carefully, since the optimism may be challenged by reality.

The Everyman can make an appearance in the form of the Green Man, rooted to the earth like the tree of life, yet the face in the great bough demonstrating how the branches rise to embrace the heavens. Grounded yet rising to heavens, in dream we feel how it expresses keeping one's feet solidly connected to Earth while we glance to the heavens. It is a necessary message to the Innocent.

The Hero or Heroine, Explorer, and Rebel. Here we may have a dream visit by Lawrence of Arabia or Joan of Arc. We may have an astronaut or deep-sea diver. We may have Gertrude Bell, who broke with the Victorian rules of her time to explore the Mideast without the sanction of formal authority! Each broke with the reigning powers, explored the unknown, and went courageously ahead, becoming inspirations. The visit of these archetypes points to a break with what is accepted to cross the line into something new.

The Creator, Magician, and the Ruler can appear in a dream as a boss, president, royalty, or deity. These archetypes point to the imaginative and inventive. This is about building something, making a dream come true and then being responsible for it.

The Lover and the Caregiver appear representing a medical, environmental, or charity organization. They may be simply represented by the archetype of the loving grandparent taking care of children, or the mother cow, like the Egyptian deity Hathor, feeding her children, offering nourishment along with love and charity. Movie idols can appear, focusing on the romantic, the relationship of human love.

The Jester. As Mark Twain represents the best in humor, so does the Jester appear to bring fun, often wisdom, in the comedy.

The Sage. Here the wise, robed old man or woman is often carrying an ancient papyrus, or a single candle points to wisdom teaching.

Each of the above can be represented by the characters of the dream. There is no clear distinction, and there is often overlap where one character may hold qualities that represent more than one archetype. The Jester may likewise play the part of the Sage, as in a play, where the Fool is often the wisest character in the performance.

As we pay attention to our dreams and the various dream characters who appear, we can become familiar with them, immediately seeing that when a particular archetype shows up, they represent something very special and unique to us. With practice, like a relationship that demands our attention, the dream characters reveal more of their identities.

CHAPTER SEVEN

The Waking Dream Revisited

The seat of the soul is where the inner world and the outer world meet. Where they overlap, it is in every point of the overlap. (Novalis 1980:48)

The dreams come. The journaling is begun. Our thoughts are recorded. It is a beginning. It is hoped that with our awakened attention, more dreams are remembered. We are on our way to becoming seasoned dream explorers. Our initial view now effectively scans and gently picks away at the surface of what initially appeared as the manifest dream content. We uncover and make relevant connections with waking-reality challenges and events. This is a good beginning, and sometimes it is enough, since the dream may not present a vast territory of perplexing or strange imagery. Yet, some dream material can be more challenging, bringing us into the strangeness that only hints at making sense. Here is where reinforcement comes in. When we visit a new place in waking reality, we often revisit through images in a book, a video, or our personal journaling of our visit. We perhaps took one trip to an exciting foreign land such as Egypt, where we only briefly visited tombs and temples. We journaled and purchased travel and antiquity books, and upon return home we browse through all these to learn more and expand our waking-reality journey. We may choose to revisit our exotic country, focusing more narrowly in our return visit, attempting to better know one particular region. It is our beginning, whetting our appetite, opening us to increasingly wider and deeper experiences. For the dream we can accomplish something similar. We can read and reread our journal, trying to remember missing dream segments and filling in more completely some of our descriptions. Yet, in the end, meaning may remain elusive. We have this incredible dream that leaves us more questions than answers. How might we fill in the missing segments?

The answer comes by reentering our dream experience through what I call the waking dream. The waking dream is our return visit to the dreamscape. Like a lucid dream, we are aware of the exercise, aware we are experiencing a dream in which we may interact and communicate with the different characters. We accomplish this by altering our consciousness, shifting our attention and focus from the waking-reality external environment to the inner landscape of the imaginal, the place where mental imagery rises. This is much like the shamanic journey, where we alter consciousness to enter onto a dreamscape in service of healing, understanding, and wisdom. These altered-state experiences and shamanic and waking-dream exercises help us work out perplexing dreams and solve problems and creative blocks, as well as enhancing our ability to remember our nighttime dreams. Furthermore, the more we focus inwardly, the better acquainted we become with the inner landscape. We gain insight and understanding, benefiting from these imaginal journeys. The waking dream joins trance, meditation, and shamanic-journey practices, which are widely recognized, revered, and honored for the healing and information received. Take the example of synchronicity, with the dreamer who sought to reenter the dream that abruptly ended as she listened to Beatles music, with the ringing of her waking-reality phone waking her. She entered the waking dream by willing herself back into the nighttime dream while in the waking state. Below we shall learn the process.

The Process of Entering the Imaginal: The Waking-Dream Experience

The intention to reenter a nighttime dream is usually pretty clear. We wish to better understand it. Like the Beatle dreamer, we may have been awakened before a dream concluded. Thus, parts elude us and possibly a resolution may be left hanging. The waking dream gives us the opportunity to revisit.

We find a dream that has left us with questions that remain unanswered, even after an exhaustive amplification process of investigating characters, landscape, and actions. We articulate our concerns. We wish to reenter the dream to see more clearly something that may aid us to better understand its message.

Although the initial dreamscape opened while we were sleeping, the waking dream is approached when we are fully awake. It is a matter of shifting our focus from our waking-reality environment to the inner landscape of the imaginal. The territory is the same; the approach is merely different. At night we put our head on the pillow and are enveloped in the evening darkness as we drift from beta, waking consciousness, to the alpha/theta of the imaginal land.

Looking at our dream journal accounts, we shall choose something that we wish to explore in greater depth. The following dream was recorded in a dream journal.

DREAM JOURNAL:

Date: February 7, 2018. The Masked Stranger.

I am in a large ballroom. It looks like my old grade school gymnasium, yet it is grander and larger. Everyone is wearing masks. It appears to be a masked ball. I do not know the occasion and think it is strange, finding it difficult to move around the dance floor when everyone is engaged in dancing. I alone seem to be wandering between the couples. No one notices me, and I am pleased with that. I touch my face and realize that I am not wearing a mask. Even stranger. After a while of wandering through the dancers, I make my way to the stage door, remembering this also gives me entry to the stairs, which lead not only to backstage but also to the door that opens outside. I push through the door, only to be shocked that a rather large Harlequin masked figure is waiting for me there. In this in-between space, he puts out his hand to me, leading me up the stage stairs.

I wake.

The recorded dream is an actual dream. For our purposes, let us have it double for any dream, either experienced or made up for a dream journal entry. Let us pretend this is our dream. We first look at it with our dreaming lens. By visiting it in this manner, we can uncover as much as we are able.

1. As we revisit our dream, one of the first questions we may ask concerns how we see ourselves in the dream. Are we an active participant or an observer?

Answer: We are a participant in that we are on the dance floor of the masquerade, and yet we seem not part of but apart from it. We are not wearing a mask. No one seems to notice our presence on that floor. We are very much active in the space outside the room, interacting with the mysterious Harlequin figure.

2. Is our dream double visible, on- or offstage, in the dream performance?

Answer: Our dream double is visible and interestingly seems to play the most important role offstage, beyond the dance floor. There is no information on age.

3. Who is the main character in the dream?

Answer: The dream double is definitely the main character, and the only one where real action takes place. While the floor is apparently filled with masked dancers, they are more like extras on the dream stage.

4. How do we feel in the dream? What emotions filled us? Are we happy, sad, angry, confused, scared, amused, bored, captivated, mystified, or upset?

Answer: The dream double's actions of wishing to leave, of feeling like no one notices them, points to a sense of not belonging. They are confused by the event, not knowing its purpose.

5. What is the major situation that stands out in the dream? How was it resolved?

Answer: The dreamer seems not to like being at the masked ball, instead threading their way to escape. They succeed in leaving the room only to be stopped and taken somewhere by the Harlequin. So yes, they have escaped. Yet to what?

6. Where does our dream take place? What is the setting?

Answer: The setting is like an old gymnasium, which is now larger in the dream.

7. What are the outstanding objects in the dream? In other words, what are the props on the dream stage?

Answer: The outstanding prop is the mask everyone is wearing except the dreamer. Perhaps the costume of the Harlequin stands out as well.

8. Who are the other characters in the dream?

Answer: The dream persona, the masked dancer/extras, the Harlequin

9. How is nature represented in the dream?

Answer: Nature is only suggested in the door that leads outside.

Conclusions: In the dream the dreamer feels alienated. He feels he is the only one not wearing a mask. He escapes yet does not achieve the goal of leaving completely, since he is led upstairs, backstage, by a mysterious Harlequin, a silent stranger dressed in a black-and-white diamond-patterned costume.

The previous example is a dream in which we understand some aspects but wish to explore others. As we read, let us pretend this is a one-act play. Does it satisfy us, or does it leave us wishing to know more? It does feel like a cliffhanger, doesn't it? So many dreams are like this, a plot ending before the story is completed. Thus, it is easy for us to see that were this our dream, we might have one really important top question: Where is the Harlequin figure taking our dream persona, and what happens next? (Naturally, we wish to know who or what our mysterious Harlequin represents.)

Thus, having reviewed our dream entry, we come up with what we most wish to know. Once we have our question, we are ready to revisit the dream in a waking dream.

The dream scenario is clear in our head. We remember the details as best as we can. Armed with our question, we take our first step in entering the waking dream.

We have the time set. We need about an hour. We need a space where we will be undisturbed and comfortable. Perhaps there is an easy chair in our bedroom or office where we can shut the door, turn off the ringer on our phone, and be left undisturbed.

We take our dream journal and in the back of the book we can dedicate pages to "Waking Dreams." We write the date and the name of each dream we are investigating. Remember, we may be choosing a dream we had several days ago. As we record dream entries each day, a revisit or a waking dream will naturally not be recorded immediately after the original entry. At the end of our journal, working backward, we can record all our waking dreams in one place. If we use a computer file for our dream journal, we have a choice. We can either open a separate file for all waking dreams, or we can go to the original dream entry and record our waking dream with a new date right at the end of the original recording. That is the beauty of computers; they make space whenever we need them. I use this technique for presenting synchronicities, the meaningful coincidences that turn up a day or two after a dream. I merely place the date and the information right beneath the original dream study. The computer just allows the "insert" by electronically moving things to accommodate the reorganization. In a book journal, naturally the little coincidences need be added along the narrow edges of the pages or pasted in with extra sheets. It still works as it always did for me, since I enjoyed physical book dream journals for years. The computer is just easier these days, so I welcomed it. I currently have all my dreams on the computer, yet for years I used beautiful books. When I travel, I still love to dedicate a physical dream book, since it is an easy way to record dreams at any time, anywhere, without depending on technology, electricity, and the internet. And for whatever reason, I really love the feel of my fingers on the pen. There is something very visceral about it, as though the words are literally flowing from my veins through the ink to the page. I never get this feeling writing on the computer, but it does still record my thoughts and help me work with the many dreams. My advice is to use whatever method appeals the most.

We have our intention upon our dream journal page:

WAKING DREAM

Date   **Original Dream Title**   **Question:**

Were the previous dream example our dream, our questions might be "Where is the Harlequin figure taking our dream persona? What happens next?"

The stage is now set.

Once we have connected as fully as possible with the dream we chose for a waking dream, we can find ourselves a comfortable position. Next, we need something to help us shift our consciousness. I recommend setting up a drumming recording on a cell phone. There are free recordings online of twenty to thirty minutes of drumming. The beating of the drum assists us in shifting our consciousness. The steady monotonous sound of a rattle or a drum signals the brain to enter alpha and theta consciousness. The shift of the drumbeat at the end of these recordings signals the return to the ordinary waking state of beta consciousness (Neher 1962:153). Used for centuries for shamanic journeying, it works beautifully assisting us in shifting our focus from waking consciousness to the inner domain of the imaginal. I well remember during my shamanic training when we were instructed to seek shamanic journeying to deepen our understanding of our dreams. While our shamanic work incorporated an understanding of nonordinary reality that is not incorporated in our waking-dream exercise, the process of achieving the altered state is greatly enhanced by the sonic drumming utilized by shamans for centuries.

We play our drumming recording and close our eyes. We use these techniques of relaxation to bring us to the space between waking and sleeping, the space where mental imagery arises. In order to honor the shift from waking to imaginal consciousness, we can picture ourselves in front of a door. We begin on one side of this door, in a room we can label waking consciousness. Beyond the door is the imaginal landscape of the dream. In our mind we see ourselves rise and move toward our imaginal door. We can see the beauty of its polished wooden surface. We can reach out to touch its oval burnished-gold knob. We hear the drumming and imagine it comes from the imaginal space on the other side of the door. We are anxious to enter and thus we touch that knob, turning it while gently pushing the door open. We now cross the boundary and enter the other side of that door. This first step honors, acknowledges our passage into the altered state. We are experiencing a different reality now. We welcome the experience as the imaginal door gently closes behind us. At the end of our experience, the drumming shall change its beat, signaling us that it is time for the experience to end and for us to find our way back through the imaginal door. We thus imagine this door once again and move from the imaginal landscape through the doorway and back into our waking-reality room. We keep this entry-and-exit scenario in our mind for each of our waking-dream experiences. We always seek to cross the portal at the beginning and end of each visit. For now, we have crossed into the imaginal realm, and it is time to experience our visit.

THE WAKING-DREAM EXPERIENCE: WHAT TO EXPECT

First we just allow images to arise, not trying to control anything. Sometimes an imaginal landscape just appears. We have crossed the portal, and we need just observe. If no imagery appears at all, it may take work to attempt to imagine we are experiencing the chosen dream landscape, revisiting it. We try to call it to mind and allow our memory to manifest all. The important thing is to be a good observer. Each image carries meaning, so we must accept all of what comes. In our mind we seek to see more, to see if we missed something in our nighttime dream experience. If we have questions, we bring them to mind, allowing the imagery to arise and shift before us. New characters may appear, and the landscape may shift as new thoughts enter. We accept everything that comes, since this is all part of expanding the original dream. This new information may show up in surprising ways, with new episodes adding and expanding the view. What manifests may seem totally unlike anything we anticipated, not at all similar to the original dream. Yet, we must remember all of it. We remain attentive to the sights, sounds, and feelings that arise.

If there is fear of falling asleep while we are listening to the beat of the drum recording, we can always hold something in our hands while we are moving into our altered-state experience. If we should begin to fall asleep, our hands will relax, dropping the items we hold, thus awakening us. We may enter the waking dream as often as we like. We should honor it as we do the nighttime dream, recording it in our dream journal with date and name and additionally identifying it as a waking dream in service of learning more of the original nighttime experience, noting the date of the original dream as well. Doing this several times will bring the hidden nature of the dream forward, helping us understand it better.

Seated comfortably, safely undisturbed, book nearby, we merely listen to the beating of the drum while our attention flows with what arises on the imaginal landscape. Armed with our intention, we relax into the experience. Our experience will flow within the twenty-minute recording with a callback. Thirty-minute recordings might be too long in the beginning. We stay aware and focused on our quest, to see more of the nighttime dream, to better understand its meaning.

We close our eyes and just keep repeating the question in our mind. Slowly, images shall appear and quickly disappear. At first, they may seem without a story line. We let them come. Images may be visual or auditory. As the drumming continues, the mind relaxes and enters the altered state. The experience manifests on its own. Images and thoughts arise. All we need to do is observe and interact with what comes. We can communicate with beings that appear. Often, we will see a shift of imagery that accompanies our questioning. The conversation is not a direct one where complete sentences come in reply to our inquiries. Yet, the images that arise have much to tell us. We just allow things to manifest. At the end of the drumming there is a change in beat. It awakens our mind to move from the relaxed alpha/theta altered state. We return to beta waking consciousness. The recording ends. We sit for a moment gathering our thoughts.

Quietly we open our eyes. We have at least a half hour left of our dedicated waking dreamtime. We open our journal and we record our experience.

In response to the previous example dream journal entry, the dreamer did enter a waking dream. The questions were "Where is the Harlequin figure taking our dream persona? What happens next?"

Here is the journal entry:

Date: *February 9, 2018*

Waking Dream: *The Masked Stranger*

I closed the door of my office. It is early morning. I seek my waking dreams before my spouse awakes. I have an hour. Where is the Harlequin taking me in this dream?

Waking-Dream Report:

Eyes closed, I am back in that ballroom, the old auditorium. I feel like this is a replay of Groundhog Day. I am making my way across the dance floor. Hmm. I remember something important now. In that movie, each replay was met by an action that shifted things, helped things move along in a more positive fashion. I am not going to repeat my moves of the recent dream. I am going to linger on this dance floor a bit longer. I know I cannot be seen, so I decide to play a joke on the masked dancers. I move among them and yank off their masks. I am not invisible to them now, yet there is no sign of recognition from any of them. We are simply strangers on this floor. I move on. I still do not wish to stay on this dance floor. Suddenly I see that only the center of the floor remains filled with the masked dancers. The others, now freed of the masks, are mingling all around the sides of the room. There are refreshments, which sit on office desks. Strange. I move to walk among them. Everyone is busy, eating, drinking, and working at the same time. I find I have files in my hand now. I see an open drawer of a filing cabinet and realize I have removed these files. I see masks dangle from them. I touch my face and realize that now, at this periphery of the dance floor, in this space where others have no masks on, I am the one wearing the mask. I yank it off. The Harlequin stands in front of me, replacing the filing cabinet. He just stands there. Completely silent and unmoving. What is he waiting for? I realize I wanted to know where he was taking me. His arms stretch wide as though to say, "Here? Here?" Where is here? I do not belong here. I know I must leave. If the Harlequin is here, then he is not going to interrupt my leaving. I turn my back and walk to the door by the stage. I stop. I still do not know what that Harlequin wants. I push open that very same door, just knowing he is going to be there. He is. Yet, that door is to the very same strange office-like space, the periphery of the ballroom. Except now I realize this is my office. I get it. I understand. The Harlequin nods. He hands me the folder I left behind. One mask is on it. Mine. I understand. I must come to terms with this. I must do something about my job.

Waking-Dream Discussion:

The waking dream alerts me to what I have not been able to accept. I feel like an alien working a job I hate. I want to leave, but I need the job. I am trying to complete a degree while I am working a job completely divorced from my interests and abilities. I believe the dream is about this. Masks all around, People with interests far removed from mine. I am wearing a mask at times to fit in. Is that Harlequin me? Silent, am I not speaking up, not coming to terms? I cannot run away from this. The Harlequin is there handing me that mask, pointing to me, hiding. I cannot stay at this job, which is interfering with my academic and personal life. I need to find an answer, a new job.

In the weeks that followed, this dreamer sought his way, placing applications for extending his education as well as working in a situation more to his interests. The waking dream showed him the way.

This example demonstrates how revisiting a nighttime dream can help clarify its meaning. Additionally, it is beneficial in increasing our experience in the altered state. The more we seek the dreaming, the easier it becomes to enlarge the imaginal domain.

Waking-Dream Review

1. Begin by devoting two days a week to revisiting dream material, in order to more fully explore aspects of the dream that remain puzzling.

2. Designate a particular room as the waking-dream room, where an hour may be spent uninterrupted.

3. Have a drumming recording placed on a phone or tablet to be used to help initiate the dreaming altered state.

4. Open a dream journal page and place date and name of the particular dream to be explored, along with a new date of the waking dream.

5. Have a question ready to explore from the chosen sleep dream.

6. Comfortably take a seat, turn on the recording, and close the eyes.

7. Focus upon the question. Let the drumming fill and block out the external.

8. Accept what comes. The scenario may repeat much of what was experienced in the night dream, or it may be surprisingly different. Keep the mind on the question and be aware of what happens and who appears. Generally, the answer to the dream question is not going to manifest in an easily understood sentence. Rather, images and thoughts arise that need study and clarification once we return to waking consciousness.

9. When the drumming recording sounds the callback, mentally say a few words of appreciation for whatever images rose. Gently open the eyes and record the experience.

Our entire experience can be completed in about an hour. We bring to mind how we felt during the original dream episode and, immediately upon waking, after it. We compare those feelings to how we feel now after this waking-dream episode. An emotionally charged dream is full of potential. Strangely enough, I have often listened to terrifying dream scenarios that were so deeply disturbing they produced enough adrenaline to wake the dreamer middream! It is an effective way of the unconscious getting our attention. Some of these dreams actually have messages, which become clear to the dreamer who is brave enough to reenter in a waking dream. The bravery comes with the assurance that in a waking dream, like a lucid dream, we are able to chase the demons. We are in charge, unlike during the nightmare, where events can whirl beyond our control.

Another example of a dream that proved terrifying to the dreamer demonstrates the power of the waking dream to clear things up! Below is the dream verbally reported to me.

In the night dream, a woman, recently widowed, found herself walking on a deserted street when suddenly a huge wave flooded the sidewalk and took her in its wake. She screamed and flailed her arms, trying to swim. She realized that along the side of this rapidly flowing current, the sidewalk was dry. There were people gathered on both sides just watching her scream. No one offered any help. Suddenly the water pushed her into a phone booth. The phone was ringing, and she picked it up, frantically screaming that she needed help. Her deceased husband was on the phone. He quietly listened without commenting as she complained that no one was helping her. As though things could not get worse, as she glanced out of the phone booth glass, there was a huge brown bear clawing the window, trying to get in with her.

She woke terrified.

We sought the waking dream in order to investigate the situation. At the very least, I instructed her in her waking ability of having control, like in a lucid dream. She could stop the flood. She could tell the bear to get lost. And in the end, she could speak to her husband, telling me how disappointed she was that he was not helping her with her problems.

She entered the waking dream and followed the instructions, yet something interesting happened. The people along the side of the road turned out to be angelic beings in her waking-dream version. The bear was no longer threatening but was a helping spirit who wished to empower her with courage and strength. In the end, her entry into the phone booth led to communication with her deceased husband. She missed him and was overwhelmed by the "flood" of paperwork left upon his passing.

The waking dream had opened the emotional outpouring that she had kept bottled up. Presenting a brave front to the world did not match her true emotions. The dream and the waking dream helped her better understand what was happening. The death was accompanied by a flood of emotions, a tsunami of paperwork in which she found herself drowning without any help. With spiritual guidance she found her way, better equipped through her understanding of the true dilemma. It would be challenging, but like the blissful marriage, the sorrowful aftermath would in time flow onward. It would eventually bring her to yet another doorway, like the phone booth, a new place of communication and of salvation. The waking dream was the real help in shining light on what at first came as a terrifying dream.

Each of us can safely use the waking-dream process to investigate our more perplexing dreams. Together with the mirror study of the sleep dream, we can uncover some of the hidden treasures that help us understand not just a little aspect of a dream, but the greater territory of ourselves and our waking-reality challenges. There is more to dreaming than simple stories.

CHAPTER EIGHT
Setting Up the Personal Dream Dictionary, First View: Perception

I have had a most rare vision. I had a dream, past the wit of man to say what dream it was. . . . The eye of man hath not heard, the ear of man hath not seen, man's hand is not able to taste, his tongue to conceive, nor his heart to report, what my dream was. Methought I was—and methought I had—but man is but a patched fool, if he will offer to say what methought I had. The eye of man hath not heard, the ear of man hath not seen, man's hand is not able to taste, his tongue to conceive, nor his heart to report, what my dream was. (William Shakespeare, *A Midsummer Night's Dream*, Bottom, act 4, scene 1)

Upon our waking, who has not agreed with Shakespeare's Bottom that what we remember of the night's strange happenings lie beyond our comprehension—too weird, too bizarre for even the most astute. Yet, be that our very first opinion, perhaps on second look we may find that beneath the strange wrappings our dream is quite revealing. Perhaps that donkey head we felt upon our shoulders really does hold something beneath its flesh. Our dream journals are filled with our dream stories and our initial attempts at understanding what each dream is attempting to tell us.

Thus, at this point we have established our ritual of seeking, recording, and studying our dreams with our method of dream mirroring. We have our dedicated practice of working with our dream journal. Now we are ready to dive more deeply.

Our dream journals should be well established with daily recordings when we move on to create a second dream book, our dream dictionary. Here is where it gets interesting. While the dream journal aims to help shed light on particular dreams and specific issues in our waking life, the dream dictionary moves beyond singularity as it opens the world of dream language to a stage expanding beyond our personal experience! It is a living vessel of wisdom arising from the depths of our unconscious. It connects us with our far ancestors and with deep visions that awaken us to a land beyond our limited personal view.

Our first view of the dream is something I call our initial perception. We write the dream as we remember it. We detail the who, the what, and the where. We go through the initial process of viewing it like a play of one or several acts. We pretend we must set up the staging, the props, and the roles of the characters. We must define the scenery and place, inside or out, fancy or plain. All this comes at the beginning. When we want to pull the dream apart for all the pieces that come together to create it, we need not go very deeply. In fact, one dream may be viewed pretty universally in this manner.

Let us return to the Harlequin dream we discussed above. This time we are going to revisit it solely for the superficial details.

Date: February 7, 2018. The Masked Stranger.

I am in a large ballroom. It looks like my old grade school gymnasium, yet it is grander and larger. Everyone is wearing masks. It appears to be a masked ball. I do not know the occasion and think it is strange, finding it difficult to move around the dance floor when everyone is engaged in dancing. I alone seem to be wandering between the couples. No one notices me, and I am pleased with that. I touch my face and realize that I am not wearing a mask. Even stranger. Finally, I make my way to the stage door, remembering this also gives me entry to the stairs, which lead not only to backstage but also to the door that opens outside. I push through the door, only to be shocked that a rather large Harlequin masked figure is waiting for me there. In this in-between space, he puts out his hand to me, leading me up the stage stairs.

In our perceptual view we are making no deep assumptions. We are merely looking at this as though it is a street map. We are reporting on solely what we see in front of us.

The first sentence is revealing. The "I" is the dreamer manifesting as what we call the dream persona. If we look through the entire short dream, we see this dream persona is the main character. We do not know if the waking dreamer matches the dream persona in age or appearance. We can conclude only that the dreamer is experiencing the dream.

The place: Things begin in a ballroom that looks like an old grade school gymnasium. Grander and larger, yet no more description is given.

The second act: The dreamer moves to a hallway where there is a door leading out and stairs leading to the stage.

List of other characters: There are couples wearing masks. No comment is known as to whether the dreamer knows these characters or if he is among strangers.

Harlequin: We may or may not be familiar with what a Harlequin represents. If we understand without looking up the word, we can say a Harlequin is a silent figure in a black-and-white costume, usually geometrical in design such as diamonds. If we have no idea, then we can merely say a mysterious person called a Harlequin. The perceptual is very much the surface of what appears to us upon our first view. The dreamer in using the term obviously understands its meaning. If we were to use the term Spider-Man or Superman, many would likewise understand completely without the need for additional clarification. The perceptual view just puts things clearly in view for our first look.

To conclude the Harlequin dream as to our perceptual inventory:

(A dreamer), couples, masks, a ballroom that looks like an old gymnasium, a Harlequin, a hallway, a door, stairs

Notice that the inventory is neutral at this point. We have not attached emotion. We have not said anything additional beyond what is written in the text.

This first objective view is what we shall refer to as the perceptual view. It is an important beginning place for the work we need to do to build our dream dictionary. Beyond the dream journal mirroring, we now need to make this perceptual inventory.

Next, let's be organized. Let us rearrange the inventory alphabetically:

Ballroom

Couples

Dancers

Door

Dreamer

Gymnasium

Hallway

Harlequin

Mask

Stairs

I purposely left out modifiers, adjectives such as "pretty," "old," etc. This is kind of a skeleton of the dream. No meat on it; just the bare bones. Now we are ready to make our first entries in the dream dictionary.

If we choose a physical book for our dictionary, then let me suggest we purchase a ringed loose-leaf binder, the kind that lets us put section dividers in it. Separators will make it easy to divide the book into sections for each letter of the alphabet. As the book vocabulary grows, it allows for inserting additional pages where needed. If a regular book is chosen, it is more difficult, since there is never a clean understanding of just which letter shall demand the most pages with the most entries. With a computer file it is definitely the easiest for room manifests as needed. Yet, choose what best suits ease and comfortability.

Next, the dream dictionary begins by allowing space under each letter of the alphabet. For the notebook, which has a set number of pages, care must be taken in allowing enough space for the letters, which logically present more words for examination than some of the less used letters, such as, for instance, "y" or "z," which may appear less. If a computer file or loose-leaf binder is chosen, less attention is demanded here, since there is always insert space.

Above we have our first entries. We place each in the appropriate sections.

We begin by placing our perceptual ordinary interpretation of what is seen.

B

Ballroom: A large room where events may be held. (Fair enough. Pretty generic. We do not describe it at this point. Remember, the first recording is pure bare-bones perception.)

C

Couple(s): Two or more people

D

Dancers: People in the act of physical movement (The dream does not mention music, which may or may not be implied.)

Door: Portal place of passage between outer and inner

Dreamer: This is the dream persona, how I, the dreamer, see myself in a dream. (At this point we know nothing more, such as age, sex, like or unlike waking.)

G

Gymnasium: A place where different sports are played; can be an all-purpose room in a school

H

Hallway: A place between rooms, leading to and from somewhere

Harlequin: An individual who is usually silent, dressed in a black-and-white costume

These entries are quite generic. They say very little other than the brief comments as to their general meaning. We can all agree that most who read the dream episode would have little trouble accomplishing the first dream dictionary entry. This just helps us dig more deeply once we have uncovered what we need to look at. We can consider this as our find while walking across a desert. Imagine walking along an ancient desert path as the sun was slipping beneath the horizon. Glancing on the ground, we notice glimmers of shimmering light. We stop and bend down to see what has captured our attention. We are amazed to find pieces of broken pottery and glass, thousands of pieces strewn along the surface of the land. We pick up a few interesting pieces. At first glance we know so little. We can conclude that a pottery vessel, something, broke and the pieces found their way here. Nothing more. Other questions may arise, yet they are for later. Questions such as the following: Who made the vessel? When was it made? How did it arrive here? How did it break? Why was its owner here? Was there a deep meaning to the journey or to the carrying of the vessel, which is now broken? Our first glance might bring up all these questions. Yet, we can all see that the task to uncover more lies ahead. It is not revealed by our first glance. The first step is the fact that we are aware. We take notice of what calls to us. We stop. We will look more deeply later. We have begun the process.

Some of my fondest memories of Egypt involve my walks along the desert. One incredibly special visit was along the old pilgrimage route to the ancient deity Khenti-

Amenti, whose name means "Foremost of the Westerners." This title was associated both with the Egyptian deity Osiris and the jackal-headed god Anubis. Both deities were associated with the necropolis, the city of those who passed into the afterlife. A few hours' ride into the desert outside the modern city of Luxor takes us to the temple of Abydos, lying on the site where it is believed the cult of Khenti-Amenti flourished. My guide that day was enthusiastic in reporting that here the ancients made their pilgrimage much as modern seekers flock to sacred sites all over the world. Walking beneath the blazing sun, we came to a clearing where we could view the remains of an ancient enclosure. Beneath my feet were thousands of precious pottery sherds. I bent down to look more closely, picking up a few that had strange imagery beautifully colored on the terra-cotta. I went further, asking as to possible dating. Were these old or products of modernity? I was shocked to learn that indeed they were believed to date to the ancient era, and that in the coming months a group of researchers would gather and spend the winter holiday collecting as many pieces as they could. They would see how the pieces fit together. They would examine the imagery still visible on some, like ones I held in the palms of my hands. It was hoped that in the end, these pieces of broken pottery would reveal stories of long ago. I knelt down and tenderly placed my pieces back in the sand. I longed to return, to spend more time with them, to seek to hear their story. Images lying naked on the sand. Their stories hidden within them. For a moment my heart beat more strongly, its strings pulled by some ancient musician calling to me, inviting me to discover his song and thus partake in his life. I turned and followed our guide back to our vehicle. Yet, that site never left the field of my imagination. The dream calls to me, for all stories lie there, in the fertile imagery that arises to whisper in our ears.

I share this since it beautifully describes our journey into the story of dreams. We begin by picking up the pieces that appear upon our dream landscape, sherds of imagery lying in the sands of the terrain. We sort and examine more closely to fit our pieces together and find the story that is waiting to be heard.

THE PERSONAL DREAM DICTIONARY

Setting it up and choosing the first entries

with a perceptual first view

1. Choose the dream dictionary wisely, understanding the challenges of regular notebooks and the ease of loose-leaf binders and computer files. If a loose-leaf notebook is chosen, carefully place the page dividers into separate sections. Let each section represent one letter of the alphabet. The loose-leaf shall allow for additional pages where they may be needed. If a computer file is used as the dream dictionary, set up a file in additional to the dream journal. If an old-fashioned journal is the choice, leave plenty of room between sections to accommodate the growing dictionary lists. I suggest keeping both the dream journal and the dream dictionary in places easily retrieved for frequent referral.

2. After dreams are entered into the dream journal, chose the characters, landscape, things, settings, and props that make up the dream, what we call the bare bones. Alphabetize and place them in the appropriate dream dictionary sections. Record their perceptual identity. To aid us in viewing our dreams, we can refer to eight basic categories that turn up in dreams as presented by the Hall–Van de Castle Content Analysis System, which presents the following for consideration:

1. Characters
2. Social interactions: aggression, friendliness, sexuality
3. Activities: walking, talking, seeing, thinking, etc.
4. Success and failure / Misfortune and good fortune
5. Emotions
6. Settings
7. Objects
8. Descriptive elements: modifiers, time, negatives
   (Calvin. S. Hall and Robert L. Van de Castle, *The Content Analysis of Dreams* [New York: Appleton-Century Crofts, 1966])

3. We keep our lists current, consistently adding to our dictionary. We are ready to dig more deeply into each item recorded. Like the pilgrim picking up the sherds of pottery from an ancient pilgrimage path, we are engaged in the mystery. We are intrigued. The amplification comes next.

CHAPTER NINE

Personal Dream Dictionary, Second View:
Amplification/Cultural/Mythic/Historical

Your vision will become clear only when you look into your heart. Who looks outside, dreams. Who looks inside, awakens.

—Carl Gustav Jung

Once an archeologist leaves the fieldwork, he or she goes to the laboratory to see if there is information on what has been found. What is known about the location, the beliefs of the people who inhabited the land? Is there information in texts or even in the oral tradition of what remains surrounding the now-deserted area? What do the present people believe of this deserted place? Why is it now deserted? Is there some belief that keeps people from it? Is it considered sacred or taboo? From a simple piece of broken pottery first perceived in a deserted place, the research widens. The dreamer, thus returned from the field of dream, likewise initially records surface perceptions that call for deeper understanding. Thus, we begin, digging more deeply. This process is called amplification. Actually, it consists of two separate tasks. One is more objective; the other, more personal. We begin with the objective exercise.

Back in the laboratory from our fieldwork viewing pottery sherds, usually the first thing we do is to locate information that might aid us in better understanding our find. Perhaps the student of archeology, history, religion, mythology, philosophy, and such has an advantage in having an internal encyclopedic resource in their memory bank. They think about the terrain and what it represents to them.

To better illustrate this, I will present the adventure of the pottery sherds as it showed up in a dream:

EXAMPLE:

April, 19, 2018: Pottery Sherds in the Abydos Necropolis. The pilgrimage route to the Shrine of Khenti-Amenti.

I find myself in a white van approaching the ancient temple of Abydos. I am excited—thrilled, actually—to be here again. It is my favorite temple. I know I am dreaming as I see Abydos without the huge modern plaza that now marks the tourist entrance area. This alerts me to the fact that I am lucid. Thus I enjoy my return to Abydos as the van pulls up in the sand a few yards away from the small concession building and multicolored tented refreshment area that once greeted visitors. I am with my Egyptian sister. Together we leave the van and make our way through the reception area, where we pause for a moment to see the English woman seated with her needlework. Her straw hat, her clear blue eyes, her porcelain skin glow. Her smile radiates her love for Abydos. We know her. Yet, no words are exchanged. I feel blessed at her presence. She who embodies remembrance. Suddenly a thought is transmitted through that watery blue gaze. Why are we revisiting? Why have we returned? What must we remember? Upon these thoughts the scene shifts. I am alone now, walking in the ancient burial grounds behind the temple. I am sure of it. This is why I have come, returned. I need to remember, to put together the memory of this place. It is important. I remember my visit, the pottery. My eyes look at the ground, which is littered with broken pottery. I stop to examine a few pieces, which are painted with turquoise-blue imagery. My eyes strain against the bright sun, which beats down upon the sands. I look around to see a small farmers hut ahead. I know it provides shelter during the hottest part of the day. Yet, it is far off and I am not going that direction. I place the pottery back in the sand. As much as I would like to take the few interesting pieces with me, I know I cannot. They must stay. Someone someday will come to study them. I wish I would be among their number. In some manner I am to be part of it all. I am, actually. That is why I have returned. For now I must go back. Suddenly I am standing with my sister, looking at the empty seat where once the English woman sat. She is gone now. I shield my eyes and see the sun is not so high now. Time has passed. The temple is before us. The temple of remembrance. We begin to walk toward it.

I wake.

Place: *Act 1 and act 3, The entry of Abydos. In the van. At the concession stand.*

Act 2: *The necropolis, desert sands*

Characters: *My Egyptian sister, the English woman, my dream persona*

Props: *The white van, the multicolored tented area, needlework, pottery sherds*

Main feelings: *Elation, thrill, importance in remembering*

The above description is what is written in the dream journal. The dream experience is built on a waking-reality experience of roughly a year prior. The pottery draws me deeply into the waking memory, something extremely pleasant. The visited area is not open to tourists, and thus it was an honor to visit. In the dream I am not only happy to be there but filled with it, as though it points me to something important.

Next we pick the terms we wish to explore more deeply. These shall go in our alphabetical dream dictionary. Below is what stands out most from the dream. Each dream we have is made up of many parts. We, the dreamer, decide what stands out.

Abydos

Desert

Egypt

English woman [* Here the adjective seems important]

Necropolis

Needlework

Pottery sherds

Temple

Tent

Van

To amplify the dream with more, I can begin like an archeologist, by fleshing out what I know about the location.

First, quite general but significant is the location of Egypt. Immediately most of us can associate Egypt with pyramids, tombs, and temples. Most of us know of the rich iconography found upon the walls of the tombs and sarcophagi. We are familiar with the many deities. Perhaps we know a bit of the famous find of the tomb of Tutankhamun. This is all very general. If we wish we can look up more. In general, the placement of dream terrain can be steeped with history and belief systems, especially concerning the afterlife. Again, pretty general, but a place to begin when we place "Egypt" in our dream dictionary. Associated with.

We next move to the more specific place. The dreamer knows of the temple at Abydos, in the desert on the west bank of the Nile in southern Egypt. It is a sacred mortuary temple of the pharaoh Seti I. It is a beautiful temple with seven chapels, as opposed to the usual three found in most mortuary temple complexes. Likewise, there is a sacred pool, the Osirian, located below the temple. The necropolis, burial ground of Egypt's first royals, is ancient, predating the temple. There is a pilgrimage route leading to the ruins of an ancient sanctuary dedicated to the deity Khenti-Amenti, foremost of the West, referring to a powerful chthonic deity of the afterlife. Since I, as dreamer, visited this temple many times in waking life, I am familiar with it. Thus, this information is something others can easily attach to my dream location. As to the canopied refreshment area, likewise it physically existed until quite recently, when the area underwent modernization. Anyone who visited Abydos in the nineties and early twenty-first century would know this.

This part of amplification, enlarging the dream with additional information, relies on material not specific to one individual, the dreamer.

There are myths associated with the chief deity of Abydos, Osiris. As time passed, Khenti-Amenti took on the name Osiris. And with Osiris comes mythology. Since I love this temple of Abydos, I am familiar with the mythology, which easily comes to mind when I think of Abydos. Sky, Nut, and Earth, Geb were parents of five children: Osiris, Isis, Seth, Nephthys, and Horus the Elder. Osiris and Isis were given the fertile black land adjacent to the Nile. Seth and Nephthys were bequeathed the red land of the desert. Envious of his brother, Seth prepared a coffin, a sarcophagus of great beauty, and, tricking Osiris to get into it, he nailed it closed, then flung it into the sea. After great lamentations, Isis recovered her deceased brother/husband Osiris and brought him back to Egypt. Yet, Seth, finding his brother returned, dismembered him and flung his body pieces along the Nile. Once again Isis grieved and searched until she recovered her beloved spouse. Since his genitals were devoured by a fish, she fashioned a magical phallus upon which she became pregnant with their son Horus. Osiris would rule the afterlife, and their son would rule the waking world. It is thus a story of dismemberment and rememberment. The temple interestingly has in a hallway the image of the pharaoh Seti I showing Ramesses II, his son, a wall of cartouches that bear the names of former pharaohs, as though the father is telling the son to remember all that came before them, to honor the past and the past ancestry. Throughout the temple there are beautiful wall reliefs of Isis tenderly welcoming Seti to the afterlife.

Learning to amplify dream images and symbols in view of meaning within specific cultures, myths, and esoteric beliefs widens our understanding of what surfaces in our personal dream. Like the initial perceptions, the amplification may be commonly shared beliefs. What is presented here is pretty general and can be appreciated by others beyond the dreamer. The myths, for instance, are not specific to the dreamer alone. The dream moves from surface story, yet it is still not limited to personal history.

Abydos now can be placed in the dream dictionary with a condensed version of the above. Our entry begins with factual information on place and history, along with some mythology.

Now, there is another story that is likewise associated with Abydos. It is halfway between the general and the personal in this case. It refers to the English woman seen in the dream. I, the dreamer, know her. She is Om Sety, a.k.a. Dorothy Eady. If in a dream the English woman appeared with a name tag, then the dreamer, if he or she remembered that name, could look it up, if in fact there was no obvious personal memory. I say obvious since our dreamer may have visited Egypt or watched a Discovery Channel program offering that tells Dorothy Eady's story. They simply have the information in dusty mental storage. Likewise, they may have read something and shelved it in memory. Or they may, as I have, a more personal relationship with our English woman. In my case, my relationship began decades ago as my interest in Egypt, in dreams, and in parapsychology merged in yielding the extraordinary story of Dorothy Eady.

Om Sety, also known as Dorothy Eady, was the only child born to her English parents. In 1907, at the age of three, Dorothy fell down the stairs in her home. A physician was summoned and upon examination pronounced the child dead. Dorothy was left upon her bed while the proper death certificates were composed. Yet, upon returning to the bedroom to remove the corpse, the physician and the family were both shocked and delighted to find the young Dorothy seated on her bed playing with her doll. The rest of Dorothy's story is quite amazing. She began to dream of another life, in Egypt. The pull was so great that in time she did marry an Egyptian and bore a son; hence her name, Mother of Sety, Om Sety. The Seti was Sety I of the temple at Abydos. Dorothy's child was named for her dream Seti, the main character in her dreams. So strong were these dreams and so real her knowledge of Abydos that she spent the last many years of her life living near the temple. Often, she was seen seated beneath the refreshment canopy, selling her needlework. She is buried in view of the ancient pilgrimage site near the necropolis behind Abydos, the terrain of the current dream. There are books written about her, since her dreams seemed to point to her memory of a past life (see *The Search for Om Sety*, by Jonathan Cott, 1987). Thus, Om Sety was a real person. I, the dreamer, knew of her and experienced her presence on previous visits to Abydos. Thus, there is both the amplification of general information, which is available to anyone who looks for it, and personal knowledge. As will be the case for many dreamers, the dream dictionary entries may easily bridge from the more general to the more personal in a fluid manner, as is illustrated by this one entry.

In the dream dictionary the entry "English woman" would thus include information on the specific connection with Om Sety for this dreamer. Because Om Sety's life was guided by dreams and past-life beliefs, that would be most important in the dream dictionary entry. For beyond the name is the reality of the importance of dreams to Dorothy Eady. The point to remember is that the image appears to bring a message of something. The more we explore each image, the closer we come to uncovering its message. It is obvious that "English woman" can have many other meanings, some which may come to light as the personal associations are allowed to arise. With this example, as we continue on the personal associations, I will share how the term "English woman" does bring up more for me. Yet, I will also share how each thought and association that arises comes with a feeling. Some "feel" like they fit what we seek in a particular dream, and others just do not "feel right." That is the exciting part of the dream dictionary. Only the dreamer can feel their way. Others who listen, even therapists, can merely suggest, yet only the dreamer has the dream. And sometimes there are so many associations that arise. What counts is listing them. Nothing is written in stone, since all is fluid as is our lives, continually moving, shifting. And it is all the journey that matters. Our continual movement. We shall know when to stop and when to move on. When something "feels" right to explain our particular dream, and when that very same entry shifts where a precious positive feeling on one dream no longer works for another. Each has its own hiddenness. It is our work to chip away at the surface, seeking to reveal a little more each time.

I use the computer for my notes, which gives me the luxury of writing whatever comes to mind, with no worry about space. The above is the long of it.

Yet, the short of it for the dream dictionary can look like the following.

Abydos: *A place important in rituals to deity of the afterlife. Associated with memory and dismemberment. Mythology of Isis and Osiris. Magical birth from death.*

Desert: *Golden sand. The Sahara, the west desert place where the sun descends, mythology of the afterlife and journey of sun god through the hours of the night.*

Egypt: *Associated with huge iconography of afterlife*

English woman: * *Here the adjective seems important. In dreams of Abydos, Om Sety, dream, past life, memories from past entering present. Remembering.*

Necropolis: *City of the Dead, afterlife. In Egypt, Abydos. The ancient deity Khenti-Amenti. Ancient pilgrimage site.*

Needlework: *Fine handcraft producing patterns, imagery upon a canvas of fabric*

Pottery sherds: *Broken pieces of handmade jugs from antiquity, important in archeological research found in Egyptian dream*

Temple: *A sacred place. In Egyptian dream, Seti I temple at Abydos. Memory. Initiation into the mysteries of afterlife.*

Tent: *The tented canopy in the Egyptian dream. Protection from the sun, providing cooling.*

Van: *A vehicle of transportation*

As we look at this one dream, we now move to another level of interpretation: our personal associations that deepen it.

CHAPTER TEN

Personal Dream Dictionary, Third View: Apperception/Personal Association

The dream is a little hidden door in the innermost and most secret recesses of the soul, opening into that cosmic night which was psyche long before there was any ego consciousness, and which will remain psyche no matter how far out ego consciousness extends.

—Carl Gustav Jung (*Collected Works*, vol. 10, p. 304)

While the transition from the more general historical, mythological, common knowledge information on our dream inventory did show the bridge to personal with "English woman," the information recorded above is mostly of the general nature. The movement to personal begins with apperception or association. Now begins the intuitive work as we allow our chosen entry images the freedom to move toward deeper personal meaning. In the process of association, we, the dreamers, allow our imagination to bring alive personal memories and associations. Here is where memory plays an important role. For we review the dream characters, places, and things and just let thoughts arise. What does each make us think of? There is no right or wrong. Sometimes something arises that does seem logical.

EXAMPLE:
Snake in a Dream
Personal Associations:
If there is a snake in a dream, our personal association may be with a childhood jump rope. The snake can leap, and we can jump through the alternating movement of the flying jump rope. We can associate our movement, the movement of our rope, and the movement of the snake. We may even connect with the visual patterns on a snakeskin with the patterned weave of the jump rope, perhaps even coloring of green and black. Thus, such an association may come easily. That seems logical. If we move to mirror such associations with our waking life, we can attempt to make connections. Is there something we wish to leap from? Is there something that threatens to leap at us? Is there fear in something, someone, who might slither unseen and then just leap and attack us? Is there a relationship, a business deal, a contract that appears to run smoothly yet could present an unseen attack? We consider all the possibilities, just from one simple image. The shape, the movement, our thoughts about that snake help us see something we may be missing in our waking-life complexities.

Yet, perhaps that snake makes us think of a vase in our mother's house. There is a beautiful hand-painted rose on that vase. The vase sits on a mantle in a beautiful setting, a comfortable living room. It seems totally disconnected from the dream image of a snake. Yet, we record it in our dream dictionary. And we let it just sit. We allow the associations to make connections. Is the worried uncertainty—the unpredictability—

of the serpentine movement at odds with the very predictable stable position of the vase? Is there a message in this? Perhaps there is something, an issue in waking life, that frightens due to its unpredictability. On one hand, we see calm, peace, and tranquility. We see stability. On the other, we see the snake that can hide and take us by surprise. Is there a concern surrounding an illusion of stability? The dream is pointing to this concern. Thus, one image can bring forth different personal associations that leap from the original perception to something that seems far removed.

The snake for another dreamer might immediately point to lawyers or legal situations where injustice rules. The image of the snake would alert the dreamer to watch out for the smoke and mirrors, the lawyers' tools that obscure truth. There may be someone in waking life not worthy of trust, and the appearance of the snake along with the personal associations would alert the dreamer to take care and choose carefully.

Snake in a Dream
General Amplification:
General amplification of the dream snake might bring completely opposite meanings. Historically, snakes were associated with transformation and wisdom. The Greek goddess of wisdom, Athena, wore a helmet festooned with a serpent. Such was considered a symbol of the creative power of wisdom. Since the snake sheds its skin, the dreamer might see the snake representing the cycle of continuous creativity, of growth and change. Since the snake outgrows its skin and slithers out of it, the dreamer might think of slipping out of their waking persona, perhaps relationship, career, location, or current endeavors, to venture into something new. Since the snake wrapped around the staff of the ancient healer, forming the caduceus, the dreamer, if touched by this stream of thought, can look for the shift in their life as something bringing healing.

Describing a snake as a zoologist would, one might come up with the definition of a snake as a reptile, rather long, minus limbs, cold blooded, with scales. They lay eggs. They molt, meaning they grow and shed their skins in preparation of growing new skins. They have sense organs on their underside, allowing them to feel vibrations. They likewise have a heightened sense of smell. The very biological traits can be helpful in interpreting the snake in a dream. It may strike the dreamer that they, like the snake, lack arms to carry some waking burden. They may feel they are left to crawl on the ground, seeking the aid they need. They may see the snake as cold blooded and associate that with something or someone in their lives.

Finally, the snake might bring up thoughts of DNA. The double snakelike helix, which carries the units of heredity in living cells. This naturally is general amplification, knowledge widely embraced. Since DNA is information, the snake dream could be pointing to some information that needs to be accessed, something that lies deep within a situation.

Thus, looking at "snake" in our dream dictionary, we see how varying, often-opposing thoughts can be included under this one entry. When we have a dream and look up an entry in our dream dictionary, finding multiple meanings, all derived from our different dream thoughts, it is most important that we search for how we feel in connecting with the one aspect that best relates to our current dream. Perhaps the current dream brings up yet another feeling or thought, in which case we add it to our dictionary. We must simply depend on our feelings to lead us. This is not a waking mental activity. It is one of gut feeling. What follows is an example of what an entry can look like.

Snake:

Perception: *Limbless reptile, cold blooded, molts, cyclically renews self*

General amplification: *Associated with DNA. Ancient caduceus, wisdom, renewal in ancient cults. Healing deities.*

Personal association: *Lawyers, "snake in the grass" hidden deceits, jump rope, sudden unexpected attacks*

With the "snake" entry we merely isolated one image without visiting a complete dream. See how one entry can move from healing deity to wretched deceiver. Immediate to a particular dream scenario feeling will lead to see which entry best relates to the meaning relating to the one particular dream. The image is never bogged down with one dogmatic meaning, but it is alive. Thus, it speaks to us, opening us up to its vastness.

Below is a dream where a snake image manifested:

August 20, 1989: The hill, the long chord, the ancient fellowship

It is a beautiful day, and I am walking in the countryside. I am familiar with this place. I have visited it in dream many times. There are flowers that grow wild, and I love to pick them and listen for their song. Today all the flowers are white. I am so aware that there are cyclic appearances of colors. First yellow, then white, and at the end blue. Each color enjoying its time. I pick up a simple field daisy and place it under the cuff of my sleeve. I am happy, carefree. The field is filled with beautiful voices, and they speak a language that shows me the healing value of the plants. I am just enjoying my visit when suddenly I come to the base of a very steep mountain. I stand there for a moment before realizing there is a serpent wrapped around my hand. I look for the daisy, but all I find now is this heavy serpent. It is glistening, each tiny sequin of scale iridescent, beautiful. I realize it is pulling me up that steep mountain. I let it draw me upward. I get about halfway before all movement ceases. I wonder what is happening until I realize that my feet feel the vibrations of movement of others coming up this steep incline. I cast my eyes to the below and see women, old and young, climbing to join me. I wait, and together we hold on to the serpent. Slowly we continue on climbing . . . I wake.

For the sake of brevity, with this one dream we shall concentrate on the one mysterious image, the serpent or snake.

We see below that our snake entries were made as a result of several previously experienced dreams. Thus, in this one dream dictionary image, entries were entered at different times, expanding meaning. We review what we have previously recorded, adding any new thoughts, general or personal. Finally we see how we feel. Which description fits our feeling of association with the above dream?

Snake:

Perception: *Limbless reptile, cold blooded, molts, cyclically renews self, healing caduceus staff*

General amplification: *Associated with DNA. Ancient caduceus, wisdom, renewal in ancient cults. Healing deities. Transformation.*

Personal association: *Lawyers, "snake in the grass" hidden deceits, jump rope, sudden unexpected attacks*

Above we presented the variety of thoughts under our dream entry.

Looking at the above dream, we can readily dismiss some suggestions as we review it to collect our feelings with a view of our recent dream:

A beautiful day. Feeling good. In communion with the environment. The flower turning into the snake, which does not yield unpleasantness or fear. Rather, it initiates a journey to the summit, one in which the dreamer is accompanied by others. The snake in the dream appears to be taking the dreamer from the bottom of the mountain to its apex. We take the feeling of this dream and think about what we already have in our dream dictionary. One entry describes the snake as "a limbless reptile." We think how in our dream the snake is actually an added arm, attached at the wrist, where the dreamer placed the flower. It pulled her up, and others came to join as well. We give a thought to that one entry. The entry is viewed as the opposite to that of the action in the dream. We think some more. The snake as an ancient symbol of transformation, ushering in the shift from one location, also resonates. It feels right and seems appropriate. We view the other entries. The more negative associations can be dismissed. We remember that images are open to many meanings, often at opposition to one another. The dream and the dream material guide us to the meaning, specific for us at a particular time in our lives. It is why our dream dictionary is so significant. No one else has our unique life. Our views, our memories, our history, our culture make up who we are and how we ultimately view things. In this case, this one entry can appear at different times in different dreams, awakening feelings within us that may awaken us to the truth of the moment. Nothing is set dogmatically. The image is alive, continually shifting between opposite meanings, all waiting for us to feel, to sense, to uncover the meaning appropriate to the time.

To look more deeply into the personal association of dream images, let us now return to our dream of the pottery sherds in the ancient necropolis. We began with the original entry in our dream journal. We chose our dream dictionary entries and gave them the general amplification expansion. Now let us expand further with our own personal associations:

Abydos:
A place important in rituals to deity of the afterlife. Associated with memory and dismemberment. Mythology of Isis and Osiris. Magical birth from death.
Personal: For the dreamer, Abydos is a place she frequently visits. Her memories arise to feelings of great spiritual connection. Her personal experiences there make this a temenos, a sacred place where she feels connections beyond the physical. The place awakens memories that resonate with her personal spiritual path. For her, Abydos is a temple of memory. Its appearance greatly resonates with the spiritual journey of remembering our true identity. Its appearance in dream is synonymous with remembering, putting together.

Desert:
Golden sand. The Sahara, west desert place where the sun descends, mythology of the afterlife, and journey of sun god through the hours of the night
Personal: The dreamer connects desert with desert hermits, with those who find truth by seeking the silence and solitude of the desert. It also brings to mind Antoine de Saint Exupéry's *Le Petit Prince* (*The Little Prince*), the story of a pilot who crashes in the desert, where he discovers the meaning of life via his meeting with a strange boy with golden hair, the little prince. So for the dreamer, it is about the wisdom found in the gold of the sands, in the solitude and silence of the hermitage.

Egypt:
Associated with huge iconography of afterlife
Personal: For the dreamer, Egypt is a place where ancient spiritual beliefs continue to dwell in the temples and tombs along the Nile. The entire romance of Egypt is part of her and her many journeys there. To see Egypt in a dream for her would be to take her home, to the real depths within her.

English woman:
* Here the adjective seems important. In dreams of Abydos, Om Sety, dream, past life, memories from past entering present. Remembering.
Personal: The dreamer immediately remembers the Queen of the Desert, Gertrude Bell, a brilliant English woman who like Lawrence of Arabia visited the lands of the Mideast and learned the language. Here, English woman would resonate completely with the desert being a place of wisdom, of deep learning beyond the

physical. In a dream it would take an entire scenario to determine if this one particular woman, brilliant, brave, adventurous, fit the feeling of the particular dream.

Necropolis:

City of the Dead, afterlife. In Egypt, Abydos. The ancient deity Khenti-Amenti. Ancient pilgrimage site.

Personal: The first time the dreamer saw an Egyptian necropolis was in dream. It was in the old area of Cairo. Her sharing of the dream with an Egyptian friend brought her to visit the site, which remains with her a deeply moving experience. The necropolis for her is a bridge between the living and those passed on. It is the doorway of communication.

Needlework:

Hand stitching accomplished by applying different stitching techniques along with different-colored threads to produce imagery on a fabric. Embroidery is an example.

Personal: The dreamer's mother was an expert at needlework. The dream would connect not only with Om Sety's needlework but likewise her mother. Since both the dreamer's mother and Om Sety were strongly connected with the dreamworld, the needlework would expand and become a powerful connector to walking the worlds between dream and waking, going far beyond threads and fabric. The dreamer, like both needleworkers (her mother and Om Sety), heavily respects her visionary dream communications in her life choices. For the dreamer the needlework would be viewed as piercing the surface of a fabric to plunge beneath it to the other side, as she plunges into the depths of dream, the other more hidden side of consciousness. Needlework would carry the personal meaning of sewing fabric beyond the obvious to amplify it, sewing the two worlds of consciousness together, bringing forward dreams to merge with waking reality. Om Sety's needlework reflected her life's devotion and commitment to the revelations of her dreams. She followed her dream visions to Egypt and spent her life honoring them. Less dramatically but equally powerfully, the author's mother honored dreams in making decisions in her daily life. The dreamer likewise honors and respects dream, incorporating the communication she receives through dreaming into the fabric of each of her breathing moments. Thus the associations brought on by needlework appearing in a dream would carry deep personal meaning for the dreamer, well beyond the art of fabric design.

Pottery sherds:

Broken pieces of handmade jugs from antiquity, important in archeological research found in Egyptian dream

Personal: Her personal attraction to pottery runs deeply within her waking personality. Her desire to study and learn from them is strong. Her experience of holding ancient sherds in her hands brought alive a connection to something hidden, as though the stories themselves remained present through the hands that once held the pieces, joining with her, touching her hands as she held the very same pieces centuries removed. Thus, the dreamer sees them as keys to opening the hidden door of the ancient people.

Temple:

A sacred place. In Egyptian dream, Seti I temple at Abydos. Memory. Initiation into the mysteries of afterlife.

Personal: The dreamer sees the temple as a temenos, a sacred place where the waking personality moves beyond the physical to reach out and connect, communicate with the Unseen.

Tent:

The tented canopy in the Egyptian dream. Protection from the sun, providing cooling.

Personal: The dreamer has personal memories of spending one special week in a tent with her family at a retreat center deep in the mountains. Thus, the tent is seen as shelter and a place of togetherness. She also has memories of the Abydos tent that once sat at the temple entry. It was a place of welcome where she first met Om Sety, along with the concession proprietor who decades later found her on visits long after the tented area was removed. The proprietor gave her the precious wheat of Osiris, a gift of remembrance.

Van:

A vehicle of transportation

Personal: In the many visits to the ancient sites, the dreamer often travels in a white van, so there is personal identity with the van in the dream. She sees it as that which carries her from the modern city into the ancient mysteries. In a dream it can represent movement from the waking reality of noise and business to an inner reality of spiritual meaning.

Notice how in the above we moved from viewing a dream, amplifying it with general thoughts that most would make, to personal associations unique to individual memory. We can also see how in time our notes on particular entries shift and bring conflicting and even opposite thoughts. In the end the dictionary is ours alone, bringing us through life, helping us grow and widen our view of our place and our journey through life. We look at particular dream dictionary entries as we experience new dreams, seeking to reach out to our former thoughts on the various characters, symbols, and items that fill the dreams. Meaning arises through our personal reactions to these notes as the entries awaken feelings within us. For a moment, thought rises like the bubble in a champagne class. It is an "Ah-ha!" moment. It *feels* right, fits the recent dream scenario. Understanding meaning demands we rely on our intuitive sense of feeling. This is not the time for mentation, for thinking. Likewise, it is not a time to present the thoughts to our faculties of sensation, which help us navigate the physical. Feeling matters most in connecting us with the meaning appropriate for the particular situation, dream, and interpretation. Time continues to flow past us as the thoughts and entries grow along with our increasing life experience. The dream dictionary becomes a companion jarring our memories, directing us on certain paths of thoughts. In a way it becomes a global-positioning tool, pointing us along a particular road, hinting at the discovery that lies at the end.

The ancients would say that each entry is a "herma," a special pile of stones that were once revered for good luck as one traveled the ancient pathways, especially entering crossroads and approaching boundaries between their here and there. Each herma was a place to stop and throw an additional stone upon the pile, adding to it, as we add to the entries of our dream dictionary. Each is meant to represent something of ourselves and our journey. The herma are our little piles of stones showing the way of the image.

The entire idea of the herma remains today in our viewing of statutes that sit in sacred places. I well remember visiting churches as a child, where my mother would place her hand upon the knee of some holy saint statue. She would tell me that by doing so she was seeking communion with the saint, assistance and guidance in some life challenge. Her hand against the knee was a sign, her acknowledgment of her presence and the unseen presence. The knees of these statues were polished and worn with the many hands that touched them. The tradition of leaving something, a stone transferred into the touch of the hand.

Most interesting was the holy cross that sat on the molding beside our front entrance. My mother would not pass that cross without touching it and kissing her fingers in acknowledgment of some hidden sacred nature that watched over the portal of our home. Each image—the statues, the cross—held meaning. Each was part of a crossing over from what was seen to what was apprehended on an imaginal level. Each was accompanied by movement beyond the boundary of the seen into the unseen imaginal. The cross is the very same as used by the first Christians in ancient Egypt. They displayed the symbol of a cross within a circle to mark the places where they would meet, the first Christian churches. We see these crosses in some of the ancient temples where the early Christians gathered. The symbol was carved upon the stone walls. This ancient hieroglyph for city center, placed where the roads converged and diverged, was an appropriate symbol for the new religion. Through time the cross took on other meanings. In the beginning it marked the center where all roads met. Yet, the center within us, where the imaginal dreaming arises to converse with the rational waking. And in our dream dictionary we see the entries, the herma, as the places that become meeting sites. They rose from dream and conversed with waking to bring forth an awakening, something to guide and accompany beyond the crossroads of our lives.

Our herma began with a few stones, perhaps small pebbles; yet, with time, with our travels and our many dream visits, they grow. We move from the here of what we believe we know of our waking and our dream realities, as we venture a little more deeply on our paths, coming to crossroads and finally braving the boundaries that separate waking and dreaming terrain.

CHAPTER ELEVEN

Empowering the Dream through Artistic Expression

To the one who knows how to look and feel, every moment of the free wandering life is an enchantment.

—Alexandra David-Neel, 1868–1969

At this point the journal is taking form, and dream elements are recorded and amplified. We sit, ponder, and allow the stories to fill us. Now is the time we cross the bridge, taking our dream imagery to the drawing board of waking reality. Like a developing relationship where we may begin by simple meetings as our paths cross, the time arises to move to the next level, shifting from the inner space to the waking daylight. In waking we might take a walk in the park to become better acquainted with a new friend. Here we take our dream images into the light of waking, allowing them to fill our consciousness, warm our hearts, intrigue and capture our attention. Giving them the increased attention helps us in our journey to become familiar with them.

The written word is one thing. Taking the time to revisit a dream by recording what we remember is a huge step in remembering more and more dreams. Yet, moving up a step to draw, sculpt, or even search for images that bring alive the dream imagery and experience takes things to another level. And putting these waking images on a place where they meet our gaze in waking helps us become increasingly more familiar with them. The images come alive. While we may be neither artists nor sculptors, we still can manifest our inner dream imagery. Our creative spirit finds a way through to the waking world via books, photographs, and vast internet resources.

We can gather a variety of images that we can cut and paste to create a collage that helps bring alive the feelings of the dream imagery. An individual in the dream may be a person from our childhood, a deceased grandparent, elder, or friend. We can locate old photos and give them a place on our nightstand or office desk. The more we allow the images and our thoughts to cross over from dream into waking, the more communication we receive in information and increased understanding. The dreamscape is alive, just waiting to share its wisdom. We must work with it.

My own process is just taking a pencil to pad. I often begin by drawing a circle, occupying the entire page as far as it can extend. I then divide it into quarters. Originally there was no thinking, no logical reason for this choice. It happened quite intuitively, and I allowed it. Yet, the more I contemplate it, the more I see it as the alchemical vessel, the alembic, waiting to emerge from the four corners of the paper, the quaternary on which the circle arises. The images emerge within the circle, and through the living process they arise, releasing their energy in my life. From the dreamscape they take on life in waiting. I am no artist. I merely bring alive something I feel. The characters may be childish, yet they do what is needed. They display feelings. I draw the dream images that stand out. There may be a book, a manuscript, a papyrus roll. There may be a prominent moon or tree. Perhaps all I remember of a dreamscape is standing before a mirror or a window. Thus, the mirror or window ends up just floating in the dreamscape I am drawing. Their location and size will be reflected by their importance, according to how I feel as I draw things. Feeling is important because I am bringing through my inner experience, my intuitive communication with the mysterious hidden part of myself. Color is a feature that takes on varying degrees of importance in the artistic expression. Sometimes I do not wish to color the dreamscape drawing. I have inks, and I sometimes just rework everything in black ink. Other times I find a gentle touch painting with watercolors, often giving silver and gold touches. Yet, since not all dreams are the same intensity, there are times when gouache is needed. Gouache is a heavy, opaque, water-based paint, like watercolor yet without the transparent light look. They are bolder colors and give a more dramatic presence. There are also colored watercolor pencils and even colored markers that make good tools for quick drawings. Charcoal and crayons also work well. For me, my various moods are reflected in my choice of medium. Not all dreams arise with the same intensity. We remember that like play scripts, all the dream scripts differ. How we present the imagery to waking will reflect the distinct tones along with our individual preferences. The important thing to remember is that none of us need to be accomplished artists to draw our dreams.

When I was deeply involved in the imagery of my doctoral work, I often felt inspired in painting more and more of the dreams, having little time for much else. Most of us do have other issues to attend to, yet occasionally a big dream may come, one that seems amazing and beyond any simple comprehension. The big dream begs for our attention. Whatever time we have, this is the dream we investigate by opening it to our creativity with dedicated attention. Other dreams may suffice with simple drawings.

Some may not wish to attempt any drawing or painting yet may be attracted to collage. Taking images from a magazine, old paper, or album, or even printing off imagery from the internet before cutting them and pasting them on construction paper, may be the manner of choice in manifesting the waking dreamscape in the tangible physical reality. Beautiful collages may manifest even for the least artistically gifted, so collage has a wide appeal. As a child I often took pages out of the old *Life* and *McCall's* magazines, arranged them, and pasted them on old boxes, after which I lacquered them and stored correspondence. I still have some of these boxes. On some, I took old rags and wet them with wallpaper paste, after which I shaped them into flowers and other images. I placed them on my wooden cigar boxes and let them dry. Afterward I painted them. Nothing of grand artistic achievements, but all outpouring of emotion, taken from dreams. Yet, these boxes traveled with me through the decades, carrying the memories of the dreams that birthed them. I still store paper clips and pencils and small post-up notepads in these boxes. Thus, there is no limit to the artistic endeavors birthed by dream. Simple collages may just fill a construction paper album, acting like a dream journal. There are perhaps ways to create collages on the computer, but I must admit that is beyond my computer skills.

Many of us are gifted with sculpting things. Using simple Play-Doh-like images may be shaped that bring alive dream characters, props, significant symbols, and things. A generic version of Play-Doh can be made at home with just two cups of baking soda, a cup of corn starch, 1.25 cup of water, and a few drops of food coloring of choice. Mix baking soda and corn starch and slowly add the water. Stir and put over medium heat until it looks like mashed potatoes. This takes about fifteen minutes. Remove from heat and cover. Let cool and then smooth. It is ready to divide and shape. It's an easy way to sculpt birds, flowers, trees, and other significant images that appear in dream. If you choose, you can leave it uncolored and then even spray color onto it or place small stones or shells or details to make your sculpture come to life. The time we put into this richly rewards us. Remember, we are not entering a contest to see how gifted we are. We are spending time getting to know our dream characters.

Another creative adventure can manifest through papier-mâché. This is another easy craft. Take 4 cups of water and heat to boil. While it is heating, take a cup of flour and slowly add 1 cup of water, whisking or beating it to bring the mixture to a smooth texture without lumps. Once the pot of water is boiling, remove 1 cup of the boiling water to pour into the cold mixture. Stir well and then add the entire mixture to the remaining 3 cups of boiling water still on the heat. Stir and allow to heat for about three minutes until it gets to a thick gluelike stage. Now is the fun part. We let this mixture cool and turn to our creative spirit. Taking strips of fabric and paper, we can shape something from dream. If it is a tree we wish to make, we can take cardboard to use as our base and wrap our fabric or torn paper around it. For fun we can use colored magazine pages . . . and in the end we can paste on flowers and leaves, all dipped in our glue. Say there is a character with a huge, prominent hat. We can create a hat by shaping something over a bowl. As it begins to dry, we merely remove it from the bowl and allow it to air-dry once the shape is formed. This can be lots of fun. And in the end, it is all about spending time with the characters, the various images that arise in the dream. Time spent well develops the relationship, which in the end helps us learn more about our unique dream cast.

Perhaps the least messy and most available to all of us is photography. Available to each of us on our phones and tablets are excellent cameras. Thus, we have no excuse in not experimenting with taking photos that inspire us to think about our dreamscapes. The camera is handy 24-7. Keeping our dream in mind, we merely need to be aware in our waking consciousness. If we are thinking of a towering old tree that appeared in our dream, and we pass just such a tree on the way for an errand, we can snap a photo. Or we may be watching a film, and there it is on the video. We can pause the film and snap the photo. The idea is to bring forward the dream cast from the dream reality into the waking reality, so both halves of consciousness may meet and expand our understanding. If we are less concerned with producing masterpieces and more focused on the actual process of spending time with the thoughts and memories of the dream material, we shall find increased success learning the inner language of our dream consciousness. We become more fluent with the flow of dream communication, that which is unique and specific to our individual personal consciousness and memories. While there is overlap with all consciousness, the refinement comes from our own memory histories. Thus, the more time we put into becoming acquainted, the more we understand.

Creativity flows even into our doodles. While pondering a work problem, we may find ourselves drawing something completely unrelated to the work. If we pause and pay attention, we may see something from dream consciousness flowing from our fingers. In the early days of my handwriting all my journal notes, I often said the ideas flowed through my fingertips, activating the ink in my pen that wrote upon my tablet. I hesitated in shifting to the computer since I worried it might interfere with the creative process. I still keep an old-fashioned paper journal for notes, along with my computer journaling. There is something organic about the paper and my ability to draw, along with the stories I compose from the dream. Naturally, those of us who are more computer literate can accomplish their creative drawings by computer art, but I am not literate in these sophisticated methods. Thus, old-fashioned note paper works for me.

If I were a beach person, I would take to drawing in the sand, playing with pebbles and shells, building my dream landscapes. It is very therapeutic, child's play that releases the tension of the waking rational brain, stilling it and allowing dream consciousness to arise. Perhaps it is only playing in sand, moving the sand into a pattern that represents the temenos, the sacred space of the dream.

We can even create fabulous dream figures with sugar cookie dough, bake them, and then eat them, taking their power within us. I create what I call blessing cakes with the image of one of my dream teachers. Springerle cookies and old-fashioned butter molds carry beautiful images, some which easily relate to personal dream characters. Thus, we can use these to honor the inner visits. And eating them, taking them into our inner temples, is an incredibly old sacred ritual. In Saqquara, Egypt, on the walls of the tomb of Unas, built over four thousand years ago, there is what is called the Pyramid text. A specific portion is called the Cannibal text by modern Egyptologists. In this text the pharaoh Unas rises in death to meet the deities in the afterlife, where he eats them. The text refers to the eating of the powers, not the flesh. This ritual of eating something physical honors the spirit and power of what is taken within, represented by the bread or cake. Ancient people often kept items belonging to deceased ancestors, honoring and communicating with them. We can do something similar in shaping cookie dough in forms that represent significant parts of the dreamscape, after which we bake them, perhaps decorate them with icing, and then eat them, asking for the empowerment and guidance of the inner beings. My baking is always a ritual of remembrance, bringing current significant individuals, ancestors, and dream beings to empower the making with increased memories of understanding.

Each dream comes with its own needs. Sometimes just writing it down seems enough, and at other times it fills our consciousness, begging for attention. It is at these times when a dream keeps returning to our waking mind that we need to do more, and that is when the creative spirit takes over to bring us deeper into the dream as we share more time exploring its hidden meanings. The pursuit should be playful. It is not work, but pleasure. It is akin to spending time with someone we find increasingly interesting the more we meet and converse.

CHAPTER TWELVE

Meeting the Images, One by One . . .

I should advise you to put it all down as beautifully & as carefully as you can—in some beautifully bound book. It will seem as if you were making the visions banal—but then you need to do that—then you are freed from the power of them. . . . Then when these things are in some precious book you can go to the book and turn over the pages and for you it will be your church—your cathedral—the silent places of your spirit where you will find renewal. If anyone tells you that it is morbid or neurotic and you listen to them—then you will lose your soul—for in that book is your soul.

-Carl Gustav Jung, Visions: Notes of the Seminar Given 1930–1934

In the preceding chapters we explored the many elements that make up our dreams, along with the manner of increasing our understanding of each. We began our dream journal along with our unique dream dictionary. It makes a great beginning. The good news is there is more. If we view each dream as a stone placed in a stream we wish to cross, we begin to understand that it is in seeking a series of dreams that we can expand our understanding, visiting each dream as we go, successfully seeing more and more. We advance from our initial view, a single manifest dream, to the deeper, more complex understanding of the hidden meanings that arise as we view several dreams as a united series. It takes many stones to give us passage from one bank to another; hence we place the dreams in a similar fashion so that we can view them as different chapters in one story, the story of what is going on in our life at a particular period when the dreams appear.

I have a well-established relationship with several inner teachers who regularly appear on my dream landscape. Likewise, I am familiar with dreamscapes that I visit often in my dream experiences. Over time, I note their appearances during certain waking challenges. Viewing them as part of the continuing story of my life helps deepen my understanding. Seeing them as tutors in particular settings helps me see connections with parallel waking issues. Such guides me in much of my intuitive healing work. On the basis of a trust built over decades, I've come to know what I must face directly, and I act upon their appearance in my dreams. My familiarity with the various appearances has facilitated the expansion of my understanding and ability to handle waking-reality challenges. This widening of my perspective rises from seeing the dreamscape much in the same manner as waking landscapes, ever-present places that are visited during special times with special needs. For example, one goes to work, to play, to celebrate, and to relax all in their appropriate times. We do not expect to find computers when we visit a retreat center or tropical beach. Neither do we look for sunglasses when we seek our beds for sleep. Likewise, the dream, along with characters and places, appears to help us with specific waking-reality needs. As we move to see them as chapters of our life moving through many pages or days, we can draw links between a series. A series of a week may thus open like a novel, which does not reveal all in one chapter. Chapter after chapter, night after night, the plot develops. Yet, we need to look for connections. Since we already have our journal and dictionary to help us along, we can look beneath the manifest to find the links beneath the initial surface appearances.

EXAMPLE:

A dream analysis client had a series of dreams over a period of a month, which in the end contained certain common links. Following the previous chapters' directives, we arrived at the common elements:

The following characters were present in each dream, along with specific feelings:

• *His dream persona at her current age. Confused, lost, fearful, anxious, familiar feelings brought up in most of the dreams over the past month prior to analysis.*

• *A male boss from a career that ended poorly over twenty years past. Anger and fear.*

• *Male and female infants, unknown and without bodies. Just the faces appeared. Anxious, since children seemed alone without parents.*

The following locations were present along with the dreamer's emotions in each:

• *Some dreams took place in a thicket, a forest in the middle of nowhere. Not like anything familiar. Loneliness.*

• *In empty concrete lots that were fenced in like prisons, with barbed wire. Feeling of being trapped with no way out.*

• *In back seat of vehicles. Feelings of being controlled, since he was never driving.*

The following actions were found:

• *Trying to find the way out of the forest. Waking up in fear.*

• *Humiliation after suffering from bullying by an old boss*

• *Fearful of bodily harm when trying to climb over prisonlike fencing in the middle of the night. Unable to make it over the circular barbed-wire tops, falling again and again.*

Although it took several sessions to arrive at the above, one glance says it all. The mirror is on the waking life. Months prior to entering therapy, the client retired from his job of several decades. He expected to enjoy life with his bride of thirty years. Unfortunately, she fell ill with an aggressive cancer, which took her quickly and unexpectedly. His wife handled all the house bookkeeping. After her passing, he was lost on all levels of caring for himself and his home. Successful in his career, he now felt incapable of taking care of himself. He had no children. His friends were mostly workers. Thus, retired and distant from his comrades, he was physically and emotionally alone. The dream scenarios focus, above all, on feelings of isolation and fear. The dream children who have no one to take care of them show up to shine light upon his feelings about himself. His wife took care of him and is now gone; he felt like an infant. He feared for his future. Trying to climb over barbed-wire fencing, he was trying to make it out of the prison he found himself in. It was only six months after his wife's passing, and he was not giving himself enough time to adjust. The dream of humiliation with his old boss demonstrated his frustration and embarrassment over his situation. He felt he should not be having any issues and was uncomfortable with his feelings.

The series of dreams allowed him to face the situation and to speak of it openly, thus receiving the compassionate support he was sorely missing.

In continued therapy the dreams shifted. The children were no longer just faces but complete beings, often successfully arranging blocks in formations of simple houses. The old boss was missing. Feelings of humiliation were gone. The forest opened to a stream, where he found himself fishing, an old hobby he enjoyed. Slowly, he began to ease up on his self-imposed waking demands. He took time to join fishing groups and made new friends. All along, the dreams shifted, with the dreamscapes opening to display a wider view, something that helped him in embracing his new life. The sorrow was still there, but the hopelessness and frustration eased. Linking together the shifting series of the dreams helped him. The dreams showed him the way.

CHAPTER THIRTEEN

Using Tarot Card Imagery to Empower Dream Interpretations

The important fact to remember is that the images are each keys to understanding. . . . *The Mystical Dream Tarot* can help us to shine light upon our hours, inviting each of us to see beyond the limited view of waking reality. Dreams, beautiful dreams. Phantasmagorial journeys beyond the ordinary.

—Janet Piedilato, "Introduction," in *The Mystical Dream Tarot*, p. 13

Images are the language of dream, and the more images that arise, the more help we have in better understanding our dreams. A method I use to increase the amplification of dreams is to incorporate Tarot cards. Their presence adds an additional perspective on waking and sleeping dream-generated imagery. In this chapter I explain the process of additional imagery, such as Tarot card images, in service of drawing forward more dream associations and amplifications. I use my deck, *The Mystical Dream Tarot*, and randomly pull two cards, which I consult after the dreaming. These cards call alive personal memories and thoughts that help expand the dream landscape and assist in interpretation. Below I demonstrate how using an image taken from an art book acts in the same manner. Thus, even randomly choosing images taken from books and magazines at hand shall work adequately. The process is explained along with examples.

Amplification of the dream with the aid of external images such as The Mystical Dream Tarot cards

1. Before getting into bed at night, shuffle a deck of cards, preferably ones with lots of imagery, such as *The Mystical Dream Tarot*. Choose two cards, turning one immediately to view the imagery. Keep the other turned facedown. Get into bed and allow sleep to come.

2. In the morning upon waking, record what is remembered of the night dreams. Turn over the second Tarot card. Look at both cards. Write down immediate thoughts. What memories arise? How do the cards relate to the imagery in the dream? Look at the dream story. How do the cards relate to the dream images? Is there overlap with the imagery? Perhaps a butterfly appeared in a dream, and a butterfly is also displayed on one of the Tarot cards. This would signify a meaningful coincidence that is important. Does the butterfly signify some special meaning? A personal connection, perhaps bringing to memory a special event or person? If there seems to be no immediate connection between cards and dream imagery, think for a moment. Sometimes the cards wish to put attention on something missing, making a compensation available that is needed. Other times the imagery may point to what needs to be released, taken

away from a waking condition. Remember, the imagery is alive with meaning, meant to awaken the hidden. If the imagery on the cards—the characters, symbols, settings— were added to the dream scenario, how would it influence the flow? Look at the cards. Do they tell a different story from the dream? Does the Tarot imagery story deepen and bring more clarity to the night dreaming? How does all of this relate to waking life and its challenges? Does it mirror waking life? Is it the opposite of life experiences?

3. Sometimes we wake and do not remember any dreams. The presence of the two Tarot cards remains. On such mornings, we immediately go into the "if I had a dream" mode. We make up a dream and then turn over the second Tarot card. We move ahead exactly as above. The two cards help in widening the morning "if I had a dream" scenario writing and in fact assist us in seeing more clearly any waking issues that need to be attended to. Giving time to enter the imaginal mindset, to enter the creative intuitive domain, helps widen and deepen our experiences. As most writers, myself included, must admit, once we begin to write, something else takes over, another voice arises, which in the end is far more knowing than we. Thus the "if I had a dream" scenario becomes a form of automatic writing where the creative inner dream voice becomes present to guide and awaken us to the hidden aspects that are usually unavailable when we are in our waking consciousness.

I take the following from my personal dream journal, since it beautifully demonstrates how cards add to understanding dream. I record dream material, usually in the middle of the night, waking and emailing myself. In the morning upon waking, I revisit my immediate recording to make notes, which I quickly write down in italics. I do this quite quickly, allowing thoughts to literally pop into my head without censoring them. I wish to capture the immediate waking response. Thus, the most-intuitive thoughts rise.

EXAMPLE:

A sample dream journal entry:

Name of dream: The Plaza Hotel, "Gather ye rosebuds while ye may." John William Waterhouse.

I am in the Palm Court of the Plaza hotel. All around me are empty tables. It is between breakfast and lunch.

I am in the place in between . . . alone . . .

I am sitting at the small table with the white cloth. EB, a lovely Palm Court waiter from my past waking-reality life, brings me the silver teapot and a silver bowl of strawberries.

Silver for the moon . . . watery, emotional, tearful . . . an offering with the red berries. The Rubedo of Alchemy.

I smile. EB is wearing a top hat; he is the figure on my ancestral Tarot*.

10 of Pentacles: La Croix, Caribbean psychopomp deity, undertaker, he undertakes to connect us with our ancestry and is involved in inheritance and family ties. He stands at the crossroad between the inhabitants of the afterlife in near ancestry as well as far ancestry, joining each with the waking residents who walk the incarnational path. He connects all family, near and far ancestors. Dressed in a black tailcoat, glossy black top hat, and dark eyeglasses, he directs our vision beyond the seen. The Baron brings manifest, gifts of family, emotional and financial support to circle around us. He is the Mercury of Rome, the Thoth of Egypt, the Hermes of Greece. He is the communicator who bridges all boundaries; by his movements he keeps things fluid, keeping doors open for easy passage and exchange. La Croix is the cross at the center of all directions, open to each that the vision is panoramic. He helps us see from different points of view and thus accept a wide understanding of nature.

(unpublished from my manuscript for the Ancestral Healing Tarot)

Suddenly I see EB as a skeleton all dressed up for a wedding.

"Be happy for me, mother," said Ignatius, my son who appeared in a vision only days after his passing. . . . "For I am wedded."

EB takes my hand and ushers me into his sleek black limo. The car takes off, moving beneath the bridge leading into Central Park. The lights of the Tavern on the Green, the restaurant in the park, sparkle. . . . EB lets me out and the Ferryman greets me and takes me to his craft . . . we shall move across the pond to the wedding on the other side.

Vehicle, sleek black, nigredo . . . ashes . . . Death, afterlife. . . . The ferryman, Chiron, moving across the River Styx, the River of Eternal Life, delivering me to the Other side.

I am dressed in white . . . with blood dancing in a swirl down the skirt. . . . Albedo . . . the white queen . . . the red . . . the Red king . . . the mysterium coniunctio.

The blood: red is my mother's mark for luck, for protection. She pricked her finger and put a drop of her blood on the beautiful dresses she designed for me. The mysterium coniunctio, the alchemical marriage of opposites . . . the soul and the soma, the moon and the sun . . .

I carry blood-red roses.

The repetition of the red is made to place emphasis upon its importance. Rubedo.

The craft moves. Suddenly I see myself in the mirror surface of the river. . . . I am a skeleton. . . . Upon my head is the crescent moon. No longer moving on the waters, the ferry is traveling among the stars.

I am moving to the Other Side, a dream of wish fulfillment during a meaningful memorial day when I am sorely missing family, all passed, all on the Other Side.

My feeling is one of joy. The red blood, a gift from my mother. My son's words of passing being wedded, wedded to eternity filling me, reminding me of eternal life past the physical. Finally, EB in dream delivering me to the Ferryman to help me journey to beyond for a visit. The dream helped me remember what is important and everlasting at a time I needed such comfort.

Now to the cards from the Mystical Dream Tarot:

Lady of Swords. Here is the priestess ushering in a deeply spiritual period with a fiery awakening and enlightenment. She embodies courage and strength, often accomplishing her goals alone. Thus, she is often a widow or a single female, fulfilling the reason for her incarnation without much help. She has survived deep loss and abandonment but in doing so has undergone a major transformative crisis, one that completely stripped her of her grounding and familiar comforts, a heart-wrenching loss, yet it allowed her to climb the spiritual ladder, knowing the high cost of sorrow and death, of dismemberment and dissolution. She is self-actualized.

Four of Cups. The Fates and destiny. All is fate, written in the great book of life. From the water of the cosmic womb, we come into being, living a life, working through the threads, the fabric of our being. We suffer. We rejoice. The nature of being is movement through many cycles. We must honor necessity, what we cannot change but that time alone shall resolve while we tend the threads, weaving our stories.

The cards confirm the need for strength to carry on until the physical end. The Fates begin with necessity, along with the spinning, measuring, and cutting of the thread of life.

In view of waking emotions that carry deep sorrows at a significantly painful memorial date, the dream shines light upon the final reunion, coming together in eternity beyond the physical. The cards awaken memory of the importance of seeing life as cycling events, happy and sad, all passing. With strength, courage, and memory, I shall cope and carry on, knowing the end will come and rejoicing will replace sorrows.

Because the above was my personal dream, I share it for the many who like me experience tragedies and challenges, which demand courage and perseverance. When I completed my write-up and study, I noticed a picture of John William Waterhouse that called to my attention. I present the following thoughts upon viewing this, as an example of using a waking image as a help in expanding dream material.

The image is of a beautiful woman. The title is *Gather Ye Rosebuds While Ye May*. The painter is John William Waterhouse. "Gather ye rosebuds while ye may" is the first line from the poem "To the Virgins, to Make Much of Time" by Robert Herrick. The words come originally from the book of Wisdom in the Bible. These lines embody the carpe diem (Seize the day) philosophy: young women should make the most of their youth and loveliness because it will not last long. The poem is about making the most of one's time; also it is about the passage of time, and the fact that as we get older, we change. Like the dream and the dream cards, especially the card with the Fates, the message awakens me to remember the many seasons of life, each passing in the waters of time.

The dream begins in the Plaza Hotel, and so in two days' time the memory of my anniversary of engagement. My beloved, in his sleek T-Bird, drove to the circle outside the Plaza, produced a double-necked red wine bottle, and asked me to marry him. Long past now, along with the joys, but not gone with the sorrows, which remain, solidly the blood that continues to flow. EB, the lovely waiter from the Palm Court, someone I do not often think of and never dreamed of before, showing up in the dream to turn La Croix, Death, the supreme teacher leading me to the Ferryman, Chiron . . . and into the sky, reminding me of the T-Bird car where it all began—the bird, like the ba rising in death to rejoin with the ka, to be elevated, enlightened, remembered in the afterlife. Death is approaching as I age, and for me, it is a celebration, a wedding. Adding this to the image from Waterhouse, "Gather ye roses," complementing the roses in my dream. The silver bowl complementing the silver moon upon my dream persona head.

And so . . . all passes, joyful and sorrowful. We merely tread water in the River of Time.

END, dream journal entry.

Note that the journal is written simply, reflecting the flow of consciousness that wishes to go beyond any grammatical rules. We are not producing a literary masterpiece in our dream journal, but, rather, speaking a living testimony of our passage through time seen through the lens of dream consciousness. The more we seek, the more that is uncovered. Note that in the above I opened a cherished art book in addition to the two *Mystical Dream Tarot* cards, amplifying the dream in view of each. I may add that even opening one's eyes in the morning, we can see what in our waking room attracts our attention, using this to widen the night dream. Is it our clock, our nightstand, a random book lying on a chair, our shoes, a photo or painting near us, the sun coming in the room, a squirrel scurrying on a branch outside our bedroom window? Each has a message, since each image contains meaning. Thus, using the Tarot cards, a beloved art book, or room imagery is a helpful way to broaden and widen our search for meaning.

TWO

CHAPTER FOURTEEN

Dream Incubation
via the Waking Dream

Throughout part 1 of *The Dream Gate*, our emphasis focused upon understanding the language of dream. We came to understand that this voice does not arise solely during the night, when we are deep in sleep, but it can arise anytime, anyplace, often far removed from the sanctuary of a bedroom. The flashes of inner visions that arise to speak as we work or relax are hints at the vibrant inner life that goes on, often ignored by our waking mind. Once we become aware of this powerful voice, we can actively engage with it. Conversations are not one sided. Like relationships, there needs be an active engagement and positive interaction. Here is where the waking dream becomes the stage for the performance. While the physical world is stage to our waking interactions, fostered by our physical senses and rational mentation, the waking dreamworld takes place on the stage of the imagination. It is an inner realm ripe and creative.

Most of us are aware of our imaginal wanderings, the generation of "mind candy." We escape our waking challenges by moving into our imagined utopia, the perfect safe place accessed by virtue of our imagination. Perhaps one of the most famous "mind candy" generators is Walter Mitty, a character created in a short story, "The Secret Life of Walter Mitty" by James Thurber, in the late 1930s. It was updated as a film in 2013, *The Secret Life of Walter Mitty*, directed and starring Ben Stiller. Walter is an ordinary man who on the surface leads an ordinary dull life, which is compensated for by an inner life of extraordinary heroic deeds. As his wife nags him about driving his vehicle too fast, Walter shifts to fantasy, where he is powering a navy hydroplane. When in waking reality, he drives past a hospital, and his mind candy produces a scenario where he is a brilliant surgeon. On it goes, with Walter producing exciting fantasies to heighten the doldrums of his mundane existence. The book and the movie offer pure mind candy, raising the spirits with a life well spiced. We can all generate these escapist adventures, which may well serve to raise our spirits, increase our endorphins, and help us pass through hours of boring tasks and weather difficult, challenging times, yet in the end these are not the imaginal experiences we seek as we attempt to learn more about ourselves and our life path by entering the Gate of Horn, of truth.

While previous chapters presented many examples of waking-dream experiences, discussing and amplifying each for possible interpretation, less time was devoted for the serious work concerning the intentional entering of this powerful imaginal state. The Walter Mitty dream episodes perfectly explain the ease in which some of us may escape our waking environment to plunge into fantasy, without intention of anything serious. For some, this can be a tool for escaping responsibilities, delaying decision-making, or simply passing time. It can serve much in the same manner as modern theater, films, and commercially presented television series. Yet, one does not usually ponder a serious issue before choosing what to watch on the big screen or theater stage. Perhaps it may be an idea to explore. What if we have a problem we cannot solve or an issue we need to clarify? Would it be possible to then choose a film, with the issue firm in mind, and through the viewing of the film find the answer to our question?

I immediately think of an issue presented by a young woman in dream analysis. In her late thirties she has spent the years after college graduation attempting to manifest the career of her lifetime dreams. Talented and highly creative, she continually struggles to find a position that satisfies her desire. She is a hard worker, unmarried, continually casting off romantic relationships, focused and dedicated to achieving her goal. Recently I recommended an Italian film based on the Cinderella fairy tale, updated into a charming modern romance. The film *Cinderella*, with Vanessa Hessler and Flavio Parenti, tells the story from a unique place. In the 1950s a talented young pianist dreams of a successful life, following in the footsteps of her musical parents. Her parents die and she is left in the hands of a stepmother and stepsisters who thwart her attempts to achieve her dream. Naturally, since all fairy tales end "happily ever after," so does our film version of Cinderella. Her true love and inspiration is her Prince, her truth to her heart's desire, giving and receiving love. Along with it comes her entry into the world of music, at the same time inspiring her Prince in his own creative talents of writing. The young dream analysand watched the film and was enchanted by it. The gloom of her personal failure slowly diminished as she mirrored her life with the film version. Both parents were deceased. No stepmother was present, yet she saw inside herself the internal stepmother, the narrow drive to this one path, diverting any attempt at a relationship. She saw her opponent: refusing love was her real rival. She is slowly allowing herself to accept what was missing from her career goal-directed life. She now questions her narrow view of what would make her happy. The movie inspired her. She does not expect a prince to save her from her disappointments. Yet, she is hopeful that a healthful relationship would allow her to have a more balanced life. One hopes that opening her heart to give and receive in a relationship will empower her creative nature and help her achieve happiness. The movie, the imagery, like that of a dream, rose to touch and speak to her. Thus, I do not exclude using such a method. In fact, the viewing of drama has been considered healing since antiquity, when healing sanctuaries included not only temples for dream incubation but also theaters upon which dramatic performances took place.

According to Pausanias, an ancient traveler, the theater at Epidarus at the healing sanctuary of the god Asclepius, constructed at the end of the fourth century BCE, was a stunning example of architectural design, perfect in its symmetry and beauty. Pausanias boasted of its capacity to host 13,000 to 14,000 spectators, offering pilgrims a sensory delight featuring music, singing, and dramatic games, all part of the healing powers that overflowed in the place that included the sanctuary and incubation process. All played a part in fostering healing for the many pilgrims who flocked to its sanctuary, home to the healing deity Asclepius. Centuries removed from modernity was the belief that the observation of dramatic shows performed on the theater stage had positive effects on mental and physical health (Pausanias 1898:1:113).

My observation of the young analysand's reaction to watching a film, which produced a shift in consciousness toward healing, is right in line with the belief found centuries ago in this ancient healing sanctuary. Yet, there is a major difference between watching the many offerings on commercial airways and the theater presented long ago. We may just hit on the right visual to help our path, as with the suggestion of the above film to one in analysis. But in the great sea of presentations, we might just as well fail miserably, often finding ourselves deeper in our depression or confusion. While it is generally agreed that watching comedies is good for raising the endorphins and immunity, the opposite may be generated by watching disturbing, tragic, or sad shows. If one is already depressed, challenged, or stressed, care must be taken in choices. I often suggest that sensitive individuals chose something to watch and then fast-forward to the last ten minutes. They can safely watch without attachment. If the movie ends badly, they can move away and choose something that is more comforting. True, they see the ending, yet seeing just the end allows them to decide if they are strong enough to watch it.

On the stage of the ancient theater at Epidaurus, there were presentations that aimed at healing. Naturally, it is unlike modern theater or cinema. Since Asclepius was the god of healing, it is believed that most of the presentations included stories about the god, his birth, and his healing, as well as rituals of offerings and ceremony.

There are many stories about the god of healing. Asclepius is said to be the son of Apollo and a beautiful mortal woman, Coronis. Upon his travels, Apollo leaves a raven to watch over Coronis in her pregnancy. Perhaps due to her unmarried pregnant state, Coronis seeks to marry another mortal, Ischys. In other stories she falls in love with Ischys and is thus unfaithful to Apollo. Yet other tales have her traveling with her father, hiding her pregnancy and birth. The myths concerning her, her relationship with Apollo, and her death vary, yet the power of her womb, her child, remains. The raven flies to Apollo to inform him of Coronis's decision, and in a rage, Apollo turns the white raven black. Hence from that day forward, all ravens become black. Apollo sends his twin sister, Artemis, to kill Coronis with an arrow. Coronis is then flung upon a funeral pyre. In various stories, her child, Asclepius, is cut from her womb by Apollo or Mercury. Other tales have her deliver safely and leave the child, so the birth remains secret from her father. The ancient myths continue in diverse ways. In one, the child Asclepius is sent to the mountains and left exposed. A goat herder finds him and brings him up. In other versions, Apollo, regretting his actions against Coronis, brings up the young Asclepius and has him tutored by the healer Chiron, a half-man, half-horse centaur. Chiron is seen as representing the above with his human head and torso, and the below—the horse or hidden chthonic qualities—might represent the mentation and sensation of the waking mind, represented by the male head and torso, while the horse beneath represents what is hidden, connecting with the depths, the intuition and dream reality. In alternate versions, Asclepius is tutored by a snake who licks his ears, teaching him secret healing wisdom.

While the stories of his birth and his parents' complicated relationship vary, all culminate with Asclepius becoming a famous healer, even raising the dead. His growing fame eclipsed that of Zeus, who, enraged with jealousy, threw a bolt of lightning, killing Asclepius, hoping to diminish his power. The lightning merely killed the man and birthed the deity, who was no longer bound to the limits of his physical form. This is important. For while he was honored in specific locations, including shrines such as Epidaurus, once he was elevated to the above, he was no longer limited to physical localities but could now be reached beyond any physical limitation. Psychologically this places him within, in the realm of the dream consciousness, available for personal healing without the need for physical movement to an isolated temple far distant from us. This brings to mind famous words of the great Western physician Albert Schweitzer, who suggested that each patient carries his own doctor inside himself.

> They come to us not knowing that truth. We are at our best when we give the doctor who resides within each patient a chance to go to work.
> Albert Schweitzer, quoted by Norman Cousins in *Anatomy of an Illness as Perceived by the Patient*, p. 78

In our work, going within through the Dream Gate we find the doctor who resides within, beyond the limitation of time and space. Asclepius, the healing deity now beyond the physical, resides inside each and every one of us.

The theater performance of the ancient healing sanctuary provided the stage and the setting, the words of entrance, of enchantment. Speaking the words that would open the inner gates, like the magical words of Ali Baba that opened the secret cave of treasures, is key to success. Inside each of us lies this sanctuary. Yet, we best approach by creating our own personal theater.

Walter Mitty merely needed a cue from his waking surroundings to take off to his inner place of fantasy. He relaxed himself and escaped his boring routines. We seek something more powerful. We do not merely take off on the wings of fantasy.

As the ancient healing temple used dramatic performance, ritual, and ceremony as a prelude to an inner healing experience, so does our journey through the Dream Gate into the waking dream begin with meaningful ritual and ceremony.

In his description of the sacred sanctuary at Epidaurus, Pausanias gives deep importance to the area of the shrine dedicated to Asclepius, located near the theater. The masses were treated to the performances in the theater, which prepared them to enter the healing incubation shrine. Preparation was necessary. This is the experience we receive after we are adequately prepared. Think of the young woman who wishes a special experience of her wedding day. Without preparation and planning, such cannot be accomplished. We need to undertake the proper preparation if we wish to succeed at meeting the healer within. How fortunate we are not to be encumbered by the necessity of the waking-reality time and expense of traveling great distances. Yet, we do need to take the steps of proper preparation.

We have different attitudes and clothes for our different activities in our physical life. We do not wear evening gowns to play a game of tennis. Likewise, we approach a day at the beach differently from a day in the office, so must we create the proper attitude to approaching our inner journey to our inner healer.

Approaching the Dream Gate for Inner Reflection and Preparation

For our waking-dream experience of dream incubation, we must see ourselves as pilgrims seeking to take the journey to a sacred place in search of healing. Like pilgrims on the waking level, we begin by asking ourselves an important question: What is it we wish healed? Why are we taking this pilgrimage? In waking life, pilgrims flock to waking-reality locations, searching for physical and emotional healing as well as seeking resolution to posttraumatic life situations, challenges, tragedies, and losses. People may journey to Lumbini in Nepal, legendary birthplace of Siddhartha Gautama, Lord Buddha, in search of peace and tranquility; to Mecca in Saudi Arabia to seek union with Muhammad, holy prophet of Islam; to the Western Wall in Jerusalem; and to Lourdes, France, where the Madonna was believed to appear to a young woman called Bernadette. Each place holds special meaning for different individuals. Each travels for a different reason.

With our understanding of the healer within, we understand our travel is within the dreamscape. Not with our feet but upon our imagination may we enter our holy place. Yet, we must have a reason for our journey.

Thus our first exercise is to decide what is motivating us to make this journey: love, confusion, physical or emotional illness, loss, tragedy, transition? All these are possible issues. We choose one.

As we move through time, our issues will shift and change and we may visit over and again, each time seeking healing information for what most troubles us at a particular time of our lives.

In time we become familiar with our inner sanctuary and the comforts it provides. Like a daily prayer, we may find we wish to enter often to receive the healing empowerment of knowing we have a sacred place to always aid, comfort, guide, and empower us. There are no limits on our visits.

Knowing we have the space and articulating our reason for seeking, our visit opens the way to our next step. Now we need to find the proper place and words to help shift our consciousness, to present our offerings, as was done in the ancient theaters.

This can be quite simple. Since we carry the healer within ourselves, wherever we are is where our healing temple resides. Yet, wherever we are is also populated with waking-reality disturbances, phone calls, chaos-manifesting interruptions, and distractions. Thus, we need to shut out the world. Whether we are home or elsewhere, we merely find a room where we may have uninterrupted good-quality time for our inner pilgrimage. We shut off our phones, turn off our computers, and shut our windows and doors. We create a space of silence and solitude. For it is in silence that we may enter and communicate with our inner healer. We find a place where we may imagine our sanctuary. I often recommend visualizing a circle of rose quartz crystals surrounding me as I begin. With my eyes open, I am already moving away from what is brought into me from my waking senses. I am shifting my vision from the waking room to the circle of stones I imagine around me. My sacred space grows as I imagine sitting in front of a candle, a stick of incense, and a copper bowl of clear water. I imagine all beautifully arranged on a dark-black velvet cloth. For me, the dark cloth represents night, the usual time one seeks dream incubation. Darkness also represents the black cave into which pilgrims were led, seeking the healing dreams of communication.

With the candlelight I imagine the stars lighting the sky at night. Slowly my imagination is crossing over from using my sense connections with the physical room to experiencing the imaginal realm I am creating beyond it all. By this imagining, I am also honoring fire, air, metal, and water and earth. I continue to connect interiorly. I see myself in the center of the cosmos. My black velvet cloth, my ritual items, and the circle of rose quartz surrounding me are suddenly all there, with the great unknown beyond it all. I am ready for the enchantment, the few words or prayer to open the space move fully. The prayer is spontaneous. It rises and can be short or long. As feelings arise, I merely allow the thoughts to form.

Above, below, within, without,
All around me
I am in the center of the great cosmos.
I honor the waking landscape, which offers me protection and
guidance in the physical world
I come now, in the center of all directions
To offer myself, my pure intentions
To do good and avoid all that is against the rule of harmony.
I seek healing for
[at which point I present the healing, the question, my reason for my inner visit]
May I be accepted as worthy to enter through the Dream Gate
To meet and receive healing from
My healer within.
AMEN

My imaginal space is set in the waking room. I have made my offering. I speak my words of petition. Next is the reading of the script, like the reading of a performance enacted in an ancient theater, that which preceded entry within the healing incubation space. I read the script, telling the story of the inner temple I seek. Alternatively, I may tape and listen to it. I place a timer beside me, setting it for twenty minutes. Then in my imagination I take a sip of the clear water, which I imagine is a gift of the inner healer, the one who invites me to partake of the ritual incubation healing. I imagine placing the copper bowl back with the candle and incense, and I then close my eyes and seek entrance and experience.

When the twenty minutes is over and the gentle chimes of the timer alert me, I do not quickly rise but I slowly retrace my steps from the inner temple through the Dream Gate and back into my imaginal sacred space. I visualize my candle, incense, and copper bowl with water, and the ring of crystal quartz that surrounds me. I take another imaginal sip from the copper bowl and give thanks for all I have seen. I make an exit prayer much like my entrance prayer.

Above, below, within, without,
All around me
I give thanks for my safe return to the center of all directions.
I give thanks to my inner experience.
I give thanks for my healing.
I honor the waking landscape, which welcomes me.
May I now bring my inner healing to manifest upon the waking plain.
May it empower and guide me through whatever storms lie ahead.
AMEN

I give myself time to write my experience and to better understand it so that I may incorporate its healing message into my life.

Following this example, each of us may experience the waking-dream healing incubation.

Yet, with the waking-dream method we seek not the external image generated by another, but we seek the theater within, the imaginal realm of our own dream consciousness. My use of the word "theater" is appropriate. Even today in some countries, individuals entering a hospital room for surgery are brought into an area designated as the "theater." The theater is the stage where one begins. In the following chapters, I offer different waking-dream scenarios at sacred pilgrimage sites. As in waking reality, they offer different energies. I suggest trying each and, in the end, choosing according to mood. Like the waking-reality pilgrimages, our taste and needs shift as we grow.

The Pilgrimage to the Waking-Dream Incubation Experience

Life, to be happy at all, must be in its way a sacrament, and it is a failure . . . to divorce it from the holy acts of everyday, of ordinary human existence. The Greeks saw in every drink of water, in every fruitful tree,

in every varied moment of their living, the agency of a God.
—Freya Stark, *The Journey's Echo.* p 141

The waking dream, moving through the Dream Gate while lucid, softens our gaze upon our waking environment while empowering our communication with the inner voice of dream. The process becomes a ritual that widens our view of our waking experiences, awakening us to see life as part of the larger picture of being. By offering our petitions, our needs, our perplexing challenges, even presenting our thanksgiving for favors received, all during a dreaming experience, we honor waking life beyond transience, acknowledging the Mysterious Hidden, Nameless Source of our origin. In entering the waking dream as a ritual, we elevate life beyond our limited physical sight.

The following waking-dream meditation presents a Dream Gate pilgrimage, an imaginal journey to the healing incubation temple within our inner consciousness. It mimics the journeys of antiquity where pilgrims traveled miles over rough terrain seeking healing information from the god of dreams via dream incubation. In antiquity the process was simple. The pilgrim arrived at the sacred place and was met by residents of the temple complex. Ushered inside, they brought their offering gifts. In places such as Egypt we find pottery sherds along pilgrimage routes, the physical remains of the once-upon-a-time pilgrimage offering. When I visit and retrace these ancient routes, I often pick up a piece of broken pottery in my attempt to connect with its maker. My dream insert in a previous chapter of this work brings attention to the pottery sherds and my attachment to this experience. The questions that arise fill me with emotion, reminding me of generations of ancestors who made their journeys along the sands of time. I believe they brought their complaints, their petitions, and their dreams along with them. The pottery vessels carried all this, their physical offering to present at the dreaming temples. An ancient writer shares thoughts on such a pilgrimage:

Today we realize we do not need to physically journey to experience the healing incubation process. We can enter the silence and solitude of our own private space and imagine the process as we shift our consciousness inwardly. We focus beyond waking like the ancient shaman, journeying upon the imagination to visit the nonordinary reality of dream consciousness. While most of the time the shaman went on behalf of others, we may take this pilgrimage to aid us personally with our waking-life challenges.

The waking-dream journey shall bring us to Charonium, the healing cave of dream incubation where we present our petition, seeking guidance with a waking-reality challenge. The waking-dream meditation will relax and foster the shift in consciousness in preparation for our personal inner experience.

PILGRIMAGE RITUAL CHECKLIST:

I present the following steps as our pilgrimage to the dream incubation cave.

1. We set aside an hour free of interruptions. Close doors and turn off phones. Leave responsible people in charge of any waking concerns that may need attention. For an hour we shall be beyond waking communication.

2. In the chosen safe place of departure, a personal sanctuary, we ready ourselves, either physically producing or imagining the following: a black scarf or piece of fabric that shall be dedicated to the incubation process; special items of personal significance such as a stone taken from a favorite place; an icon, a small image of a deity, saint, or angel; and, if meaningful, an image of a plant (totem) or animal (power spirit), or both. Additionally, a bowl with a small amount of water alongside a stick of incense and a candle. Remember, we do not need these physically. If we wish, merely imagining their presence is enough.

   Sometimes I wish to enter the incubation space and I have none of these ritual props with me. Easily I shift gears as I imagine all before me. The ancient Egyptians believed in enchantment, calling something present. And in their voice offerings, the calling brought eternal gifts, which were not physically present. They were powerfully present in the imagination. And, most importantly, they were considered incorrupt. The imaginal offering would not decay and thus was a perfect gift. We realize that since we do not need to physically travel a distance to the dream incubation temple, neither do we need all the physical ritual tools. Additionally, I always have my dream journal present to record the date, my petition, and afterward my incubation dreaming experience. I recommend a tablet, a physical journal, any surface that may be used for recording notes on the experience. These may be placed in a convenient place for use immediately upon returning to waking consciousness.

3. Once we are physically settled in, we quietly focus on our intention, the reason we wish to travel to the inner incubation temple. We need to formulate a clear intention. Below are some suggestions. Journeying imaginally, we approach the Charonium, seeking help with any of the following issues.

4. Remember to take time to be with the ritual items, allowing them to help shift consciousness from the waking environment to the imaginal realm. This helps produce the liminal space of hypnagogia, consciousness between waking and dream. It is a softening of consciousness. Even if the items are physically present, we wish to soften our view of them, taking them internally, allowing them to dwell beyond the physical moving, alive within the imagination.

5. The following is a list of possible healing issues. Use it to help clarify the reason for the pilgrimage:

- Healing for self or for another
- Creative inspiration
- Communication with afterlife
- Guidance through blocks and transitions
- Helpful support in carrying difficult issues of change and loss
- Planetary communication for harmony and peace worldwide

Once the reason is decided on, the question needs to be formed. We do not seek a yes or no. We seek healing, clarity, and information to help shed light on a situation. The following examples are given. Formulation of the question:

- Shall I do this or that?
- Who shall I trust or seek for aid?
- Where shall I go in my decision-making: location, career, relationship?
- How may I uncover the truth in my dilemma?
- How may I better understand my life purpose?
- When will I heal my current hurt?
- How may I best aid another in their difficult time?

6. Once our petition is formulated, we write it down in our journal beneath the date. We are ready. We get comfortable, and, breathing deeply, we seek to focus inwardly on our journey.

7. **The Incubation Dream Experience.** We read and reread it. We become familiar with it, taking our time to imagine it, feel its texture, smell the incense, and feel the heat upon us as we imaginally prepare to enter its space. If we wish, we may read it aloud, recording it on our phones or computers, after which we can listen to it over and over again. We want to become familiar with it in the same way as we would attempt to learn and become acquainted with a physical-reality place we plan to visit. If we wish to record the script to play during our experience, then we must carefully follow the below directives, which allow for personal visionary time.

8. For some of us, entering the inner journey space may simply require sitting quietly with eyes closed for about twenty minutes, during which time the Dream Gate opens inside, allowing access to our imaginal waking-dream experience. For others, a twenty-minute recording of drumming, chanting, or rattling with a callback shall aid the process. Shamanic altering of consciousness makes use of monotonous drumming quiet effectively. Drumming recordings are available online for download. I recommend trying both ways to find what best suits. Personally, I find that mood dictates whether I wish complete silence or drumming. Often quite spontaneously, I find myself chanting to open the Dream Gate, which ushers in my experience. Other times I spontaneously shift consciousness in response to haunting music like that of Erik Satie. We must

accept our personal differences in the mode of shifting consciousness, our shamanic journeying. We travel on our imagination, the faculty that allows us to see imaginally what is missing in our proximal external environment. Yet, as the shaman thinks of his drum as his horse, his eagle, his vehicle of transition to the nonordinary reality of the dreamscape, so can we choose our personal vehicle. We can alter our consciousness by sheer desire to do so, in silence and solitude, or upon the beating of the drum, rattle, or chant, or to a piece of meditative music. We could set a gentle chime on our phone to alert us to the twenty-minute time span if we choose quiet. If we use a drumming tape, the recordings announce the approach of the chosen time frame by shifting the beat. This announcement allows us to offer thanks for all that transpires and to make our way back to our place of departure and return. Like waking-reality visits, we end where we begin, leaving and returning home from our visits.

9. When the vision ends, we treat the experience as a dream, writing and deciphering its many elements to source its reply to the petition. It may take more than one visit to expand and to finally understand the message. Like the pilgrims to the ancient Oracle of Delphi, the key to all is to "know thyself." The answer lies within, often given in a puzzle.

These instructions will be used as a guide for each of the waking-dream incubation pilgrimages. Place a red ribbon to mark the pages to help with each visit. Eventually, after many journeys it will become a well-known ritual. Yet, the discipline of following a ritual elevates the inner pilgrimage, empowering it with sacred meaning. Thus I strongly advise following this, becoming an initiate into the mysteries of the inner realm of incubation healing.

The Waking-Dream Script

In the following chapters, the incubation scripts may be read prior to seeking the incubation experience, or they may be read and recorded, after which they remain available for frequent visiting. There is a choice in how we listen if the script is taped. We can listen as we soften our hold on waking reality, envisioning the shifting from our encircled sacred place to the inner healing place, or we may recline and listen to the tape as we experience the inner vision. If this is the chosen scenario, then the taping should include a twenty-minute period of silence (indicated in the actual written scripts that follow), after which the remainder of the script is recorded. In this manner, we have a recorded version that ushers us into the experience, leaves us twenty minutes of private personal visionary communication, and then resumes to help us reach the end.

CHAPTER FIFTEEN

The Journey to Charonium, the Dream Incubation Cave

On the road between Tralles and Nysa is a village of the Nysæans, not far from the city Acharaca, in which is the Plutonium, to which is attached a large grove, a temple of Pluto and Proserpine, and the Charonium, a cave which overhangs the grove, and possesses some singular physical properties. The sick, it is said, who have confidence in the cures performed by these deities, resort thither, and live in the village near the cave, among experienced priests, who sleep at night in the open air, on behoof of the sick, and direct the modes of cure by their dreams. The priests invoke the gods to cure the sick, and frequently take them into the cave, where, as in a den, they are placed to remain in quiet without food for several days. Sometimes the sick themselves observe their own dreams, but apply to these persons, in their character of priests and guardians of the mysteries, to interpret them, and to counsel what is to be done. To others the place is interdicted and fatal. (Strabo, *Geographia*, XIV, p. 44, 1903)

The above text comes from the writing of the ancient philosopher, geographer, and historian Strabo. Born around 64 BCE, he lived into his eighties, producing volumes of text. In the quote above, he describes an extraordinary place, a sacred cave named the Charonium. Interestingly enough, Charon was the mythical ferryman, the psychopomp, who ferried the newly deceased to the afterlife. He is the brother of Thanatos (Death) and of Hypnos (Dream). In the shamanic experience, the initiate shaman undergoes what is called a dismemberment, a death. He is remembered, made new, as he embraces his role as shaman, walker between the worlds of the physical and the imaginal or nonordinary reality. Here in this sacred cave, the Charonium, we are given the hint at the experience one sought within its depths.

IMAGINAL PILGRIMAGE TO THE INCUBATION TEMPLE WITHIN CHARONIUM, THE SACRED CAVE

We begin, using the Pilgrimage Ritual Checklist.

PILGRIMAGE SCRIPT:

We sit in the sacred space of our personal temple, the home that gives us shelter and warmth, protection from the storms of life. We are grounded, the earth beneath our feet, our hopes soaring to the heavens.

Fertile earth beneath us. Give us stability.

Vault of the heavens above us! Shine light upon our path.

Air around us. Fill us with the essence of breath.

Water within us. Moisten us with new growth.

North, South, West, and East

Above, Below, Within, Without, and All about Us

We stand in the center of all directions.

Welcome us as we come with purity of heart.

We come seeking truth. Banish the darkness of our ignorance.

Open the Dream Gate that we may find wisdom and understanding.

We honor the physical realm, which feeds our form and gives us protection.

We now ask to enter beyond the seen.

We offer ourselves in purity of mind and spirit.

Hidden One guide us safely . . .

Ancestors rise and be with us.

We present our petition:

[Here we articulate the reason for entering into this journey.]

We seek healing, wisdom, and strength. Around us is the circle of being, all that manifests and roads on which we travel. We honor all directions and all being, joined in unity, birthed from common origin, destined to return to a common home. Traveling in the domain of time, we are all on this pilgrimage experiencing the transient physical. All this we acknowledge as we pause to fully embrace our position in the center of all, sitting in this temenos where past, present, and future collide.

The colors of the rainbow fill us, as does the fragrance of their presence. Rose filling our hearts, moss running through our veins, wood nourishing our hunger, and clear waters quenching our thirst. The sweet sound of birds calls us to the beyond. We listen and are filled with its gentle cadence. Memories flood us and draw us to the beyond.

The breezes gently move through us, filling us, giving flight to our feet as we begin to dance, turning gently like devout dervishes, entranced as we circle round and round. Shifting sands of time carry us beyond the present. Round and round we continue to turn, noticing the softening of our physical environment. Round and round the great wheel of the cosmos turns. Round and round it opens the chiasm that brings entry to Charonium, the sacred incubation cave.

We see the mountain peaks reaching into the blue heavens above. We have arrived. The fragrance of sweet incense fills the air along with something undefinable, exotic, intoxicating. Our head spins and we must sit and find our balance. We have taken a long journey, through the halls of time and beyond. And we, not alone, have arrived with the many who seek counsel, healing, and strength through the Great Hidden One, beloved beyond name and form, the Inner Voice of Charonium. We have completed our journey. We have arrived. We are officially welcomed as we hear the words of greeting: "Blessed are you who seek counsel, supplicants of the Hidden One. Come."

The swirling spiral of fumes continues to flow from the mouth of the cave, calling us. "Remember, remember. . . . Remember the long journey that brought you here!" Memories rise, filling us, memories from childhood. Memories of long ago. Like a picture show, our lives march upon the recordings of our consciousness. Important, significant, joyful, sorrowful scenes manifest, many acts in the play of our life. This is the long journey that brought us to Charonium. This is our pilgrimage of life. We have endured. We have survived. We have soared to the heights of joy and descended to the depths of sorrow. This is who we are, the sum and strength of the long road that led us here, the often-arduous life journey. We come to Charonium, famed dream incubation healing cave. We come to consult the Hidden One. An awareness stirs within us, an understanding that here, in dream consciousness, we shall communicate with the Inner Voice of the Hidden. Here, in incubation, we shall commune with the Divine Oracle. We shall gather the courage, strength, and wisdom provided. Here we pray we shall find answers to important questions that fill us. We realize that our vision, our thoughts, and our memories rise in response to our petition. We must allow each thought to arise, and we must remember that the message comes as a puzzle. Later we shall find the gem hidden deep within the memories.

We sit for what seems like an eternity. We relive our lives. We hardly notice the sky and the movement of the heavens as the wheel turns and day becomes night. Tiny lights appear at the mouth of the cave as white-robed guardians, priests, and priestesses emerge. They are both familiar and unfamiliar. Among them are ancestors, beloved family, and friends who once for a time walked with us on our physical life journey. Others, while strangers, offer compassionate smiles. Each of us is greeted by a robed guardian who joins us in our waiting. "What do you remember?" the robed one asks. "What memories fill you?" Slowly our stories fall from our lips. Slowly we relive moments, flashes of our life. And then we present our query along with our offerings. Sacrifice is necessary. We realize it is an essential part of this experience. What of ourselves are we willing to give in return for this incubation knowledge? Shall we promise our loyalty to truth? Shall we promise devotion, dedication to the path? Shall we offer a particular service, the gift perhaps of a special talent, which we shall use for the good of all? We ponder and finally we give response. We humbly ask it to be accepted.

"We offer all that is good and pure to the Hidden One, that we be purified and made acceptable to enter into the holy presence in Charonium, the sacred dreaming incubation cave. We promise to act with integrity and good will toward all the manifest. In the end we seek to do good, avoid evil, and conduct our lives within the code of harmony and justice."

Our presence, our petitions, and our offerings are accepted. The robed ones take our hand and help us rise. They bow before us and hand us a sprig of fragrant rosemary. They whisper:

"Welcome to Charonium. Your offering is accepted. Receive this herb of remembrance, that you always remember your offerings, honoring your vows and commitments."

We form a procession moving toward the cave. How strange it is that the cave that initially appeared so close is now at a distance. Beyond us we see spiraling threads of iridescent vapors curling and reaching out to draw us to our destination. Closer and closer we move. The threads weave cloth of light for each of us, shimmering robes that adorn our spirit.

The robed guardians step aside to invite us to move within the mouth of the cave. Inside we find a great pool of clear water, upon which floats one single lotus blossom. We gaze into the pool and then accept a goblet of its fresh water of remembrance. We drink and return the goblets to our guardians before moving into the tiny rooms that line this central space.

We find our tiny niche, a humble bed of linen-covered straw waiting for us. Our guardian helps us lie down and covers us with a blanket of soft, shimmering blue light. Our eyes become increasingly heavy. From some distant place we hear music playing, lulling us to relax.

"Remember your petition. Speak it aloud. Enchant it. Ask and find the way to the Hidden One and the voice of the Divine Oracle within. Remember . . . Blessings be with you."

The air is charged with light as we begin our inner journey for reunion while our guardians remain at our side, guiding and protecting us as we journey within to offer and to incubate our petition, seeking help, healing, truth, understanding, guidance, love, strength, and perseverance. We seek the answer to our waking challenge. We feel all form dropping off us, freeing us from the weight of waking-reality challenges. We rise to move beyond all trouble, to experience the healing of the cave. We feel an extraordinary sense of peace as we turn within.

[Twenty minutes of quiet . . . the time for personal memories and thoughts to rise in answer to our petition. * If recording this script, let the recording continue here in *silence for twenty minutes before resuming reading the remaining text that follows]*

The soft music plays and catches our attention. Slowly we wake as though from a long, restful sleep. We are filled with the vision of the cave. Our guardian removes the blanket of light and offers us assistance in our return from our adventure. We watch as the guardian raises a hand to catch a crystal that manifests in the air above us. Saying one word, "Remember," we watch as the many facets upon it send blinding light in all directions. We blink and in that one moment the crystal appears resting upon our outstretched palm as a memento of our experience. "Remember." The word echoes in our tiny niche. The guardians turn, leading each of us back into the central cavity of the cave. Our pilgrimage group gathers, and for the first time we realize this cave is formed from precious crystal. Floor, walls, and towering dome are multifaceted. We are enveloped and filled with its radiance. We are transfixed by its power and beauty.

The guardians speak: "Remember. Remember all that has transpired here. Take back the memories and learn, uncover your truth. Unlock the mystery of your being. The path is now open. Life is a journey toward remembering, remembering the truth of your incarnational being, of becoming whole. In the end you shall accomplish this knowing."

With these words we are led from the cave. Slowly, one by one we process. Unhurriedly, we part, moving from this center of inner wisdom, this sacred space of dream. Gradually our consciousness shifts, and we find our waking room coming into focus. We are safely returned to our place of departure. We allow our eyes to adjust to the shift, and, slowly giving thanks, we turn to locate our journal. "Remember." We remember the rosemary, our intention, our vows, and our offerings. We remember the sacred space we created around our waking room of departure, the cloth, the vessels, icons, incense, and candles either physically or imaginally present. We call to them, releasing them, thanking them for their presence.

Fertile earth beneath us.

Vault of the heavens above us.

Air around us.

Water within us.

North, South, West, and East.

Above, Below, Within, Without, and All about Us.

We stand in the center of all directions.

Welcome us home, back to our temenos.

We give thanks for our experience.

We shall remember as we now return to the waking domain.

Above, below, within, without,

North, south, west, and east,

In thanksgiving we close this sacred space, which shall be ever present

outside time and space, waiting for our return.

We inhale the scent of our waking room and adjust our consciousness to return to waking. We move to locate our journal, in which we begin to record what we experienced. When we are ready, we shall move to uncover meaning in the same fashion as our sleeping dreamwork. We can return over and over again to incubate our challenges to expand our waking consciousness with the help of the inner incubation cave, the Charonium. We will remember more and more as we expand our consciousness. We can expand our meaning by the addition of Tarot or other art imagery as we wish, since each shall broaden our understanding of our experience and its relationship to our dream incubation query as well as our waking challenges. We may return as frequently as we desire, since the dream incubation cavern is within our imaginal center. The road is before us and the way is made clear.

CHAPTER SIXTEEN

Approaching the Temple of Telesphorus: The Healing Asklepion for Personal Healing

Telesphorus, Blessed One! Giver of Necessities!

Accomplisher, Bringer of Completion!

Greet me! Accept my petition.

Come forward!

Free me from my malady.

Bring light to shine upon my dark paths.

Telesphorus, Bringer of Light!

Visit me in dream!

In this section we seek in the depths of our being, our healing in the healing temple of the Telesphorus. This waking-dream meditation is most powerful in seeking to heal a long-standing problem, helping us deal with disturbing blocks that keep us tied to challenges instead of opening doors to resolution. Telesphorus is son of Asclepius and brother to Hygenia. It is before Telesphorus that we place our petitions. Yet, this trinity of healing deities remains together in their work, producing the cure for what ails us. While many of the ancient incubation temples and public rituals officially honored Asclepius, Telesphorus cults were believed to be more of a quiet, more personal nature and therefore appropriate to be sought in the privacy and solitude of our waking-dream process. Telesphorus is the god most intimately concerned with convalescence and completion. This refers not only to physical or emotional illness, but most importantly to disturbing issues of a continuing nature, blocks that keep us from moving ahead and accomplishing goals. One goes to the incubation temple of Telesphorus seeking resolution, seeking to end one chapter of our lives so that we may successfully enter a new, more productive phase.

This waking-dream meditation will relax and foster the shift in consciousness in preparation for the personal experience of presenting a petition of a long-standing challenge that it may be healed. Here we receive healing, not only through the intervention of Telesphorus but also from that of Asclepius, his father, and Hygenia, his sister. Thus, we are reminded that healing does not occur in isolation. Mind, body, and spirit are interwoven like the threads of an exquisitely crafted tapestry. A weakness of one thread threatens the integrity of the entire cloth. Thus it is with our being. Mind, body, and spirit need to be balanced, and thus the three deities of healing work together to produce the harmony needed.

We begin using the Pilgrimage Ritual Checklist.

PILGRIMAGE SCRIPT:

We find ourselves walking quietly along an unpaved path. We, pilgrims, seek the route to the incubation temple of Telesphorus. None of us have journeyed there before, and thus we travel with uncertainty of direction, merely led by the herma, the small, unpolished gray stones that act as markers, set apart from one another along our path. We have traveled for a distance now and grow weary, since it has been some time since the last herma greeted us. We know these markers are placed by the Great Communicator, Hermes. Hermes, he who wishes to facilitate our passage and arrival to the great healing temple. Yet, weary we are for the long journey. The heat of the sun is relentless. Our feet are calloused and sore. Our sandals offer little protection with their thin soles. Dust seems to permeate our every orifice. We are hungry and thirsty, yet we do not rest until we reach the next herma. And we are reminded that if we do not accomplish this soon, we must return back to the last one and revise our journey, for perhaps we have not taken the correct road.

Lost in our thoughts, we walk through the silence. How long have we been traveling? When did this pilgrimage begin? Is its origin so far distant that we fail to recollect? Are we carrying this sorrow, this issue, this nagging burden, since our very birth? In silence we contemplate, seeking to reach back in memory. Born of the waters of Lethos, of forgetfulness, is this the reason for such difficulties? Or do we know exactly the time and place our problems germinated and grew? We continue to walk, stumbling, struggling to continue on, when slowly, in the distance, there appears a glimmer of light shining from an unseen origin. Is this the light radiating off the herma stone? We squint our eyes, shading them from the sun. Can we hope? Is this light a sign of our future success? After this torturous journey, dare we hope?

Our steps hasten to close the distance. One by one we move ahead in silence except for the sound of our sandals pounding the dry earth. One stumbles, and a hand reaches out to steady the imbalance of the other. We reach out to help the weak among us. Together we are stronger. Together we shall make it to this herma. Thus on we go, together, walking to meet the herma stone.

As we approach, we are overcome as our exhaustion gives way. We collapse upon the dry earth as we reach the small herma. Light emanates from the stone, and the warmth falls over us like a soft welcoming blanket. We drift off somewhere between waking and sleep. Anxiety is replaced by peace. Time seems to pass. We do not know how long we lay there. Only slowly do we realize that while our bodies lie, spread out like fallen birds upon the parched land, our sight descends upon the scene from above. Looking down upon the herma gives us the peaceful understanding and wise perspective on our own struggles. We see how in truth all is manageable. The part of us that worries, that is

---

burdened by life trials, lies sleeping upon the dry earth while our spirit, knowing truth, sees all as passing. More than hope fills us. We are bursting with surety, knowing our journey this day is already working its healing magic. With these thoughts we find ourselves returned to the ground surrounding the herma. The light radiating from it blinds us, and for a moment we close our eyes. And then slowly we hear the words drifting from the stone:

"Welcome, pilgrims, you who have been initiated by me, the herma of memory. Your arrival here was foreseen in the halls beyond time, where you joined in the eternal procession. Like the others, you come, tired, weary, and thirsty for the waters of life. Come near and take from me the goblet of the waters of remembrance. It shall quench your thirst and cool you."

We opened our eyes, slowly, shielding them from the expected ferocity of light. Yet, the light was gone. Only the raw stone remained. But what was revealed was the goblet that sat alongside it, water dripping from an aperture in the stone. One among us, an elderly woman, bent and feeble, approached and hungrily drank from the goblet. For a moment she appeared enraptured by some unseen visitation. Although she remained bent, there was a strength about her that was not present previously. She did not return to sit but took up her bundle, her heavy sack of challenges, as though it were merely filled with air, and glancing once at the herma, she bowed and begin to walk on the road ahead. There was determination in her step.

The second approached and then the third, and the one who was fourth brought forth the rest of us until we each drank of the sacred waters of the herma.

Like the old woman, we each were changed, no longer lost in our fatigue and anxiety, no longer unsure of the path ahead. And so the line of our pilgrimage moved ahead with great determination. We knew this herma had taken up over the invisible line between the profane and the sacred. We knew we were now walking upon sacred earth.

Beneath us the sand glistened like gold. Above us, the sky darkened only to give birth to the shimmering stars. On we continued. In our mind we carried our petitions, which were no longer heavy burdens. They were changed now, as were we. For now we see truth. Each burden is an offering, as we offer our journey to becoming whole.

On we walk. A song arises spontaneously, and we, earth and sky, human and divine, join in with this enchantment:

"We are children of the herma, initiates of the inner way.

We have risen to great heights, seeing beyond blindness.

We have partaken the waters of Memory.

The herma has initiated us as children of inner knowledge.

We are devotees of the herma, initiates of the inner way.

We seek the inner temple of Telesphorus . . .

We go to complete our healing.

We go to be remembered.

Shine the light. Shine the light.

Open the inner gate to the sanctuary."

The darkness grows and the stars disappear. We have entered through another invisible border. Song of the depths ushered us in. For now we navigate solely by our feelings, our deep connection with the internal domain of this, the inner pathway to the sacred temenos, to the incubation sanctuary of the deity Telesphorus.

Our feeling reaches out to guide us, and somewhere along the way we realize we are being led forward, connecting to an invisible grid of knowing. On, in silence, we walk. We feel the moist earth beneath us and the towering ceiling of this inner space. Off in the distance we sense a presence, hearing distant chanting. We remember. And we walk on, softly navigating the earth.

There is an earthy aroma that suddenly arises. We sense the fragrance of bread and beer. In the halls of memory the thought of beer-fermenting grain fills us. We see the beer giving rise to the golden domes of rounded loaves. On we move, now hungering for a taste of the sweet newly baked. Slowly we arrive at an inner cavern. In the very center there is a domed oven. Beneath it we see the rising flames. Above it the rising moisture from the open oven, its fragrance filling the space, filling us. There is a hooded figure in black tending the fire. He watches over it and the loaves. Around him are robed figures, each in white. We are invited to sit upon the earth, and in doing so we form a circle around the oven. We wait in quiet. We put down our burdens, laying them beside us.

We watch as the loaves begin to brown. Our attention so taken, we are surprised when the white-robed ones approach us with refreshment. We remember the water of the herma and we nod. This shall be another sacred drink. We sense the rising perfume of fermented mead, an ancient drink. We take it to our lips and let it slowly roll to the back of our throat, cascading down our esophagus, where it bursts with life, filling us.

We grow tired, and the white-robed ones take our hands and slowly move more deeply into the sanctuary until we come to small cubicles, in which are the incubation sleeping tables. One by one we enter along with our guardians. One by one we take our place in these incubation rooms. They are small cubicles with domed stone ceiling and walls. The floor is earth. There are no windows and no light. We see merely by our feelings, as though we move by some internal sonar. We feel protected, welcomed, and safe as we enter. How strange, but we feel as though we have reentered the womb, that liminal space that gave us shelter before ushering us into the waking reality. And now, we feel returned to this space between all. Slowly we lie down upon the waiting bed. Shaped from the stone, it feels surprisingly soft, perhaps a clue that things are rarely as they seem to be. The robed ones cover us with a linen coverlet. They then take a bowl of clear water and, with a clean linen cloth, wash our face, hands, and feet before anointing us with sacred oils. Satisfied with the purity of their ritual, each speaks, their words drifting from our individual dreaming cubicles to join beyond separation:

"Initiated by the Herma of Remembrance

Welcome to the sacred incubation chamber

You have drunk deeply, twice,

Once from the sacred herma,

And once by the fires of transformation.

Now your thirst is sated.

Your third drink is that of sleep,

For in sleep you shall drop your burden into the lap of Telesphorus

And he shall fill your thirst for healing with the light of his lantern.

He shall turn the lead of your burden into the gold of your memory.

Now sleep, and together let us go and seek the welcome of Telesphorus."

[Here each of us brings the issue we most wish to present for resolution, for healing. And in quiet, setting a timer for twenty minutes, we allow the inner images to rise, meeting Telesphorus and accepting what comes. If taping this script, let the recording continue for twenty minutes of silence before completing the recording by reading the below concluding text.]

The air around us is filled with light. We shake off sleep slowly, stretching our limbs. Lazily we rise. How is it, we wonder, that we did not notice the light within our incubation cubicles? Naturally it was not there before. It could not have been! We stand and fold our linen cover. We look down upon the stone bed and marvel at its comfort. The robed ones are waiting by the arched portals of each cubicle. They welcome us to return with them to the domed oven. Energetic and refreshed by our experiences, we move without delay and once again sit around the huge oven. The loaves have baked all through our incubation. And as the guardian removes them, we see that each carries a name. Our names were placed on these holy loaves, put into the fires of transformation, and allowed to grow golden overnight. One by one we accept our holy bread. One by one we break off a piece and place it in the fires as an offering in thanksgiving of our incubation healing. One by one we stand by our burden sacs. We notice they have taken on a different appearance. For a moment we are back at the herma, looking at the old woman, the first to partake of the initiation of the water of the herma. We suddenly realize that she was never a part of our group! Yet, naturally she is part of each of us, the wise part that although fatigued by life and sorrows is over and over again strengthened by the inner voice of healing. We remember. We are remembered, put back together, healed by this knowledge. We take up our sacs of challenges. They feel lighter and easily slide on our backs.

Together we give thanks for the keeper of the fire, the guardian of the sacred oven, and the many robed ones who kept watch over us during our incubation.

They lead us through the winding tunnel into the light. It is a new day, and each of us takes the road that leads us home.

We are remembered. We have received healing. We shall write this story in our book of days, remembering our visit. All these thoughts fill us as we journey back to the Dream Gate. We pass the Herma of Remembrance, and for a moment we pause and give thanks for the guidance given here.

Sun high above, we finally reach the fork in the road and separate to continue to our final destination, our waking-reality sanctuaries beyond the Dream Gate.

Entering within, we give thanks for the earth below, the heavens above, the air around, and the waters within. We are returned. We say our prayer of thanksgiving and of grounding:

"Fertile earth beneath us.

Vault of the heavens above us.

Air around us.

Water within us.

North, South, West, and East.

Above, Below, Within, Without, and All about Us

We stand in the center of all directions.

Welcome us home, back to our temenos.

We give thanks for our experience.

We shall remember as we now return to the waking domain.

Above, below, within, without,

North, south, west, and east,

In thanksgiving we close this sacred space, which shall be ever present

outside time and space, waiting for our return.

We slowly open our eyes to our waking environment. We take note of the very first thing that comes into view. In quiet we contemplate what we see before our eyes with what we experienced with our inner vision. Did we see a clock? Is this a message that the time is ripe for us to accept this inner healing and move to honor it in waking reality? Did a bird land upon our windowsill, singing a sweet melody of welcome? Are we now balanced by the music of the inner in perfect synchrony with our external reality? Let us ponder all. Waking reality shall rise to welcome us with these meaningful coincidences, where the boundaries between waking and sleep are perfectly aligned. We must be aware of such messages. And so in quiet we contemplate all as we move to locate our journal in order to record what we experienced. When we are ready, we shall move to uncover meaning in the same fashion as our sleeping dreamwork. Like archeologists we shall dig beneath the manifest to uncover the hidden gems. And the light shall shine through to aid, comfort, and guide us in healing. We can return over and over again to incubate our challenges to expand our waking consciousness with the help of the inner incubation temple of Telesphorus. We will remember more and more as we expand our consciousness. We can expand our meaning by the addition of Tarot or other art imagery as we wish, since each shall broaden our understanding of our experience and its relationship to our dream incubation query, as well as our waking challenges. We may return as frequently as we desire, since the dream incubation cavern in within our imaginal center. The road is before us, and the way is made clear.

CHAPTER SEVENTEEN

Approaching the False Door for
Afterlife Communication:
Incubation Dreaming for Special Intention

I have mourned you, and I will not forget you.

I will not be inert until the voice comes forth for you every day . . .

that you may live as a god.

Oh [beloved deceased].

May your body be clothed so that you may come to me.

—R. O. Faulkner, trans., Utterance 690, in
The Ancient Egyptian Pyramid Texts, 1998:2117–19

This waking-dream meditation is a pilgrimage to the False Door, where the shifting light of the afterlife shines brightly, inviting communication with beloved family and friends who have passed away physically but who live eternally in spirit.

We begin by speaking the utterance taken from the Pyramid texts, hieroglyph incantations engraved upon the walls of ancient tombs. The most famous is the Pyramid text of the pharaoh Unas. The small pyramid sits in the shadow of the Step Pyramid of Djoser in Saqqarra, Egypt. It is an amazing gift to all who enter it.

Let us imagine the journey there, for it shall prepare us for our waking-dream incubation visit seeking communication with a beloved who has physically passed away.

Together let us leave our private sanctuaries as we open the Dream Gate.

From the waking-reality room of our physical environment, we soften the hold of our senses, awakening the light of the inner world to open to us. Slowly the room fades away, inch by inch its colors melting into oblivion. A glittering circle of white crystals surround us, and we, in its center, are now in the temenos, the sacred liminal space between waking and dream consciousness. We utter a sacred prayer for safe transport to the beyond. We ask for the four winds to carry us forth north, south, west, and east. We honor the four elements air, fire, water, and earth. We, in the center of all, ask to be carried beyond the Dream Gate. In quiet, all becomes still. The gate appears before us as all shifts.

We walk along the sand, seeking to enter a small white van that shall carry us to Saqquara. It is early morning, and together we watch the sun rise over the sacred land. We imagine how the ancient Egyptians welcomed the sight of the great golden globe that flooded the land with light, banishing the shadows of darkness. Our van travels along and finally stops in Saqqara. We are quiet as we begin to walk to a causeway. To our right we see the towering Step Pyramid, marvel of the ancient world, built by the demigod Imhotep. We pass it, our eyes upon the white causeway that leads to a considerably smaller pyramid, the tomb of Unas. As we walk we see his cartouche; prominent is a rabbit image. How can we not think that like the rabbit, we move today to follow Unas down the rabbit hole into his tomb? Do we not imagine the children's tale of Alice in Wonderland? Because following the rabbit down the hole in the earth, Alice, like an ancient shaman, entered another world, a Wonderland, unlike waking reality, a world apart. Did not Unas once walk upon this same causeway, look upon the waking world, wear a body? Are we not the same as he? Naturally, Alice is an imaginary character, and Unas was once an ancient Egyptian pharaoh. So there are differences, and yet . . . Both traveled into another land, accessed via the faculty of the imagination. And so we, living upon the earth, do seek to have a glimpse of this other world, that which lay beyond the physical senses. The ancient shaman, altering his consciousness, traveled through a cleft in the earth, traveled down the roots of the tree of life, traveled down to the depths of the great ocean, all in search of another world, the world of nonordinary reality. There is a lineage here. There are ancestors here, connecting us beyond time, space, and physical heredity. We, pilgrims, are empowered by all that came before us. All that is experiences birth and death. Life outside our physical remains mostly a mystery. And yet, there is a way to connect, to remember, to put together what we forgot. To remember to put together communication with our beloved deceased.

Oh [beloved], I have come, and I bring to you the Eye of Horus . . .
Horus has filled you with his complete Eye.

—R. O. Faulkner, Utterance 29, in
    The Ancient Egyptian Pyramid Texts, 1998. p. 31

We remember the ancient symbol of healing, the magical and powerful Eye of Horus, son of Osiris, Lord of the Otherworld. Words spoken, one chanted in the tomb in honor of the pharaoh, for Unas, but today, instead of King Unas, the names of our beloved deceased are called out. For each who make this journey to the Otherworld, the land beyond, are joined in glory. And so we address those we have lost. . . . We remember each by chanting their names, for in remembering we bring them forward, calling to them, announcing our presence.

All these thoughts run through us as we await the opening of the tomb, the pyramid of Unas.

We approach and we wait. We stand upon the sand, looking at a small wooden platform that leads down an incline to the door and entry into the tomb. A guard stands erect. The door is not yet open, and thus we have time to contemplate the tomb and Unas, this pharaoh who passed over four thousand years ago. His monument remains. His name is spoken. His essence is ever present beyond the temporal form he once inhabited.

This fills us with hope. The blinding sun warms us and reminds of the ancients who so loved this glorious sunrise. The sun is far more than the physical fire in the sky. It is the light beyond the shadows of unknowing. As this tomb lives on, so does he whom it honors, Unas, now risen beyond the physical. Unas, now joined with the gods of the afterlife. We remember the purpose of our journey. We mourn our deceased, our beloved family and friends. We come to remember, to recollect what we have forgotten, the truth of our existence before we entered the physical, beyond our departure from the land of form.

Re [through the arrival of the sun] is gracious to you, and he conciliates the Two Lords for you. . . . Graciousness is what has been brought to you, graciousness is what you see, graciousness is what you hear, graciousness is in front of you, graciousness is behind you, graciousness is your portion.

—R. O. Faulkner, trans., Utterance 44, in
   The Ancient Egyptian Pyramid Texts, 1998, p. 34

Is it not symbolic that the door of the tomb opens, welcoming us to enter? We leave waking and we enter the narrow birth canal, bending low to make the passage from the land of the waking to that of the beyond. And we remember Re, the sun rising in the sky, brilliant, alive with light as we enter the womb of the afterlife. It is not symbolic that the light perceived by our senses merely hints at the brighter light of the afterlife, which appears only as darkness?

Our eyes adjust to the black interior of the tomb. We pass from the anterior chamber into the room with the vaulted ceiling, beneath which rests an empty alabaster sarcophagus. Here once rested the discarded form of the great pharaoh Unas. Unas has risen. He has joined the gods. Hope surges within us.

> *The doors of the sky are open.*
> *The doors of the firmament are thrown open.*
> *I am pure. I am conveyed to the sky,*
> *Thereby I remain more than human.*
> *I appear in glory for the gods.*

—R. O. Faulkner, trans., Utterances 563 and 565, in
   The Ancient Egyptian Pyramid Texts, 1998, pp. 1408 and 1423

We stand in darkness, which is no darkness at all, for the room fills with light. Before us there appears a door, which is no door at all, but a portal of enormous beauty, brightly colored with elaborate imagery of an offering table laden with ripe fruit, round loaves of bread, jugs of beer, bolts of linen, and mugs of alabaster. We are struck by the vivid colors, the purple, the turquoise, the field green, and the brilliant gold. The hieroglyphs come alive and we hear them calling to us:

Oh you who walk upon the earth
You who come to do honor to the ancestors.
Make this voice offering of all things good and pure
Say the name of your beloved.
Open your heart to sing of your love.
Give thanks for their physical presence.
Once in time for a time, companion, friend, lover, guide.
And now place your heart at your offering
As a gift of constancy.
Come forward and take rest beneath this portal.
Call to your beloved.
Announce your presence here,
Here at the false portal,
The door that opens not into a waking room
But the door that opens to the afterlife.
State your intention.
Why have you come? What is it you wish?
Call to your beloved family, friend, or lover.
"Open your heart and let your heart speak."
Beloved! Beloved!
Come to me! Come to me!
Let me caress your face! Let me hear your voice!
Come! Come! Come!
The door to the afterlife is before you.
Rest! Let the sun rise inside you!
Close your waking eyes and enter the Gate of Dream.
See the False door open . . .
Welcome the beloved . . .
Unite in the beyond . . .
Be remembered, rejoined with eternity.

The walls of the tomb begin to move, the hieroglyphs upon them moving, sending ripples of movement through the space around us. . . . Together we chant, four times, each time turning, like the arms of a wheel, turning, north, east, south, west, and north again!

Arise, O great reed float.
Bring forth our beloved.
Open to us, s(he) who is like Wepwawet, Opener of the Ways.
Bring s(he) who in passing is now remembered, made whole.
Arise, O great reed float.
Bring forward our beloved.

S(he) who departed not dead
But departed to greater life!
Arise! Open the door.
Let the communication commence!

All quiets. We lay our petition asking for communication at the base of the False Door.
We feel tired from our journey, and thus we close our eyes and await the opening of
the door to the afterlife, awaiting our vision of what lies beyond the Golden Fields.
We await communication with our beloved, s(he) who passed, alive not dead.

[Twenty minutes of silence (or rattling, drumming). Callback with the tape or with
a gentle alarm chime.]

Oh, Beloved. We give thanks for your arrival.
We, who walk upon the earth, give thanks.
For our vision, for our time seeing beyond the False Door.
We give our thanks making an offering.
We offer a thousand loaves of bread, a thousand jugs of beer,
roast meat, and delicate sweets.
We offer the finest of linen and alabaster.
We offer the gold of truth. We, who were blind to the hidden,
offer ourselves and our sight,
that we remember forever that we are remembered
as this day we remembered our beloved,
seeing that which was forgotten in the birth waters of forgetfulness.
We remember. We are rejoined with truth and with the knowing
of our eternal nature.
We give thanks.

We stand and for a moment we are filled with the silence of knowing. Then slowly we
turn and we bow low to pass beneath the birth canal that gave us entrance and now
facilitates our exit, our return to the sands outside this tomb. Slowly, one by one, we
walk up the incline, seeing the portal to the exterior. In quiet, so filled with our vision,
we walk down the causeway and pass the image of the rabbit, the cartouche of Unas,
announcing his name and his living presence. And we continue on to find our white
van. It moves ahead, like a white rabbit, this time to bring us to the final gate, the
Dream Gate that takes us to the center of all directions, in the middle of the circle of
quartz. We turn round and round before we exit through to waking reality, back to
accept our awareness of the waking-reality room. We are moved to look upon our
right hand, upon our palm. It is only now we notice our lifeline, over the very edge of
the palm, seeking to move beyond our sight, like our lives, never ending, merely
disappearing over the ridge of the horizon, ushering us to continue on shining like
the sun, powerful like the great hidden mystery that birthed us. Alive. Alive. Alive.

We are returned to waking consciousness. We seek our dream journal so we may begin to record what we experienced. We may not comprehend everything immediately. Time shall reveal hidden messages. We can return over and over again to incubate at night or during waking, communication with one passed. We can expand our meaning by the addition of Tarot or other art imagery, since the more attention we give to our experiences, the more we shall understand. Most importantly, this method of seeking afterlife communication keeps alive the bond once so cherished when the physical presence was a joyful companion. Experiencing a personal connection is an extremely powerful way of piercing the veil of unknowing that shrouds our understanding of the afterlife.

CHAPTER EIGHTEEN

Pilgrimage to the Great Clearing
in the Hidden Forest of Possibilities

The mist was very dark . . . white and wet, and the cobwebs festooning the gaunt tree trunks were weighed down with thousands of shimmering, pear-shaped crystals. But it was not cold. Only still and secret and private, a hushed world within a world . . . and after a while . . . a clearing not open to the sky but clear on the ground. Long, wet grass stood there, and pine needles lay dark around the feet of the surrounding trees. In the centre, a well of water bubbled up and trickled away through the grass in two little channels already grooved in the spongy turf.

—Pauline Gedge, *The Eagle and the Raven*, 2007, p. 68

As we travel through life we are not always certain of our path. For a time, in time, we may feel we are in a comfortable place where change seems far from our domain. Then, like a stroke of lightning in a flash, the thunderbolt strikes, and we are left cut off from all that is familiar. Like travelers cast to sea without oars to steer our raft, we are left to the rages of sea and sky. Perhaps it is a turn in finances, relationship, or career that places demands on us, rapidly requiring decisions to be made, contracts to be signed, or heart-wrenching choices to be set in place. None of this is easy, and so often we feel isolated in our life-changing moments. Transition is rarely easy. The fairy-tale "happy ever after" ending that is projected upon the transition from youth to adulthood, as the hero or heroine accomplishes a task and wins their prize, is merely one act in the many acts of our life story. Thus, to live fully, each of us experiences the heights of the joyful along with the depths of the more difficult. We may reach out to family, friends, advocates, or whomever we can speak to as we attempt to find our grounding and our path ahead.

The time of transition, especially one that comes from the dark and takes us by surprise, is a time when we need to seek the wisdom of silence. For the dream voice arises to comfort and guide us through the storm of uncertainty. The questions fill us: Where do I go? What do I do next? Whom can I trust? When should I make my first move? How may I clear up the confusion that devours me? What do I watch out for?

At these unstable times we should pay special attention to our dreams, seeking to interpret them, for they remain our constant guidance, awakening us to the pitfalls and detours of our possible choices. Yet, sometimes the chaos and stress of instability and worry interrupt our sleep and sweep away any memory of our dreamscapes. In these times it is especially helpful to seek a waking-dream incubation to remedy this loss in communication with our deep inner voice. We can remedy our situation by taking the waking-dream pilgrimage beyond the Dream Gate in order to find clarity.

This is a very significant step in our acknowledging the importance of the dream reality as a companion guide to our waking actions. Here, then, we begin by an act of purification. Setting aside the time for this is as significant as the spiritual rituals performed by our ancestors as they brought their waking-reality challenges to the Hidden Divinity. Whether they entered a physical pilgrimage to a distant place or visited a local tribal sanctuary, temple, church, or mosque or even visited a place within their dwelling, an image, icon, or statue representing the Divine in a physical form, in the end each was seeking help from what is not physically present but psychically manifest. In some traditions, a certain period of time, noted by the appearance or disappearance of the moon, the marker of cycles, put the boundaries of sacred space around their intentional incubation petition. All was begun by bathing, cleansing oneself of all obstacles. Thus, we begin our incubational journey by taking a ritual bath or shower, making the intention to purify ourselves so that we enter our incubational waking dream cleansed. If we have a special shawl, scarf, or piece of jewelry, we put it on. In some spiritual rituals, individuals cover their heads and remove their shoes before entering a holy site. All this helps us move apart from the waking reality, honoring the temenos, the sacred space, that we enter. Our voices hush, and quiet fills us. We respect the passage from the profane into the sacred.

Thus, in the center of our chaos we take time for ourselves. Wrapped with the sacred that fills us, we continue. We find our quiet space. We turn off our electronic devices, close our windows and doors, and light the inner candle of intention. We bring to mind our troubling situation and formulate what it is we seek that would most help us cast light upon the path ahead of us. We seek this in tiny steps. We are not looking for the year ahead but merely the days and weeks from our current situation. We are looking to get our footing on the rocky incline. For it is difficult to climb from our place at the very bottom of the mountain. We cannot see the view from the top.

We think about what would be most helpful to us in the coming days. We review our dilemma and formulate our question: Where do I go? What do I do next? Whom can I trust? When should I make my first move? How may I clear up the confusion that devours me? What do I watch out for?

The query set in our mind, we sit and we begin our journey, setting aside at least an hour for this experience. We review and accomplish our Pilgrimage Checklist and we are ready with journal, timer, and recording, if used.

We sit in the center of our temenos. We imagine the shimmering light of the rose quartz circle around us, our boundary insulating us from the chaos of the waking world. We breathe in the air, delighting in its sweetness, which fills us with warmth. Our mind drifts back to our bath. Thoughts come to mind, fleeting yet sure, surfacing before disappearing, again and again. Each dancing before our inner eye, each a tiny bubble rising from the hidden depths of the pool of unconscious. Finally, one thought arises and gains stability. We see an elaborate portal on a beautifully painted wall. Green ivy leaves and white belladonna flowers wind their way up the salmon-colored stucco wall, forming an archway framing the sturdy wooden door. We look down to see an earthen jug and pair of crystal-studded red slippers resting by the right side. The door has a window covered with mashrabiya. Intricate wooden latticework opens to a series of multicolored veils. Taking one last look at this entry, we remember our need, our reason for seeking our way through the Dream Gate. We bring to mind our query. We ask to be given entry. We close our eyes and say a few words of prayer.

> Earth beneath us
> Heavens above us
> Air that surrounds us
> Water that flows through us
> In the center of this sacred space
> We make an offering of ourselves.
> Purity of intention, harmony of actions,
> Accept our gifts!
> Give us entry!

We see the door drift open, and in the shifting light from within we find ourselves crossing the portal. The door quietly closes behind us, and for a brief moment we are enveloped in the warm glow of light and exotic fragrance. We close our eyes to absorb it fully. Every pore of our being seemed infused with the power of the moment, as though we are submerged in a faraway spring where the water rains upon us from a high waterfall while we stand within the caress of its mystery. We breathe in deeply before reluctantly we open our eyes. What greets us is not far from our vision, a magical, peaceful dwelling filled with the light of a thousand heavenly stars.

Enchanted, we find ourselves bathing in a well-worn yet beautifully hand-hammered copper tub. The light drifts upon its surface, dancing, mesmerizing us with the patterns formed in its wake. The water caresses us as we soak in the warmth, the fragrance, and the beauty of this enchanted space. Above us is the dome, open to the heavenly stars that shine down upon us, stirring each fiber of our being. Our soul reaches upward, stretching, yearning for union with something so powerful yet utterly mysterious, remaining beyond our comprehension. We rest and yet we seek to rise, to go beyond this copper vessel that has seduced our senses, awakening us to something that calls to us. Yet, we rest and continue to allow every cell of our consciousness to wake and soak in this wondrous bath. We raise our hands from their position resting along the smooth copper ridge that circles the tub. Gently we dip first our fingertips and then slowly our hands, submerging each up to our wrists. We watch the rippling movement that circles around our hands, two circles widening and meeting, joining, merging. Lazily we repeat the action, captivated by it. We close our eyes and sink more deeply into the warmth. Steam rises, increasing our sense of protection, taking us deeply inside a mysterious place that remains a distant yet articular memory. We feel called to sink more and more deeply into this hypnotic state. Eyes closed and then opened. We are beneath the water. We can breathe. We accept this thought as though it is not unusual but purely natural. Without thinking, we begin to swim, moving at great speed, flipping over, tumbling, stretching, playfully enjoying what greets our eyes. Before us is a water spirit, a cosmic serpent with the torso and head of a human and a long tail of a fish. We remember the ancient tales of merfolk, creatures from the hidden depths who come from the cosmic womb to befriend humans, to guide and accompany us on our adventures beyond the seen. Eye to eye, we remain as the world of the hidden begins to reveal itself. We see a lamp in the land of the merserpent. Its light is golden, casting a shimmering net over our underworld surrounding. Fish of every size swim close to us, alive, intelligent, making eye contact as well. What do they wish to show us? The merserpent begins to swim, beckoning us to follow. We follow. Time seems to stop, and in slow motion we observe above us a school of fish moving slowly in a circular fashion. Below us we see the darkness of the fathomless depths.

We find ourselves drifting without effort as we gaze at tiny bubbles in which small, delicate beings tumble and laugh. So free, we find this a place where being is all that matters. There are no problems. And yet, suddenly without warning, we find we are merely resting upon a mossy field beneath the noonday sun. We remember our intention. Before us we recognize the giant being who beneath the waters appeared as a merbeing. Now this powerful one holds a trident in one hand. Lord of the watery depths, of the Sea of the Unconscious, is Poseidon, he who knows many things. He is our guardian, taking us through the waters of the depths, cleansing us of our worries so we may approach the Hidden Forest of Possibilities to enter the incubation clearing, where we receive answers for our questions.

We rise, shielding our eyes from the great globe of the sun. Poseidon towers over us, casting his shadow that rides above us like a great canopy, protecting us from the scorching heat. In silence we walk. Poseidon, shrouded in mystery, digging his trident into the sands, guiding us, ushering us forward.

In the distance we see a towering forest silhouetted against the bright sky. It plays with us, one minute a primeval thicket of flickering green shadows and then, in a flash, a fortress of enormous proportions, massive stone walls, towers with turrets and flying banners, all a play of light and shadow and mounting heat. It is mesmerizing, seductive.

We yearn to reach this mysterious place. Can it be that after our long journey we shall soon be welcomed to the hidden sanctuary, the clearing within the Forest of Possibilities? Is our destination imminent? Our limbs hasten to accomplish our desire. We yearn for this, hoping our arrival shall bring us close to our incubation ritual. Such are our thoughts as we speed onward beneath the steady shadow of Poseidon. Our thoughts turn to Poseidon. We cannot help thinking how he seems so at ease upon the land, beneath the scorching sun of Zeus. Poseidon, lord of the watery depths, showing us the way.

A voice rises. All movement ceases. The air stands still, the forest ahead vanishes, and even our guide, Poseidon, disappears. Only the voice that fills the void:

I, Spirit of the Depths, have neither form nor name.
There are no boundaries to confine my nature . . .

I am Mystery risen from the Primeval Waters.
I am the Cosmic Womb of all Being.
Cast into the belly of the cosmos, I am hidden.
I rise to accompany seekers, pilgrims yearning for truth.
I appear in many guises.
Today, as Poseidon, I lead you to what you seek.
Without my presence you would neither perceive nor enter
The Forest of All Possibilities!

We are frozen in isolation. Without the canopy of Poseidon, we are burning with the heat of the sun. There is nothing but blinding heat. We cannot see!

In a flash, great laughter fills the void and with it the reappearance of our companion and his protective canopy.

The world of the sun
Is the world beyond what we seek.
Know that. Remember well.

The voice fills us, working its magic. We feel revived, filled with new energy, ready to complete our journey. Our steps are strong as we move forward. Soon we arrive at the end of the barren land, crossing over a narrow bridge. The gurgling of the water below fills the air. There are goldfish, shimmering as they rise to the water's surface, dancing in welcome to us. Above us the royal-purple wings of dragonflies fill the air. We smell the moist moss ahead and catch sight of lizards and toads sitting at the water's edge. Here is a place bursting with life. As we raise our eyes to view the towering boughs, we see swallows and nightingales looking down upon the bridge, watching our arrival with great interest and welcoming approval as they sing sweetly. All this along with the cool that now brings refreshment as the sun disappears behind the forest.

Poseidon is first to set foot upon the other side of the bridge. His stature grows, and we see that it is he who is the portal into the forest. His legs are now fishtails, between which we enter beyond. With that, he disappears. We are inside the mysterious forest.

There is no path, and yet, upon our approach, the trees bend and open a clearing to us. Slowly we move forward. We are surrounded by the support of this ancient dwelling. Upon the ground ahead are tiny mushrooms sprouting up to lead us. With each step they move ahead of us, and together with the brush, trees, and welcoming song of the birds above, we feel safe, happy to finally be near the ancient clearing where sacred incubation is sought. We finally arrive beyond the thicket. Before us is the Great Clearing. It is a sacred temenos surrounded by great oak trees. In the very center is a polished gray stone, on which sits a simple basket filled with acorns. Beside it stands an elderly man. His hair is matted and pure white, tangled, falling to his shoulders. His clothes are fashioned of leather, sewn with spider silk. He holds a staff, around which rests a slender serpent, its blue-and-gold diamond pattern beautiful and regal in contrast to his simple appearance. He nods his head in welcome. His eyes, blue and deep like the great ocean, holds a wisdom hidden by his physical appearance.

We circle around him as he directs us to turn around. We see our incubation beds, mounds of earth covered with white linen cloth. At the foot of each is a jug of water and a bowl. We remove our shoes and instinctively place our feet in the cool water, cleansing them of the journey's dust. We pour water over our hands, cleansing them as well before we dry all with the awaiting linen cloth. And then we lie down upon our beds. The sky above us sparkles of a sprinkling of stars, one shining most brightly: Sopdet, the ancient one who comes to announce the coming of the inundation, the rising of the waters of the unconscious, to welcome us and give rise to our incubation healing. At this time of transition, we seek guidance to shine light upon the future. We bring to mind our troubling situation and formulate what it is we seek that would most help us find our way in the coming days and weeks. With our intention in mind, we close our eyes.

The Dream Gate is above us. We see it as an opening in the fabric of the sky above, a portal through which Sopdet, the great eternal star who has now descended from the great heights to meet us, offers us passage to the great Hall of Wisdom in this, the clearing of the Forest of Possibilities. We look up and marvel, yearning to move through the portal. Slowly we realize the portal grows larger, as though Sopdet is descending. Yet, we do not realize that the waters of the unconscious upon which we arrived are rising, rising to reach the portal, rising to give us entry to the beyond, to the great Hall of Wisdom, where we may communicate our petition to seek guidance.

The light overwhelms us. The joy fills us. After the long pilgrimage, we have arrived. Our personal communication begins.

[Twenty minutes of silence, drumming, or rattling, for the personal visitation and private incubation healing, after which we resume reading and recording the rest of the script.]

We give thanks for our vision and we see the portal open once again. One by one we drift through it, watching Sopdet receding to the great heights as we descend to return to our mossy beds circling the great stone in the center of the forest. Our guardians welcome our return, and we accept refreshment from them, an elixir of herbs from the sacred forest, which ensures that the memory be retained of our journey here, along with the route we took so that we may forever return when there is desire and need.

Refreshed, we turn and see the tiny spirits of mushroom ready to open the thicket for our journey back to our place of beginning. We follow in silence, our feet never touching the earth but merely drifting above it, so light and joyous from our experience beyond in the Hall of Wisdom.

Poseidon awaits us at the forest's edge and with one huge breath calls upon the waters to safely drift us back. Slowly we become aware of the great dome of the heavens above, the fertile earth below, the air around and within, and the waters from which we take our origin and our destination.

The waking reality welcomes our return. We shift our consciousness and move to quietly record our visit, honoring all we saw. In the hours, days, and weeks ahead, the visit shall yield information to guide and nurture, to comfort us. Our return visits shall assist us in our time of transition, empowering us to move beyond fear and reluctance. Change is difficult, but accompanied by the inner voices that rise in the incubation, we understand we are never without help.

CHAPTER NINETEEN

Journey to the Mansion of Many Rooms on the Isle of Remembrance Waking-Dream Incubation to Revisit and Expand the "Big Dream"

The beginning is light.

The end is unified darkness . . .

. . . the secret plan . . .

is not known by any person save a few.

In the secrecy of the Netherworld, unseen and unperceived.

Whoever knows this . . . will be a well-provided Akh spirit

(one fully aware, truly whole).

Always will he leave and enter again the Netherworld

And speak to the living.

A true remedy, (proven) a million times.

—Erik Hornung and Theodor Abt, "Closing Text," in *The Egyptian Amduat: The Book of the Hidden Chamber*, translated by David Warburton, 2014, p. 424

We lay our heads upon a pillow and sink into the depths of dream, entering a dreamscape where we observe or participate, alone or with others, in a place either familiar or foreign. We awake and we remember, part or all. We are often left with questions, missing endings, intrigues that we wish to revisit. Perhaps we awoke in the middle of the night and found ourselves wishing to return to the dream. We may even attempt to fall back to sleep but are unsuccessful at reentering our desired dreamscape. In part 1 of this text, the waking-dream method was presented for ordinary dreams that end leaving questions that beg for additional information. The dream presented was of an ordinary dream.

Sometimes we have a dream that just remains with us, calling to us like the sirens in mythology. It is what I call the "Big Dream." This dream demands special attention. The Big Dream has a numinous nature. It stirs the soul and touches us deeply. We intuitively know it means something far more than what appears on the surface.

I can give an example of a dream I had over thirty years ago:

In the dream I find myself in a library where bookshelves go on endlessly, both vertically climbing beyond any visible height as well as horizontally in spoke-like aisles that stretch in all directions from a beautiful central labyrinth. I stand in the labyrinth and can see the books as well as a hidden chapel nestled behind all. I walk into the chapel, and there is a curtain to the side of the altar, behind which sits a veiled lady holding a book, seated by a spinning wheel. I exit the chapel and begin to walk down one of the book aisles, stopping to remove one book from a shelf at eye level. I open it, only to find every page displaying a sketch of a landscape with one word beneath each image. I place the book back on the shelf and take another. The same images over and over again, until my last attempt to replace the book on the shelf is unsuccessful. Indeed there is no room. I walk to the labyrinth, thinking how strange this all is, sliding down the wall of books to land upon the stone labyrinth floor. The book bounces on my lap and opens, and suddenly characters rise into the air and dance before disappearing.

I wake. I write the dream (which was much longer with far more happenings that my shortened version above). The one word in the dream books had me intrigued. I knew it meant something important that my unconscious wished me to understand. I looked it up in one of my library books (there was no internet at the time of the dream). Temenos. Sacred space. From that moment on, I took that name, Temenos, to be my own, the name I would use for my spiritual shamanic work. Arisen from the unconscious, it called to me. Thirty years later I find myself living on the very landscape displayed in that dream. I live in a house of books, the former home of a publishing company, a residence visited by great authors such as F. Scott Fitzgerald Ernest Hemingway, and Sir Winston Churchill. I have the endless aisles of books. I have the labyrinth and the chapel. Thirty years later, the dream still calls to me. And during all this time, it has come to me in many dreams, expanding what I understand. Entering this space is and shall always be for me sacred, *Temenos*. This is a "Big Dream." By numinous, I mean spiritually stirring. Those of us on spiritual paths may experience a vision or waking-reality event that is the "Big Dream." If we wish to expand upon it, the following incubation journey to Temenos, sacred space honors it, giving it the special place it deserves.

We can create the time to reenter this "Big Dream" while awake. Like a lucid dream produced during sleep, this return visit produced during waking allows us to have one foot in waking reality and the other in dream reality. We turn our attention inward, yet 1 percent of our consciousness, what I call our critical observer, remains aware of our waking-reality body and room. At night in the lucid dream, we know we are sleeping, experiencing a dreamscape. We know our perception is of dream, not waking reality. In the waking-dream revisit, we are aware of our waking conscious state while we focus inwardly on the imaginal landscape of the return visit to our dream.

We may explore the dreamscape more fully, communicate with a dream character, seek a missing ending, or resolve a perplexing scenario in need of clarity. Since the "Big Dream" is one that shall take us through many years or decades of our life, as in my example above, we can expect many visits both during sleep as well as in the waking-dream revisit. In the end, such a dream is of enormous value since it is the golden thread that connects the two realities of consciousness, making us whole, helping us see how the inner and outer work in harmony to guide and to accompany us. Such dreams expand our understanding of the big questions of life.

Whoever knows this . . . will be a well-provided Akh spirit
(one fully aware, truly whole).
Always will he leave and enter again the Netherworld
And speak to the living.
A true remedy, (proven) a million times.

Thus, in the center of our chaos we take time for ourselves. Wrapped with the sacred that fills us, we continue. We find our quiet space. We turn off our electronic devices, close our windows and doors, and light the inner candle of intention. We bring to life our "Big Dream." Honoring it, bringing it alive. We can read our notes. We can embody our feelings of awe at the experience that filled us. We may not comprehend its meaning. Yet, we feel deeply and are touched by it. We wish to revisit the domain, communicate with the spirit of the dream. This is our intention.

Since this is a very special incubation, I suggest dedication of something special to be taken to mind, noting something symbolic of the numinous nature of this event. Perhaps we choose a crystal, an amulet, a tiny statue—in reality or in the imaginal treasury of the mind—to place upon our sanctuary to honor this dream. For this is about far more than a simple dream providing guidance for a few days or months of life. This is going to be a map for, at very least, a significant period of our life. Since my several "Big Dreams" are ongoing, still expanding, they play a continual role in opening me to better understand the many aspects of my life and my relationship to the cosmos. I might add, my oldest "Big Dream" first arrived when I was a small child of around four years of age, and continues to teach me still. It remains my oldest memory, a hypnagogic dream, I believe, although even in memory I see it as happening as I was awake, sitting up on my bed. I always remembered it as a "real" physical waking-reality event. I might add that at the time, it frightened me so deeply that my father blocked up my bedroom window where the dream manifested. It is amusing—he placed a mirror over it, which was merely another place for the numinous to appear, and appear it did, in another form much more benevolent! Only with time did I comprehend its spiritual significance. I tell this story in my book *Pieda's Tales*. So deeply ingrained is this, a "Big Dream," that it endures as part of the story of my life. Thus, we must remain prepared to accept a "Big Dream" as a major opus, a stunning contribution to the growth of our understanding of the big picture of life.

Following the general rules at setting-up time and space to work quietly, reviewing the Pilgrimage Checklist, we are ready.

THE INCUBATION JOURNEY TO THE MANSION OF MANY ROOMS ON THE ISLE OF REMEMBRANCE

Eyes closed, we drift from the waking-reality room. A circle of fire forms around us, its flames rising high, sending warmth to fill us. We stand in the center on a bridge connecting north to south by a narrow road and west to east by a running stream. The fires blaze high before sinking into the earth, leaving a golden rope that rests on the white ash left behind. We smell the burnt offering. Its aroma fills us with the scent of frankincense. Sacred. Precious. A fitting offering for the journey we seek to take. We look down upon our double, our spiritual body that shall make this journey on our behalf. Radiant and strong. Clothed in white robes of white linen, we draw the gold cord more tightly around our waist. Hanging on the chord is the knot of union, that which connects our physical and our spiritual being as one unity. This journey we know is about union, about seeing the hidden path that shall take us to our destiny. We remember our vision, our "Big Dream," understanding it is only a glimpse of the depth of treasures it contains. Years shall bring us through the chapters of our life, and this experience shall help us cast light upon our path.

As we stand on the bridge, we notice a craft slowly gliding to dock beneath the bridge. It is made of pure gold, with elaborate imagery displayed on its golden body: plants, animals, and sacred beings. In the very center there is a shrine, with veils hiding its interior. A being steps out onto the dock and looks up to us. We realize he is a baboon wearing the crown of the crescent moon upon his head. He walks erect, and as our eyes meet his, we sense his wisdom. There is more to this being than what meets our gaze. He beckons for us to join him on the shore beneath the bridge. Thus we begin our journey, walking slowing downward to the vessel beneath the bridge. As we approach the water, we notice time has moved forward. From the bright light of day, the veil of night has cast its indigo cloak over the heavenly dome. There are no stars and no moon to light our way. Slowly we move, to watch our step. The descent is steep and uneven. Slowly, carefully we move, ever remembering our mission to learn more about our path, our destiny, working through the mystery of our dream.

We reach the shore, and for a moment as we step upon the dock, time ceases and a flash of light races across the sky before falling gracefully like a great spray of stars, briefly lighting the sanctuary chapel on the golden craft. Each tiny light rests for only a brief moment before slowly disappearing. We think this auspicious, an invitation that we may make our intention known prior to setting foot in the craft. We realize we too must make an offering. And thus we chant our offering prayer:

> *Oh Hidden One,*
> *Great Being in Your sanctuary,*
> *We praise You beyond our sight.*
> *You are the source of light.*
> *You opened the darkness.*
> *Your heavenly light bids us welcome.*
> *You, font of mystery,*
> *are the source of all the manifest.*
> *You know the secret ways.*
> *You know the question in our hearts.*
> *We praise you in Your hiddenness.*

We beg you accept us and give us passage.
That we may enter the mansion of many rooms
On the Isle of Remembrance.
Aid us that we uncover the secret light of our destiny.

All shifts and we move forward, stepping from the dock into the golden craft. Our offering prayer accepted, we now take our seats in the golden barque. Where the star shower caressed the golden shrine, blue lotus flowers manifest. Their fragrance is intoxicating, filling our senses and relaxing us as though for a long sleep. We rub our eyes, lazily attempting to fight sleep, which calls us. We see at the four corners stand four stately baboons. We recognize the one that welcomed us, since his eyes betray his identity. While the four appear very much alike in stature—tall, elegant, and alert— only our host displays a sharp sense of knowing, a wisdom not only strangely unusual for his species but also greater than what is held by any human. Again we have the thought that his appearance hides a greater identity. Upon his head is the crown of the crescent moon. We realize that this, too, sets him apart.

As we rest we feel the craft begin to sway to the movement of the water beneath us. It rocks much like a cradle, and again we try to fight sleep. Yet, it is not to be. The darkness, the gentle rocking, and the fragrant blue lotus have their way of us . . .

Through the dark waters of forgetfulness, the golden craft glides. . . . Unseen oars held by unseen beings move us along. Yet, we sleep, a deep dreamless sleep. Outside time and space, the movement continues. Silence enfolds its wings about us. Only the gentle lapping of the water against the sides of the craft speaks of the voyage through the darkness.

We have no idea of how long we slept, yet the sleep was deep and peaceful. We wake and it is still dark as we arrive at our destination on the Isle of Remembrance.

Our host and his three companions move the craft to position before helping each of us move onto the shore.

We are met by a guardian, a female goddess called "She who loves silence." Her finger to her lips, she bids us welcome by inviting us to silence. For in silence, we shall find our way to our personal mansion of many rooms. She opens her hand and scatters seeds upon the earth. Each seed bursts open, and from each a tiny benevolent snake manifests. She invites us to follow these guides, for each shall lead us to the very place we need to enter. Slowly we move from shore. Slowly we move up a steep incline and then down into a deep valley, where we see many mansions, dwelling places built into the side of the cliffs, opening into long corridors that run far beyond our seeing. We walk, and slowly, one by one, we find we connect with our house, our mansion of many rooms. The exteriors are all deceiving, for inside each opens to the landscape *of our desire, opening, expanding, revealing to us more of our "Big Dream."*

As we enter we see a pail of pure crystal salt by the entrance of each. We take a handful of salt and spread it over the portal, honoring our passage in purity, seeking knowledge. The salt sparkles like crystal. Satisfied, we enter to experience the sacred dream in this, our mansion of many rooms. Here we shall reconnect with the sacred messages of the hidden.

[Allow twenty minutes of silence, drumming, or rattling, for the personal visitation and private incubation healing, after which we return to the rest of the script.]

We find ourselves at the portal once again. For a moment we hesitate to leave. This dwelling is so familiar, and we feel so connected to all that is within. We stand and turn for a moment to gaze at the interior. This is our true home. Here we know we are accepted for our true identity beyond the seen. We glance at something within that calls to us. We shall remember this, which upon our return we will honor, perhaps finding an image or drawing something that reminds us of this moment. We do not wish to leave all this here behind, hidden in this dreamscape. We must communicate all this in waking reality. We understand that is the purpose of our journey. We must reunite this part of our being with our waking life. With these thoughts we turn to the doorway. There is a copper bowl on the floor, by the portal. Within it is salt. Again, we take a handful and sprinkle over the portal floor. We stand and we give thanks for our vision here. We make the intention to return. We know we shall visit many times. Slowly we exit and we join the others who emerge from their visits. We form a procession and are met by Meretseger, "She who loves silence." She hands each of us a small velvet sac of salt. This is to connect us with this place. This is to take us home whenever we wish to return. We know we shall manifest this, the black velvet of the cloth, the white of the salt, the gold of the ribbon wrapped around it. She does not need to ask this of us. We understand, and we shall do this in memory of this visit. We shall keep it in our private sacred place as a memento of this Isle of Remembrance and our reunion with our mansion of many rooms. We bid her farewell as we reach the golden vessel and our royal baboon host. One by one we move onto the craft and take our seat around the central sanctuary and its Hidden Occupant. The sky remains inky black as we push off to glide across the sea, guided by the invisible presence of oars and oarsmen. Again, we are overcome by the sweet fragrance of the blue lotus and the deep cloak of night. Our eyes close and we move on. We sink into the deep cushion of sleep, warming and comforting us.

The craft moves along the surface of the water. Above, from its hidden place, the thin crescent of the moon slowly makes its appearance along with its companion star. The baboons look up and smile, for it is their patron and his daughter gracing the heavens. And the craft continues on as we, its residents, sleep, unaware of the celestial event.

Water laps against the vessel. The winds pick up and the veils of the shrine blow open to reveal the Hidden One. Yet asleep, we do not gaze into the interior. We do not piece the veils that cloak the Hidden One. And so the night continues on to open to dawn. The baboons become excited and, bowing low, chant their greeting as they watch the eastern horizon. The sun is not yet risen, yet they feel its presence, sense its movement from beneath the horizon. Day is about to break. The cycle of time moves forward, and we, hearing their chant, are roused from our sleep. We have arrived at the bank of the river beneath the bridge at the center of all directions. The air stills and the veils move securely back in place. Our baboon guardians, joyful at our arrival along with the new day, bid us farewell and help us to the dock and upon the land. Our host smiles at us, knowing we shall return. He has much to reveal to us. We understand this is only the beginning. Our "Big Dream" is like the mansion of many rooms. There is much to explore. We hold our black sacs of salt securely to our breast. We must take them with us, manifesting them in waking reality. We move up the incline and onto the bridge. We look down to bid farewell to the golden craft and our guides. Yet, the craft is already gone, disappearing into the far distance.

> *Whoever knows this . . . will be a well-provided Akh spirit*
> *(one fully aware, truly whole).*
> *Always will he leave and enter again the Netherworld*
> *And speak to the living.*
> *A true remedy, (proven) a million times.*

In darkness we entered the hidden mansion. In light we bring union and remembrance. We stand in the center of directions and allow ourselves to see the circle of winding rope that surrounds us in this temenos; flames rise from it, reminding us of the transformation that has begun. Slowly the Dream Gate appears in the center of the bridge. With sadness at our departure, we pass through it, holding the memory of all we experienced along with our sac of salt. We shall return.

Shifting sands of time our consciousness returns to the waking-reality room. We adjust to the waking environment, and then we pick up our journal and record our visit.

The "Big Dream" shall endure through the years, much as mine, which has been with me since childhood. Thus, its dreamscape will expand with time, both in sleeping dreams and in the incubational waking visits, where with intention we go to better understand its connection with our waking reality. In the end this is a most powerful journey, honoring the sacred nature of the union of dream and waking reality in service of guiding us to the successful attainment of the role for which we incarnated.

END OF THE IMAGINAL INCUBATION

So begins our quest to explore dream consciousness, while asleep or while awake, expanding moments when the Dream Gate opens to reveal the mysterious world beyond the seen. Through the Dream Gate we remember ourselves, healing the brokenness of seeing solely through the eyes of waking. And thus, I end the current work with my wish for each to open the Dream Gate and begin or intensity the dream quest, the place of reunion, memory, and healing. The journey shall not disappoint, and the territory shall never become boring.

My presence shall linger along with the characters that float upon the page, yet, beyond these, let us plan to meet in dream. Let our parting be temporary as our separate quests take a rambling route, giving meaning to our incarnation role. Ultimately all roads merge at the center, the place of our origin and our destination. Since dreams remove us from time and space, there is infinite opportunity to share a dreamscape in our reunion, since together we make our journey to decipher the riddle of our lives, ultimately comprehending the dictum "Know thyself."

Thus, until we reunite beyond the Dream Gate, blessings and sweet dreams . . .

> To all, to each,
> a fair good-nigh
> and pleasing dreams,
> and slumbers light.

"L'Envoy, to the Reader" —Walter Scott
In John Barlett, Familiar Quotations, 10th ed., 1919

APPENDIX

Additional Travel Guide Prayers for Your Waking-Dream Incubation Pilgrimage

PRAYER OF PETITION

Finding the reason to take a waking-dream pilgrimage

Life is complicated, and choosing the right reason for a waking dream is essential. In waking life we have various reasons for our journeys: our travel adventures, which determine what we seek to gain, mere fun vacations, or learning experiences. Likewise, when we choose to enter a waking dream, the question that leads us must be just right or we may not find what we seek.

> Beloved, Voice of Dream, help me cast my eyes upon what is
> Essential for my soul's growth.
> Lead me from ignorance into the light of wisdom.
> Awaken in me the question that is the cornerstone
> Where I must put my attention, where I must direct my steps.
> Help me capture the focus that will be the light upon the road.
> There are many challenges, struggles, and hardships ahead.
> Direct my vision in singling the most important issue for me here and
> now
> That I may clear the way for fulfillment.
> AMEN.

**ENTRY PRAYER AT THE BEGINNING
OF A WAKING-DREAM JOURNEY**

The inner dream space is filled with sacred wisdom, and thus it is akin to entering a temple, cathedral, or mosque. Honoring the shift in focus with prayer demonstrates the desire to move from the mundane to the sacred. It is standing before a sanctuary portal, exiting from the bustling exterior of waking chaos to enter the quiet of the inner holy place.

Beloved, Hidden One residing in my heart.
I seek entry into the Dream Sanctuary within.
Guide me safely that I may enter and receive support.
Aid me in expanding my knowing that I may attain the grace, peace, and wisdom
That will set me on the road of discovery.
Support me on my path that I may find my way.
Until the end of my physical incarnation,
Be with me. Steer my steps.
AMEN.

WAKING-DREAM MANTRA, COMPANION PRAYER

This prayer is said before and often during a visionary experience, giving voice to the desire and the devotion to the sacred pilgrimage.

From the Great Above of my waking room
I seek the Great Below of Dreaming.
From my eyes that see around me
I seek vision of what is within me.
From the Great Above of my waking room
I seek entry into the Hidden depths.
Beloved, Welcome me. Open my sight to
The Great Below inside the sanctuary,
Fill me with the wisdom of the Dreaming Womb.
AMEN.

PRAYER OF THANKSGIVING UPON COMPLETION OF PILGRIMAGE

Each time we exit our waking dream, we give thanks for all the imagery, the memories, the experiences that formed our visionary experience. Entering with prayer, we honor all by exiting with prayer.

Beloved. Voice of Dream.
You received me into the Great Below.
You shared with me the hidden treasures.
I rise now richer for my entry.
I bring to the Great Above
Your Gifts from the Great Below.
I am thankful for your welcome.
I shall honor all You have shown to me.
I shall return over and again
To quench my thirst for knowledge,

And to clear the blindness of waking sight
With the light of the inner dream truth that lies beyond the seen.
AMEN.

RITUAL OF HONORING THE WISDOM RECEIVED FROM A DREAM OR WAKING DREAM UPON ARRIVING BACK TO WAKING CONSCIOUSNESS

After experiencing a dream or waking dream, writing in our journals and dream dictionaries we often are left wanting more, filled with the richness of the experience that we now seek to honor in a deeper manner. Honoring the gifts, the communication of the dream state in waking, is an important step in dreamwork. Traveling into the dream and experiencing its extraordinary revelations does not end by leaving all to the recordings in our dream journals. It must be honored by bringing its richness into our lives in a more concrete manner. One way is to create a ritual that makes present the dream material in the light of waking reality.

In the ancient texts we read the holy prayer of the Angelus. It tells the story of the angelic messenger who announced to a young woman, Mary, that she was chosen to be mother to her Lord. It is the story of the Annunciation, leading to the birth of the Christ child and the story of Christmas. Yet, we can look at the Angelus, this beautiful prayer, expanding it, examining it more closely to reveal something hidden and meaningful beyond a singular event. We can embrace it as we do many beautiful ancient stories, seeing what is hidden, not diminishing it but expanding it to embrace a more personal meaning.

"The angel of the Lord declared unto Mary." So begins this ancient text. The angel, an angelic being not from waking but from dream reality, speaking to Mary, the physical embodied waking being who can receive this communication. The voice of dream may appear in many forms, for the language of dream is that of images. Each of us has in dream communication an image that arises on the dreamscape, a being, deity, angel, or archetypal figure, whose appearance speaks to us of hidden truths. Just as Mary was visited by an angelic being messenger, so are we visited by our dream communicators.

The Angelus continues: "And she [Mary] conceived of the Holy Spirit." And so each of us who communicates with dream has the seed planted within our depths, our dream womb, seeds ready to germinate and bring forth something extraordinary, something beyond the physical, something deeply spiritual. Like the Christ energy, enlightenment, dream wisdom can bloom, the coming announced by the dream messenger of the hidden.

The Angelus continues with one of the most beautiful spiritual responses, the Magnificat, Mary's consent to be a tool of the Divine.

"Behold the handmaid of the Lord, be it done unto me according to Thy word. And so . . . the word was made flesh . . . and dwelt among us."

We plummet the depths in our dreams, and implantation takes place. Yet, the child of dream needs to be brought into the light, to dwell among us, to shine upon the path forward. We accept this role when we dedicate ourselves to honoring the angelic message of the Hidden, of the dream. It becomes our task to birth the child of light, to elevate the dream from the depths into waking. We must make the word flesh.

One way we can do this is to bring forward the dream by creating a ritual space honoring what we receive in dreams. It becomes our sacred temenos, our dreaming holy place where we place tokens that represent our dream pilgrimages. We visit this place often, and as such we repeatedly seek its sanctity to say our prayers. Our visitation and prayer ritual are incorporated into our everyday life, honored as an integral part of our incarnational journey, one that includes honoring both the waking and dream consciousness.

The temenos, sacred space, we set up may be as simple as dedicating a drawer or even a small box to our dream honoring, a place where we keep our dream tokens, small images or items that remind us of our dream communications. Not everyone will have a grand space to devote to something elaborate. Our temenos need not be fancy. I began by gathering small stones and tiny crystal beads that I placed in an old cigar box. A feather, a coin, a small icon found their way in, each connecting me with various dream images. I placed the box by my bed, and it was the first item I touched in the morning after recording my dreams. I had it with me when I began my day with my prayers, which not only included my beloved living and deceased family and friends but grew to include what I called my dream family, all that arose in my visionary dream life, all those whose appearances so enriched my waking life. As I slipped into bed at night, I would open the box and tenderly touch the token items, each one bringing up a memory of the dream visits. And then I would go off to my nighttime pilgrimages, always hoping to reconnect during the night. I now have tiny ritual spaces everywhere in my home, since I cannot bear being without the physical tokens, amulets, and icons that remind me of my powerful visionary experiences. My dreaming temenos now includes a dedicated chapel and full-size labyrinth of stone in a Garden of Remembrance. My beloved husband supported my desire to create these monuments to my dream devotions. Yet, large or small, the important thing is to find time for the ritual honoring, for personal prayer in appreciation of dream, the often-hidden, underappreciated side of consciousness. My dreaming is as essential to me as my breathing, possibly more so, since my breathing shall someday cease, while I believe my dreaming eternal, unending.

When time permits, we extend our daily ritual honoring. We each can do this, even if we live in an apartment in a large city. We can take time to place a metal goblet of water, a crystal heart, a candle, and a stick of incense on a dedicated prayer cloth (any clean silk, velvet, or cotton cloth, scarf, or fabric square will do), during which we honor earth, air, fire, water, and metal—our waking world, along with our dreamworld, giving thanks that the two communicate with one another, allowing us to walk with our vision empowered by the sharing between both worlds. We can end the process by taking the water outside to pour onto the land, along with the incense ash, remembering that the physical shall disappear into the river of time while the dream reality shall endure beyond forever. Even in the city there are tiny plots of soil beneath city plantings. We can pause for a moment and say a short prayer of remembrance, such as the below, holding the dreamworld close to our hearts, thus honoring it in waking, elevating it beyond the pages of our journals.

DAILY RITUAL PRAYER HONORING THE DREAM REALITY

From the Hidden Depths
From the Great Hall of Eternity
Voice of Dream your presence awakens me to truth
Your companionship empowers me to endure
The passing suffering of the physical.
Beloved, Source of Truth abiding in
The dreaming depths of my heart.
I am servant to Your wisdom.
I am child of Eternity.
May all my days begin and end
With the wisdom of dream guiding
The hand of the waking.
May the word be made flesh
As the below is honored in the above
Shining light upon all dark corners of my being.
Voice of Dream you are spouse of my soul.
AMEN.

BIBLIOGRAPHY

BOOKS

Barlett, John. *Familiar Quotations*. 10th ed. New York: Blue Ribbon Books, 1919.

Castaneda, Carlos. *A Separate Reality*. New York: Simon and Schuster, 1971.

Cott, Jonathan. *The Search for Om Sety: A Story of Eternal Love*. New York: Warner Books, 1987.

Eliade, Mircea. *Shamanism: Archaic Techniques of Ecstasy*. Princeton, NJ: Princeton University Press, 1992.

Falconer, William, trans. *The Geography of Strabo*. Book XIV. London: George Bell & Sons, 1903.

Faulkner, R. O., trans. Utterance 690. In *The Ancient Egyptian Pyramid Texts*. 2117–19. Oxford: Clarendon, 1998.

Fitzgerald, F. Scott. *The Last Tycoon*. New York: Charles Scribner's Sons, 1941.

Gedge, Pauline. *The Eagle and the Raven*. Chicago: Chicago Review Press, 2007.

Harner, Michael. *The Way of the Shaman: A Guide to Power and Healing*. New York: Bantam Books, 1982.

Holecek, Andrew. *Dream Yoga: Illuminating Your Life through Lucid Dreaming and the Tibetan Yogas of Sleep*. Boulder, CO: Sounds True, 2016.

Hornung, Erik, and Theodor Abt. "Closing Text." In *The Egyptian Amduat: The Book of the Hidden Chamber*. Edited by Erik Hornung and Theodor Abt, 424. Translated by David Warburton. Zurich, Switzerland: Living Human Heritage, 2014.

Housman, A. E. *The Oracles*. 1959.

Jung, Carl Gustav. *Collected Works of C. G. Jung*. 20 vols. Princeton, NJ: Princeton University Press, 1990.

Jung, Carl Gustav. *The Red Book*. New York: W. W. Norton, 2009.

Jung, Carl Gustav. *Synchronicity: An Acausal Connecting Principle*. Princeton, NJ: Princeton University Press, 1969.

Klinger, Eric. *Structure and Functions of Fantasy*. New York: Wiley-Interscience, 1971.

Mishra, Rammurti. *The Textbook of Yoga Psychology*. New York: Julian, 1967.

Pausanias. *Pausanias's Description of Greece*. Edited and translated by James George Frazer. Cambridge, UK: Cambridge University Press, 1898.

Piedilato, Janet. "Introduction." In *The Mystical Dream Tarot: Life Guidance from the Depths of Our Unconscious*. By Janet Piedilato, 13. London: Eddison Books, 2019.

Schweitzer, Albert, quoted by Norman Cousins in *Anatomy of an Illness as Perceived by the Patient*. New York: W. W. Norton, 2005.

Stark, Freya. *The Journey's Echo*. New York: Harcourt, Brace and World, 1963.

Strabo. *Geographia, XIV*, p. 44. New York: G. P. Putnam's Sons, 1903.

Ullman, Montague, and Nan Zimmerman. *Working with Dreams: Self Understanding, Problem-Solving and Enriched Creativity through Dream Appreciation*. Los Angeles: Jeremy Tarcher, 1979.

Wangyai, Tenzin. *The Tibetan Yogas of Dream and Sleep*. Ithaca, NY: Snow Lion, 1998.

Winkelman, Michael. *Shamanism: A Biopsychosocial Paradigm of Consciousness and Healing*. Santa Barbara, CA: Praeger, 2010.

Yuthok, Choedak. *Lamdre: Dawn of Enlightenment*. Canberra, Australia: Gorum, 1997.

ARTICLES

Fox, Kieran C. R., Savannah Nijeboer, Elizaveta Solomonova, G. William Domhoff, and Kalina Kristoff. "Dreaming as Mind Wandering: Evidence from Functional Neuroimaging and First-Person Content Reports." *Frontiers in Human Neuroscience*, July 30, 2013.

Neher, Andrew. "A Physiological Explanation of Unusual Behavior in Ceremonies Involving Drums." *Human Biology* 4, no. 2 (1962): 153.

Novalis. "Aphorisms, from *Pollen and Fragments*" (1798). Cited in *News of the Universe: Poems of Twofold Consciousness*. Chosen and introduced by Robert Bly, 39. Translated by Charles E. Passage. San Francisco: Sierra Club Books, 1980.

Schmidt, Markus H., and Helmut S. Schmidt. "Sleep-Related Erections: Neural Mechanisms and Clinical Significance." *Current Neurological Neuroscience Reports* 4, no. 2 (March 2004): 170–78.